More praise for COLIN POWELL

COLIN POWELL

Soldier/Statesman
Statesman/Soldier

Howard Means

BALLANTINE BOOKS • NEW YORK

Copyright © 1992 by Howard Means

All rights reserved under International and Pan-American Copyright Conventions, including the right of reproduction in whole or in part in any form. Published in the United States of America by Ballantine Books, a division of Random House, Inc., New York, and simultaneously in Canada by Random House of Canada Limited, Toronto.

Library of Congress Catalog Card Number: 92-53079

ISBN 0-345-38381-8

This edition published by arrangement with Donald I. Fine, Inc.

Manufactured in the United States of America

First Ballantine Books Edition: September 1993

To Candy

ACKNOWLEDGMENTS

Grateful acknowledgment is made for permission to quote from the following works: *About Face: The Odyssey of an American Warrior* by David Hackworth and Julie Sherman, reprinted by permission of Simon & Schuster (copyright © 1989 by David Hackworth and Julie Sherman); "Call to Service: The Colin Powell Story" by Carl Rowan, *Reader's Digest* (December, 1989), copyright © 1989 by The Reader's Digest Assn., Inc.; *The Commanders* by Bob Woodward, reprinted by permission of Simon & Schuster and Bob Woodward (copyright © 1991 by Bob Woodward); *Ethnic America: A History* by Thomas Sowell, reprinted by permission of Basic Books, a division of HarperCollins Publishers (copyright © 1981 by Basic Books, Inc.); *Every War Must End* by Fred Charles Iklé, reprinted by permission of Columbia University Press (copyright © 1971 by Columbia University Press, New York); *Keepers of the Keys* by John Prados, reprinted by permission of William Morrow & Company, Inc. (copyright © 1991 by John Prados); *Panama: The Whole Story* by Kevin Buckley, reprinted by permission of Simon & Schuster (copyright © 1991 by Kevin Buckley); *President Reagan: The Role of a Lifetime* by Lou Cannon, reprinted by permission of Simon & Schuster (copyright © 1991 by Lou Cannon); *The Rise and Fall of an American Army—U.S. Ground Forces, Vietnam: 1965-1973* by Shelby L. Stanton, with permission granted from Presidio Press, 505B San Marin Drive, Suite 300, Novato, CA 94945-1340 (copyright © 1985); *Triumph Without Victory: The Unreported History of the Persian Gulf War* by the staff of U.S. News & World Report, reprinted by permission of Times Books (copyright © 1992 by U.S. News & World Report); *Two Nations: Black and White, Separate, Hostile, Unequal* by Andrew Hacker, reprinted by permission of Charles Scribner's Sons, an imprint of Macmillan Publishing

Company (copyright © 1992 by Andrew Hacker); *Under Fire: An American Story* by Oliver L. North with William Novak, reprinted by permission of HarperCollins (copyright © 1991 by Oliver L. North); *Vietnam: A History* by Stanley Karnow, used by permission of Viking Penguin, a division of Penguin Books USA Inc. (copyright © 1983 by WGBH Educational Foundation and Stanley Karnow).

A NOTE TO THE READER

This biography of Colin Powell is based on more than one hundred twenty interviews, including ones with General and Mrs. Powell; with General Powell's family members, childhood friends, and college classmates; his early Army comrades and commanders; and his colleagues, bosses, mentors, and friends from more recent times; as well as with experts on subjects ranging from West Indian culture to electoral politics to military history and strategy. The author also has made extensive use of the voluminous public record on General Powell—magazine and newspaper articles, television appearances, and his own speeches. Of particular help has been an extensive interview with Colin Powell conducted by Kenneth Adelman for the May, 1990, issue of *Washingtonian* magazine. (Adelman graciously provided the full transcript of that session.) All quotes taken from sources other than the author's own interviews have been credited to those sources. Where no source is identified, the quote was made directly to the author. Some of those quoted in this book go unnamed at their insistence. Military people especially have an uneasy relationship with journalists and writers, even in noncontroversial matters; and those in government service are frequently wary of giving quotes for the record. But wherever possible those quoted are named. Unattributed quotes are from people whose general veracity is known to the author.

The author would like to express his thanks to General Powell's staff, including Col. Frederick "Bill" Smullen and Capt. David Roth, who has since returned to civilian life, and Capt. Robin Crumm. Thanks also go to *Washingtonian* editor Jack Limpert for granting the author leave to pursue this book; to my agent, Mildred Marmur, and to Don Fine; to Col. David Hackworth, who gave generously of his hard-earned wisdom; and to those too numerous to name who took time from extraordinarily busy schedules to answer questions about Colin Powell. On a more general note, the author also would like to thank the many, many soldiers—active-duty and retired—who rendered their counsel and sage advice. It makes for a good joke, but the term ''military intelligence'' is no oxymoron.

—Howard Means
Bethesda, Maryland
May, 1992

CONTENTS

INTRODUCTION

"I Ain't Done Bad."

January 29, 1991

NBC news anchor Tom Brokaw had misidentified him earlier as
"General Clayton Powell," after the late, flamboyant Harlem
congressman, Adam Clayton Powell; but to the millions of
Americans watching George Bush's State of the Union address,
Colin Luther Powell needed no introduction.

Above him, his wife, Alma, shared Barbara Bush's special
viewing box with the First Lady and Brenda Schwarzkopf, whose
husband, Gen. H. Norman Schwarzkopf, Jr., was then half a
world away in Riyadh, Saudi Arabia. To either side of Powell,
in the well of the House of Representatives, sat the president's
cabinet; the nine members of the Supreme Court, irreverently
known to the Washington press as "The Supremes"; the foreign
ambassadorial corps, with the notable exception of the Iraqi
chargé d'affaires; and the leaders of the various military
branches. Members of the House and Senate sat behind Powell
in tier upon tier. Ahead, on the raised dais of the House—flanked
to the rear by Speaker Tom Foley and Vice-President Dan
Quayle—stood the president, who had jumped Powell over more
than thirty senior military officers to make him both the youngest chairman of the Joint Chiefs of Staff and the first African-
American to hold that position.

State of the Union addresses are neither mandatory nor, often,
particularly stirring. Indeed, for 112 years, from the administra-

-1

tion of Thomas Jefferson until Woodrow Wilson revived the custom, the nation survived without such addresses. But the one of January 29, 1991, was delivered in extraordinary circumstances. "There was a tension," Alma Powell recalls. "It was not a bad tension; it was electric." Part of that tension was broken early on in the address when George Bush introduced his wife's special guests, to a standing ovation. "It was a total shock to me to be introduced," Mrs. Powell says. "My first reaction was to look around and say, 'What should I do?' But then I realized that there were too many people watching me. So, okay, stand up, hold your head up, and smile. That was about it, but a lot of things happened for me standing up and smiling." Later, the applause would grow thunderous when Bush delivered his brief hymn of praise to the nearly half a million American troops then based in and around Saudi Arabia:

"There is no one more devoted, more committed to the hard work of freedom," the president said, "than every soldier and sailor, every marine, airman, and coast guardsman—every man and woman now serving in the Persian Gulf."

Fifteen years and nine months after the humiliating withdrawal from Vietnam, Americans finally had a war they could cheer. For an armed force that had been riven by doubt and nearly broken in spirit in the aftermath of Vietnam, it was a remarkable comeback. In Colin Powell and Norman Schwarzkopf, the nation also once again had two military leaders it could call heroes. "If you had gone to central casting and said, 'We're going to have this war. We want two people to personify what we're trying to do,' you couldn't have asked for two better characters," says Lawrence Korb, a former assistant secretary of defense now with the Brookings Institution.

As field commander of U.S. and, later, Allied coalition forces in the Persian Gulf, Norman Schwarzkopf's first duty had been to provide for the defense of Saudi Arabia and its vast oil reserves from possible further aggression by Saddam Hussein's army. To that end, Schwarzkopf was seemingly well prepared. The Central Command he headed was based at MacDill Air Force Base, near Tampa, Florida, but its theater of interest was the Middle East, and in the obsessive planning of the Pentagon there is a contingency scheme for almost everything. Seven months before Iraqi forces began massing at the Kuwaiti border,

Schwarzkopf had ordered a computerized update of a 1983 plan for protecting the oil flow from the Arabian peninsula. In the weeks before Iraq invaded Kuwait, the computer model and real life began to merge. "It was something like Twilight Zone," Maj. John Feeley told U.S. News & World Report. (Feeley's comment is cited in U.S. News's excellent history of the war, *Triumph Without Victory*.) What Schwarzkopf's plan did not have, though, was an offensive capability. In October, 1990, the general was ordered to come up with one, and here the terrain grew far more shaky. Was Saddam Hussein's army the fourth largest in the world or the sixth? And what did that size mean in practical terms? Did he have the capacity to wage biological or even nuclear warfare? And would he? Were the Republican Guards the crack unit they were widely assumed to be, ready to battle to the death for Saddam and his newest cause?

Although it was not specifically Schwarzkopf's problem, there was also the question of Saddam Hussein's ability to carry through on his threats of worldwide terrorism. As Bush delivered his State of the Union address, the Capitol was ringed by its own 1,265-person police force, with officers stationed every twenty feet. Security guards had scanned guests with hand-held metal detectors and videotaped their arrival. At one entrance a new $40,000 Entry-Scan Mark II bomb-sniffing machine had made its debut. Even as Bush spoke, bomb-sniffing dogs and their Secret Service and FBI handlers were circulating through the halls and cloakrooms and even the ladies restroom. In keeping with custom, one cabinet member had not attended the address to assure that if a monstrous catastrophe were to befall the gathering someone would be left in the constitutionally mandated line of succession to assume control of the government. That duty rotated among the cabinet members. On this occasion it had fallen to Interior Secretary Manuel Lujan, a one-time congressman from New Mexico and generally considered among the least effective of George Bush's cabinet members.

In hindsight, the questions are easy to answer. Saddam Hussein had a demoralized army and, by the time the ground war began, a thoroughly battered one; his worldwide agents-in-place, if they existed at all, never surfaced. But at the time, answers were in short supply. No U.S. intelligence agency had a reliable source within the tightly held ruling circle in Baghdad; more to the point, perhaps, Saddam was a mostly unreadable book.

Colin Powell's role in Operation Desert Shield and, later, Desert Storm is harder to put a face on. By statute, he was the nation's highest-ranking military officer, yet he commanded no troops directly. He was the military's liaison to the civilian world, the principal adviser to President Bush and Secretary of Defense Dick Cheney, yet neither was under any statutory obligation to accept his advice. He had been a soldier for thirty-two years when Saddam Hussein's army invaded Kuwait, yet Powell's effectiveness as chairman depended as much on his political acumen as it did on his military skills. Armies, the Prussian military theorist Carl von Clausewitz wrote, always had to contend with "the fog of war"; Powell had to contend, in a sense, with the fog of his own authority. But he brought formidable talents to the fray.

Powell had resisted a quick U.S. air strike against the occupying Iraqi army. On its own, an air strike could not undo the occupation of Kuwait, but it could rile the unpredictable Saddam to more aggression. As August spilled into the fall, Powell appeared to favor a defensive posture for the U.S. troops pouring into Saudi Arabia. His first preference, in an ideal world, was to let the economic blockade of Iraq do its job. Eventually, so the scenario went, hardship would be so widespread in Baghdad and elsewhere that Saddam would be toppled from within and Kuwait freed. Like most military leaders—and like nearly everyone who has seen warfare firsthand—Powell considered the exercise of force a last resort, and a dire one. If the United States military was to mount an offensive to expel Iraq from Kuwait, he believed, it had to do so from a position of such massive strength that the outcome was inevitable no matter how valiantly or recklessly Saddam's forces fought.

But Powell knew that superior military power was only part of the equation in waging modern American warfare. A Vietnam veteran who had ingested more fully than anyone else in the Bush war council the lessons of that sad conflict, Powell knew that without a fervid American public behind it and without quick success, Operation Desert Storm could turn too quickly into Operation Desert Morass. Kuwait, after all, was a remote, autocratic oil sheikdom. To many Americans, it seemed as distant and insignificant to their daily lives as South Vietnam had thirty years earlier. Powell knew, too, that to whatever extent possible Congress had to be brought along as well—not only to grant George Bush war-making powers but to avoid second-guessing once the combat began. If the Vietnam War had taught one ineluctable lesson, it was that when political objectives become muddy and politicians become generals, the cause is lost.

By January 15, 1991—the day the United Nations deadline for Iraqi withdrawal from Kuwait expired—all the elements were in place. Three days earlier, Congress had authorized the use of military force in the Persian Gulf, pursuant to United Nations Security Council Resolution 678. The authorization, preceded by a lengthy and much-followed debate, carried by five votes in the Senate and sixty-seven in the House. Simultaneously, Bush's incessant portrayals of Saddam Hussein as an Arab Satan, Hitler in a Republican Guards beret, had brought American war fever to a pitch. In Saudi Arabia, a half-million-strong international force—including units from the United Kingdom, France, Egypt, Kuwait, Syria, Saudi Arabia and the Gulf Cooperation Council, as well as the United States—had moved into place on the ground. A little after midnight on January 17, 1991, the air war against Iraq began. It would prove a technological tour de force. F-117A Stealth fighters eluded enemy radar; "smart bombs," only a fraction of the total munitions dumped on enemy targets, nonetheless caught the public's imagination as carefully controlled news footage showed them seeking out smokestacks and front doors. Reportedly U.S. military hackers even succeeded in introducing a computer virus into the Iraqi military communications system. To many Americans following the war on CNN or the major TV networks, it seemed less a military exercise than a super-Nintendo game gone awesomely right.

If anything, the potentially far more dangerous ground war launched officially on February 24 would prove an even greater success. By February 27, George Bush could declare: "Kuwait is liberated." Four days later, Norman Schwarzkopf met with his Iraqi counterpart in a tent set in the desert of southern Iraq, and the Mother of all Wars was over. Of the nearly half-million Allied troops stationed in the Persian Gulf, 244 would be killed in action, including 146 Americans. Little wonder, then, that H. Norman Schwarzkopf, Jr. and Colin Luther Powell would become the most celebrated and admired U.S. military leaders in nearly half a century.

* * *

Colin Powell and Norman Schwarzkopf had been born three years apart in the middle years of the Great Depression. Both had married in the 1960s as America slid into the abyss of Vietnam; both had fathered three children and risen to the rank of general in the United States Army. Each proclaimed the other a valued colleague and boon companion. Apart from surface details, though, they could hardly have been less similar.

Schwarzkopf had been born to military privilege. His father, H. Norman, Sr., was a West Point graduate, as his son would be. By turns, the senior Schwarzkopf served as a general during World War I, as the head of the New Jersey State Police during the 1930s, again as a general during World War II, and later as host of the popular radio series "Gangbusters." While he was state police commissioner, Schwarzkopf had overseen the arrest and prosecution of Bruno Hauptmann for the kidnapping-murder of Charles Lindbergh, Jr., the two-year-old son of writer Anne Morrow Lindbergh and her celebrated aviator-husband.

The younger Norman followed in the father's shoes. Raised in Iran, Switzerland, Germany, and Iraq, he was eventually enrolled at Bordentown Military Academy near his parents' home in Trenton, N.J. From there Schwarzkopf went on to the United States Military Academy and into military legend. Said to have an I.Q. of 170, he spoke French and German fluently, was a devotee of opera and the ballet and a member of the International Brotherhood of Magicians. The sounds of both Pavarotti and Willie Nelson could be heard coming from his sleeping quarters at the command center in Riyadh—the same sleeping quarters where he kept a stationary cross-country skiing machine, a loaded shotgun, a camouflage-covered Bible, and a TV with tapes of Ken Burns's Civil War series for PBS. In a Parade magazine poll released in early 1992, respondents judged Schwarzkopf the second smartest man in America, behind only the all-purpose savant Carl Sagan. In full-dress uniform Schwarzkopf wore three Silver Stars on his chest—two with Oak Leaf clusters—as well as the Legion of Merit and the Purple Heart. The third Silver Star had been awarded for walking through a mine field on the Batangan peninsula in South Vietnam to help a wounded private.

Known to the press as Stormin' Norman and to many of his military colleagues as Bear, Schwarzkopf wore his heart on his sleeve. He raged at underlings and was open in his scorn for the

Pentagon's army of "armchair generals." (His comment later in the year in a speech at West Point that armchair generals were "military fairies" would earn him an "Oh, Norman, you bitch" award in *Esquire* magazine's annual "Dubious Achievement Awards.") His *Who's Who* entry listed his avocations as hunting, fishing, and skeet and trap shooting. Yet Schwarzkopf was equally capable of tender sentiments—the Bear nickname stood in part for Teddy Bear—and soul-searching candor. Twenty years earlier, in C. D. B. Bryan's *Friendly Fire*, Schwarzkopf had entered the national consciousness in a supporting role as the commanding officer of an Iowa farm boy named Michael Mullin, killed by a U.S. artillery round in Vietnam. In the years since, Schwarzkopf had talked often and on the record about the pain that war and his reception back in the States had caused him. "When they get ready to send me [to fight] again," he had told Bryan in the 1970s, "I'm going to have to stop and ask myself, 'Is it worth it?'" Presumably, over the years, he had concluded it was. By the conclusion of the Gulf War, Schwarzkopf would háve a 93 percent "favorable" rating, according to polls, higher even than George Bush. His March 15, 1991, interview with Barbara Walters on ABC's "20/20" would set an all-time viewer record for the show.

As it turned out, Operation Desert Storm was to be Norman Schwarzkopf's final military adventure. Within two months of riding beside Colin Powell in a massive victory parade down the heart of Manhattan—cheered by an estimated 4.7 million people—Schwarzkopf had turned in his uniform. Courted as a senatorial candidate in Florida, he had signed on instead to write his memoirs for a reported $5.5 million advance. He had served as co-host for a fiftieth-anniversary TV special on the attack on Pearl Harbor and had crossed the country giving speeches for an estimated $50,000 to $75,000 each. Indeed, by year's end, Schwarzkopf seemed to have been everywhere and said nearly everything he had to say. A little more than a year after sweeping to the world's center stage as commander of coalition forces in the Persian Gulf, Norman Schwarzkopf seemed to many overexposed. Among those who appeared to believe that Schwarzkopf had stayed on too long at his dance with celebrity was Colin Powell, according to a high-ranking Pentagon official who had talked to him about the matter in November, 1991.

"I know," this official says, "that Colin feels Schwarzkopf has overplayed his hand."

Colin Powell was by birth, by nature, and perhaps by intent Norman Schwarzkopf's opposite. The son of Jamaican immigrants, born in Harlem and raised in the Bronx, Powell had built a reputation as a man with no bluff about him. Schwarzkopf's Saudi Arabian press briefings during the Gulf War had been theatrical exercises. Powell's Pentagon briefings were almost haiku-like by contrast, studies in compaction and terseness. "Our strategy for going after [the Iraqi] army is very, very simple," Powell had told reporters near the conclusion of a January 23, 1991, briefing. "First, we are going to cut it off. And then we are going to kill it." In Powell's flat, inflectionless delivery, it seemed a simple statement of impending fact. Those who have known Powell for many years say it was the pure man, both public and private.

"He writes his speeches," says his friend Harlan Ullman of the Center for Naval Analysis. "They're all simple. Every sentence is about ten words long: bang, bang, bang. It's elegant in its straightforward nature. There's no great Kissingerian framework, but it's entirely solid and without fluff. It's entirely him. His speeches are the way he speaks and thinks."

Conciliatory where Schwarzkopf was confrontational, Powell had survived for the better part of twenty years in the claustrophobic confines of official Washington, making peace and finding common ground with a succession of armchair generals and administration and congressional defense and national-security overseers. Where a duck blind seemed Schwarzkopf's natural home, Colin and Alma Powell had become regulars at the gatherings and receptions indigenous to the nation's capitol. Alma Powell would even be judged one of 1991's ten best-dressed women in the world in the fifty-first annual International Best Dressed Poll of fashion executives, designers, and writers. Norman Schwarzkopf was an open book waiting to be read. Colin Powell was an enigma in the cloak of a hail-fellow-well-met.

He wasn't rich; only when he earned his fourth general's star did his salary climb into the very low six figures. He was barrel-chested and ruggedly handsome but far from a matinee idol. Yet in an *Esquire* poll that asked one thousand randomly selected American men whether they would rather be Powell or Kevin

Costner—then riding the crest of enormous Hollywood fame and wealth—fully thirty-seven percent had chosen Powell.

He had never run for office, never been elected to anything, yet he had the quality of a political star. Jesse Jackson was present at an honors ceremony held in early 1992, sponsored by the Joint Center for Political and Economic Studies, Washington's only black-run think-tank. So were Atlanta mayor Maynard Jackson and others. "But it was Powell everyone wanted to be seen with, Powell everyone wanted to have their photograph taken with, Powell everyone wanted to shake hands with," says one attendee. "He has charisma. He was like a movie star."

"He has that quality," says a woman who has been seated with him more than once at formal gatherings. "When he walks into a room, all the eyes turn toward him."

For all his ready charm, Powell could be thin-skinned and unvarnished in the best military fashion. "He has been known to pick up the phone and chew generals and reporters out alike, and with equal venom," says Fred Francis, the veteran Pentagon correspondent for NBC-TV. "One time he'd been talking about how great intelligence was during the [Gulf] war, and I said on the air, 'Well, Colin's wrong.' Three or four days later I saw him, and he said, 'What is this shit about Colin's being wrong? What do you know about it?' But at the same time he doesn't hold a grudge. . . . It's not a long-lasting anger. He has a short fuse on some things, but he lets people know. You don't have to guess where you are with him."

For all his calm in the face of crisis—what Ernest Hemingway celebrated as "grace under pressure"—and for all his stern public demeanor, there is also a boisterous side to Powell. At one Washington embassy dinner, according to a guest at the party, Powell, his former boss and mentor Frank Carlucci, and Kenneth Adelman, the former head of the U.S. Arms Control and Disarmament Agency, were all seated at the same table.

"Their joking got very loud," this person says. "After twenty minutes Marcia Carlucci came over and said, 'Hold it down.' Twenty minutes later Alma Powell went over and asked them to hold it down. Another twenty minutes later, Carol Adelman tried to calm them down."

"He's a very funny guy," Ken Adelman says. "He loves to cut up. He's not controlled. It's a wonderful trait."

Powell relaxed on weekends when he could by tinkering with his beloved old Volvos in his Fort Myer garage. Indeed, he seemed to run something of an unofficial used-car lot. Hardly anyone, it is said, can come within shouting distance of the garage without Powell's trying to strike up an auto transaction. Among those he's tried to sell a Volvo to: Lynne Cheney, head of the National Endowment for the Humanities and the wife of Defense Secretary Dick Cheney. "It wasn't entirely unasked for," Mrs. Cheney explains. "Dick and I were playing tennis at the officer's club at Fort Myer. Often when we finish, we'll see Colin out in his garage working on a car. The one he was working on this day was very good-looking—I admired it excessively."

Although it is never paraded for inspection—and he often seems to have no life other than his very public life—Powell also is a devoted family man. Michael, the Powells' oldest child, was born in 1963 while his father was serving in South Vietnam. Michael would receive an appointment to the United States Military Academy at West Point, but he would choose to attend the College of William and Mary in Williamsburg, Virginia. "I was happy with his decision," Alma Powell says. "I think you get a more well-rounded view of life at a liberal-arts college than you do at a military academy." In college Michael would join ROTC, as his father had done a quarter century earlier at the City College of New York. In 1987 Michael was riding in a military jeep in Germany, in heavy rain on the Autobahn, when the driver lost control and the jeep flipped, throwing out its three occupants. The jeep bounced on Michael, crushing his pelvis—he would spend months healing in U.S. military hospitals. Later, out of the Army, he became a civilian employee of the Defense Department. Linda, the Powells' second child, followed her brother to William and Mary and then became an actress. She had a role as a law student in the movie *Reversal of Fortune* as well as a minor part in "The Human Factor," a late-season, spring 1992 replacement in the CBS Thursday night lineup. Annemarie, the Powells' youngest child, graduated from William and Mary in May, 1992.

Colin Powell has lived in a city of towering vanities—a nation's capital in which elaborate deference is expected and insistent self-importance is more often the rule than the exception—yet he often seems to be a man with virtually no vanity at all. "It's a trait that serves him so well," says Fred Malek, manager of the 1992 Bush-Quayle campaign and Powell's boss in 1973 when he was on loan from the Army to the Office of Management and Budget. "Colin Powell doesn't have an ego. He's not burdened with an ego. He's comfortable with himself, secure in who he is and what his abilities are, and he doesn't let his ego get in the way of doing his job. It's part of the reason he can work so well with people."

A key player in the most political city in the nation, Powell has had no publically professed politics—even many of his friends pleaded ignorance of his views on domestic issues, if he held any. Partisan views, they say, come up only rarely in the daily ebb and flow. "He lives politics every day," says his friend Vernon Jordan, the civil-rights leader and Washington power-lawyer. "I live it every day, too. And when we get together, I drink my bourbon and he drinks his rum-and-coke, and we don't waste that time talking about politics."

High-ranking military officers are expected to avoid partisanship. They have to serve whomever becomes commander-in-chief; they have to appeal to both sides of Congress for budget allotments. But Powell, a registered independent, seemed to carry his lack of partisanship to a near-fetish. On a segment of CBS-TV's "60 Minutes" that aired in January 1992, Powell told of being stopped by an Alabama highway patrolman.

"I came back from Vietnam in 1963, and my wife was still with our young son in Birmingham while I was setting up a home in Fort Benning, Georgia," Powell told correspondent Ed Bradley. "So I used to drive back and forth from Birmingham to Fort Benning on the weekends in a little old German Volkswagen, which were not that common in 1963. And I had my New York state license plates because I'm a New York resident, and I had a political bumper sticker on the bumper which was not the prevailing political sentiment around Sylacauga, Alabama. And I thought I was being stopped for a traffic violation, for speeding, which would have been quite legitimate."

Instead, Powell went on, the highway patrolman was "handing out political bumper stickers of the other persuasion. And so he looked down at me, this young black soldier driving this foreign car with New York license plates and with the wrong bumper sticker. And he just looked down at me and said, 'Boy, you ain't smart enough to be around here. You need to leave.' I said, 'Yes, sir,' and roared off to Fort Benning. That was the last time I ever indicated any kind of political preference as an active-duty officer.''

What Powell would not or could not bring himself to say, despite Bradley's best efforts, was that the state trooper was handing out Barry Goldwater stickers and that the sticker on the back of Powell's own VW read "All the Way with LBJ."

In fact, says retired Army Col. James G. Garvey, who served with Powell at Fort Benning in 1964, "we used to talk about the [Lyndon Johnson-Barry Goldwater] election all the time. Colin was very adamant about his beliefs in Johnson and civil rights. . . . I think even then he was apolitical, but he had his beliefs. He felt Johnson was going to do the right thing. I did not agree with him."

Asked by the author about Powell's political affiliation, Democratic Party chairman Ron Brown says, "I know he's a Democrat." (Powell, Brown, and their wives, both Almas, have a social relationship.) But so cautious is Powell not to express a preference that even Brown's flat assertion needs an instant qualifier: "At least as a younger man, I know he identified himself as a Democrat," Brown adds.

Still, in spite of Powell's determined nonpartisanship and his protestation that "I have no political fire burning in my belly," it had become almost commonplace in Washington to hear the general talked of as a vice-presidential or presidential candidate. Some scenarios had him replacing Dan Quayle as Bush's 1992 running mate. South Central Los Angeles was still on fire on May 3, 1992, when a Jeff MacNelly political cartoon in the Chicago *Tribune* showed a frantic George Bush screaming into the telephone: "Get me Vice-President Colin Powell—*yes*, you heard me right . . ." In the cartoon Bush is being hauled away by looters from a shattered store called "The New World Order." Other scenarios foresaw a Powell run at the Oval Office in 1996, under either political party's banner, perhaps after serving a partial term as governor of or senator from his native New York state.

"It would be fantastic, but I hope he's a Democrat," says Richard Betts, director of the Center for War and Peace at Columbia University, "because I've given up hope that the Democratic party can find someone who can surmount the race problem with Jesse Jackson and the national-security wimp im-

ge. I have no idea what his politics are, but from that Machi-
vellian point of view, I hope he's the Democratic Eisenhower.''

A ranking Republican administration official had his own ideas
or Powell. ''If I were George Bush, I would put him on the
icket [for 1992] and change the entire focus of the Republican
arty. He'd deliver half the blacks.'' Had Bush done so, this
ame official says, Bush could have closed out the Republican
residential field for 1996: ''Quayle is challengeable and there-
ore Bush is not having an heir apparent. Quayle doesn't deter
nyone from getting in the race in 1996.'' Powell, he clearly
mplies, would deter everyone. Not since Dwight David Eisen-
ower has there been a potential national candidate that both
olitical parties seem so anxious to call their own.

Even Dan Quayle's wife, Marilyn, seemed to be uncon-
ciously joining the bandwagon of the man who might someday
ontend with her own husband for the presidency. In *Embrace
he Serpent*, a novel about the overthrow of Fidel Castro that
he had co-authored with her sister, Nancy Northcott, one of
he heroes is a black one-time military leader then serving as a
unior senator from Georgia. Quite naturally, the hero-senator
s a conservative Republican.

A central figure in some of the biggest political slugfests of
he last half-decade and before that a supporting player in many
ther moments of high and bitter controversy, Powell also had
irtually no known enemies—in a town where everyone of con-
equence is disliked by someone else of consequence.

Trouble did not so much surround Colin Powell as it seemed
o summon him to it. He began his second tour in Vietnam in
une 1968 as the executive officer of a brigade of the Americal
Division, three months after a unit of the same brigade, led by
t. William Calley, had committed the massacre at My Lai.
During the Carter administration as then ex-Governor Ronald
Reagan was crisscrossing the country decrying America's lack
f military preparedness, Powell was working in the office of
ecretary of Defense Harold Brown. Later in the same admin-
stration, as fuel prices spiraled upward following the seizing of
J.S. hostages in Tehran and tempers flared once again at the
ation's gas pumps, Powell moved on to become administrative
ssistant to Secretary of Energy Charles Duncan. In the admin-
stration of Ronald Reagan, as the nation went into staggering

debt to fund the weapons buildup, Powell was serving as military assistant to Secretary of Defense Caspar Weinberger. In the same capacity Powell had directed the Army to provide TOW missiles to the Central Intelligence Agency for transshipment through Israel to Iran. Powell was acting at the direction of Weinberger, who in turn was following orders from Ronald Reagan. In time, the complicated missiles-for-hostages-for-covert-funding business would become known as the Iran-contra affair. Yet, though he had been deposed by, among others, Arthur Liman, chief counsel for the select Senate committee investigating the scandal, Powell was spared the potential embarrassment of having to appear before the committee on televised hearings.

Among the final recommendations of the joint congressional committee was that active-duty military officers not be appointed to the politically sensitive post of National Security Adviser to the president. Adm. John Poindexter was cited as an example of the dangers of mixing political allegiance with duty to uniform. Yet on the same day the recommendation was voted on, Reagan named an active-duty officer—Colin Powell—to that position, to succeed Frank Carlucci.

All of that, of course, says nothing more than that Colin Powell has been heavily involved in the history of his times; he is a "player" in the sports parlance that Washingtonians are fond of using. Yet it would be difficult if not impossible to find another major player in current events who has suffered less abuse among the usually jaundiced Washington press corps. There are, perhaps, questions, if not about Powell in particular, then about the messages that a career path such as his sends down the line to young officers just starting their service. Powell has risen to the top of the military mostly through Pentagon and White House postings, not field commands. The moral for young officers, says retired Navy Adm. Eugene Carroll of the Center for Defense Information, can be found in a Gilbert and Sullivan lyric: "If you be the ruler of the Queen's Navee, never, never go to sea." Powell was also relatively untouched by the controversy that emerged over whether he had confided his preference for economic sanctions against Iraq to Washington Post reporter Bob Woodward—for his book, *The Commanders*—without similarly pressing his preference in the high war councils of the White House or with key senators and congressmen. (As will be seen later, Powell disputes Woodward's account.) Even when the inevitable revisionism set in after the glow of victory in the Persian Gulf War—Saddam Hussein, after all, remained in power in Baghdad—Powell appeared mostly immune to the sting.

"An awful lot of people are totally unable to feel that there can be a completely unvarnished, favorable picture of anybody," says Powell's former boss, Caspar Weinberger, "so they're always looking for anything bad to say. But Colin is a person about whom there *is* nothing bad to say."

"You have to be a mean son of a bitch to criticize him at all," Admiral Carroll admits. "One of the reasons people always call me is that I'm one of the few people who will do it for attribution."

If Ronald Reagan had been Teflon-coated, Colin Powell was bulletproof—unassailed and unassailable. About the worst thing one could read about him was a small item in the January, 1992, *Washingtonian* magazine, noting that Powell supposedly had snubbed the wife of a State Department official at a diplomatic reception. Predictably in the hypersensitive environment of the nation's capital, no sooner had the offending item hit the newsstands than Lynda Webster, the wife of ex-CIA Director William Webster, wrote columnist Chuck Conconi to say that his item contained "incredibly false information about a truly kind, delightful, personable, good person." Mrs. Webster forwarded a copy of her letter to Powell.

"I think he's one of the most warm and gentle and kind human beings I've ever met," Mrs. Webster says. "Whoever that woman was, the fact she may have been overlooked is just too bad. He's very genuine; his eye contact is good. He's very attentive when you talk, whether you have anything interesting to say or not . . . He's the type of guy I'd like to have for my neighbor. He'd bring over steaks, and I'd bring over cookies."

As for the gossip-column item on the snub, Mrs. Webster says, Powell "shrugged it off. He said, 'Well, I guess out of the ten thousand people I meet a day, I didn't smile back at someone.' I was more heated about it than he was."

In a society still far from color-blind, perhaps the most inescapable fact of Colin Powell is that he is a black American.

"Racism still exists in this country," Powell told a group of Vancouver, Washington, students in late 1991. "It is not something in history. I have been thrown out of hot dog stands in Georgia when I was a young captain just coming home from a year in Vietnam. So that still exists in this country. And the way I deal with it is, 'I'm going to beat you. I don't care what you think of me; I don't care what you think about my background or whether I'm black, I'm white, I'm yellow. You're going to have to beat me, as they say in basketball, in my face.' ''

Yet if Powell has refused to use his race as an excuse, it has been the source of both irony and occasional unease. Raised in a household where, he says, Jamaica was considered home, he was the chief military adviser to a president intent upon interdicting and returning black would-be immigrants from another Caribbean nation—Haiti. Appearing on Black Entertainment Television's "Lead Story" in January, 1992, Powell was asked if the Haitian refugees would have been treated differently had they been white Europeans. "We were trying to apply immigration rules as they were written by Congress," answered Powell, who is rarely impolitic and was certainly not so in this case.

The first African-American to hold the position of chairman of the Joint Chiefs of Staff, possibly some day the first black to be elevated to the nation's highest rank of five-star general, Powell also found himself having to defend the military against charges that it was putting too many black lives on the line in Operation Desert Storm.

"I was challenged on more than one occasion to justify why there was such a disproportionate number of blacks [serving with the military in the Gulf War]. And I was often asked, 'Isn't that wrong?' '' Powell told the August, 1991, national convention of the Tuskegee Airmen, the all-black crew of World War II fighter pilots. "My answer was, 'No.' The Armed Forces of the United States offer an opportunity for anyone willing to serve—opportunities not found in enough of the other sectors of our society. I'm glad that all kinds of Americans seek that opportunity to serve, and especially black Americans. So I'm not apologetic about it at all. I'm damn proud of it, and you should be also. My answer to the charge of disproportion is simple. Don't criticize the military. Go ask the rest of institutional and corporate America, ask them why they have not learned from the Tuskegee Airmen and our black Desert Storm heroes that men and women of color can do anything if they are given the opportunity, the training.''

Yet with the collapse of the Soviet Union and domestic pressure to reap a budgetary "peace dividend" from downsizing the military, Powell did find himself charged with partially closing the gate he had passed through.

Black Americans and their often stormy relationship with the military Powell serves in are clearly subjects that bring the inner man close to the surface. Kenneth Adelman recalls being at a spring, 1991, Washington seminar for the Young Presidents Organization when Powell was asked for his reaction to the fact that the Congressional Black Caucus—the group of black lawmakers in the House and Senate—had voted unanimously against military intervention in the Gulf. "It was very wrenching, you could see," Adelman says. "It was like Kissinger when people accused him in office of being unsympathetic to Israel, of hiding his Jewishness. Colin gave some reasons—the leadership was still in the 1968 period and so on. But a lot of noises were saying, God, it hurts."

Powell found himself, too, serving an administration that many black Americans were at odds with. Powell was a jewel in the crown of a president who had fashioned part of his winning 1988 campaign out of the racially inflammatory issue of Willie Horton, the escaped black convict who had raped and murdered a Maryland housewife. Privately, Powell was said to be upset by the way the Willie Horton episode had been exploited by Bush's campaign planners—one acquaintance of long standing says it is "very valid" that Powell was troubled by the matter. Jesse Jackson adds that Powell's "distaste for the Willie Horton campaign is fairly well known. He has a sense of dignity that he doesn't negotiate away." But Powell's reserves were private, not for attribution. His rabbis in government service—the mentors and watchers who had helped move his political career along, who had consistently called him back from military postings to ever more important administration positions—were mostly white Nixonian Republicans. His "godfather of all godfathers," in Powell's words, was Frank Carlucci, whose G.O.P. service dates back to the Eisenhower administration.

As much as Powell seemed a man without politics, or a man of all political persuasions, so too he seemed to much of the public a man without a race, or a man of all races. He was arguably the first black ever to rise to national prominence who was thought of primarily for what he did, not what he was racially. In terms of cultural and social evolution, he was a dramatic step forward for American society.

"In the eyes of white Americans, being black encapsulates your identity," the political scientist Andrew Hacker wrote in *Two Nations*, his 1992 study of race in America. "No other racial or national origin is seen as having so pervasive a personality or character. Even if you write a book on Euclidean algorithms or Renaissance sculpture, you will still be described as a black author. Although you are a native American, with a longer lineage than most, you will never be accorded full membership in the nation or society."

Yet in Colin Powell, America seemed to have passed beyond that. Here, perhaps, and at long last, was a black person the public was ready to judge on merit alone. Here, perhaps, was the fulfillment of Martin Luther King, Jr.'s dream: "that my four little children will one day live in a nation where they will not be judged by the color of their skin but by the content of their character." Others in public life had come close: Ralph Bunche, the United Nations delegate; perhaps Massachusetts Sen. Edward Brooke. But none had done so as convincingly as Colin Powell.

"He's totally transcended this issue of race," says Oklahoma Rep. David McCurdy, a member of the House Armed Services Committee. "You don't think of him as anything other than a four-star general, and a damn good one. He's such a tremendous role model from the standpoint that his race is not his identity. It's not the role he's played."

Powell seems to be the opportunity-society come to life, fulfilled to promise. "You've done well," Maryland Rep. Beverly Byron said to Powell, after he had testified before a subcommittee she sat on.

"I ain't done bad," he noted.

"Where did it come from?" Powell's friend Harlan Ullman asks. "You have this black kid who was born poor in the Bronx who goes through City College, and all of a sudden you have this extraordinary persona who can charm Mikhail Gorbachev, Ronald Reagan, and members of Congress. Where did it come from? How did he get it?"

One place it came from is today as mean a patch of urban turf as exists in the United States of America.

CHAPTER 1

Fort Apache

> "See, this isn't a police station, Captain. It's a fort in
> hostile territory."
>
> —*Fort Apache, the Bronx*

Of all the hard-boiled police films of the last several decades,
David Susskind's *Fort Apache, the Bronx*—the 1981 urban *noir*
movie starring Paul Newman and Ed Asner—may be the most
dispiriting. The good people can't escape: Isabella, the hard-
working nurse played by Rachel Ticotin, dies of a massive, self-
administered drug overdose near the movie's end. The bad
people are beyond resurrection: an angel-dust addict who kills
without motive or even awareness, a policeman who pitches a
teenage boy from the top of an apartment building with neither
provocation nor remorse. The setting—the Hunts Point section
of the South Bronx—seems far closer to modern Beirut than to
anything domestic: block after block of burned-out tenements,
field after field of raw rubble. John Alcott's bleak cinematog-
raphy paints a hell for modern times, an apocalyptic streetscape.
If anything, the script—from Heywood Gould's novel of the same
name—is bleaker still.

"You got a forty-block area with seventy thousand people
packed in like sardines, smelling each other's shit like cock-
roaches, and that's Dugan's fault," Dugan, the retiring precinct
captain (played by Sully Boyar), tells his replacement, played
by Asner. "You got the lowest income per capita, the highest
rate of unemployment in the city, and that's my fault. Why aren't
I out there getting all these people jobs? The largest proportion
of non-English-speaking population in the city—Dugan's fault.
Why aren't I out there teaching them to speak English? . . .

Families that have been on welfare for three generations. Youth gangs. Junkies. Pimps. Hookers. Maniacs. Cop killers.''

The movie opens and closes with the same aerial view—looking southwest over the top of Hunts Point to the gleaming towers of Manhattan in the distance. Had the cameras turned east instead, they would have come to another New York landmark perhaps more familiar to the people of the South Bronx—Rikers Island, off the tip of Hunts Point, and the vast city prison that sits on it. And although the new captain vows to clean up the precinct, the message is still unmistakable: the young people of Hunts Point have far less chance of making it to the financial temples of Manhattan than they do of making it to the human warehouse on Rikers Island.

''Fort Apache'' is the nickname for New York's Forty-first Precinct headquarters, the Simpson Street station. Colin Powell grew up a few blocks away, at 952 Kelly Street. Only four decades before the Powells moved to the South Bronx—to Fox Street in 1940, when Colin Powell was two years old, and then a short distance to Kelly Street in 1942—the area had been farmland and country estates for city capitalists. Within fifteen years of their leaving—Powell's parents to Queens in 1956 and Powell to the Army two years later—the South Bronx had become the nation's worst inner-city nightmare. In less than a century, the area had managed to squeeze into itself an entire history of urban America, a model of everything that can be right and everything that is often so terribly wrong with the American urban experience.

The Bronx—the New York City borough that became the springboard for immigrant ambitions and, later, their black hole—was named for Jonas Bronck.

''It was referred to as the Bronck's Land,'' says local historian Robert Kornfeld. ''He's a somewhat enigmatic figure who was thought to be probably Swedish. He bought something like five hundred acres, which was in the South Bronx. He built his house, Emmaus, on the Harlem River, where Brook Avenue now meets the river. Bronck bought the land in 1639 and died several years later. Then it was bought by the Morris family.''

The Morrises—later to produce Gouverneur Morris, a leading financier and signer of the Declaration of Independence—are only one of the notable names of the early colonial period associated with the Bronx. Anne Hutchinson, one of the founders of Rhode Island, bought much of what is now the East Bronx in 1642 after the death of her husband and set herself up in farming. Within a year, though, she was killed by Indians. In the Massachusetts Bay Colony, from which she had earlier been expelled for questioning the Puritan orthodoxy, the murder was hailed as an act of "divine providence." Her name survives today in the Hutchinson River and a parkway that cuts through the East Bronx headed for Westchester County. Hutchinson's land, in turn, was bought by Thomas Pell, whose direct descendant Claiborne Pell has been for many years a United States senator from Rhode Island and chairman of its Foreign Relations Committee. Two decades later, Edward Jessup and John Richardson bought from the indigenous native Americans a peninsula that they had called Quinnahung, for "long, high place"; five years after that, in 1668, Edward Jessup's daughter, Elizabeth, was married to Thomas Hunt, from whom the Hunts Point area of the South Bronx derives its name.

A little over a century later, according to Prof. Lloyd Ultan of the Bronx County Historical Society, occurred the first recorded incidence of what would later become a commonplace of the South Bronx—a mugging.

"In November 1783 . . . the British were evacuating Westchester County," Ultan told reporter John Lewis of the New York *Daily News*. "They had notified the governor of New York State, but he did not get the letter until three days later and during the interval there was no government there at all. A militiaman, Israel Honeywell, came down from Westchester with a group of horsemen and encountered a sixty-year-old member of the Hunt family. They barged into his house and demanded ten dollars. 'I haven't got ten dollars,' Hunt replied, so they beat him, broke his furniture, and left him there. I would call that a mugging."

Toward the end of the next century, as the population of New York City swelled geometrically—from 515,394 in 1850 to 942,292 in 1870 and again to 1.4 million in 1890—wealthy Manhattanites such as the Tiffanys, Foxes, and Simpsons, families whose presence there survives now only in street names, began buying up the farmland of Hunts Point and cutting it up into weekend and summer estates, where they could escape the teeming bustle of Manhattan. Yet by 1900, only four decades before the Powells would move into its tenement-packed streets,

Hunts Point and the whole of the South Bronx were still largely as they had been for decades.

"Hunts Point at the turn of the century was beautiful," Edward J. Duffy, whose father had been a local dairyman, recalled for the Bronx County Historical Society Journal in 1965. ". . . It consisted of large estates with well-kept mansions and grounds . . . At the end of the old, rambling Hunts Point Road was the old Hunt mansion built in the early part of 1700. This mansion, as I remember it, was partly built of rough stone and lumber. At the east end, there was a tower about forty feet high that resembled a fort. It had windows on several sides which were probably used as lookouts to guard against raids by Indians or by pirates on the [Long Island] Sound."

About 1906, Duffy recalled, P.S. 39 was opened at Kelly Street and Longwood Avenue in Hunts Point—a few blocks from the apartment where Colin Powell grew up and his elementary school. Among the children in the community were two boys whose father was a warden on Rikers Island. They "had to row a boat about a mile across the East River and then walk about eight blocks to school."

Southern Boulevard, still a central local route in the South Bronx, "was the main thoroughfare at that time," Duffy recalled, "and it was a dirt road up to 1907. By that time the traffic was getting heavy with the farmers coming down from Hunts Point, Union Port, Classon Point, and other parts of the Bronx with heavy loads of vegetables. The dirt road made it tough pulling for the horses. Therefore the city had the road paved with asphalt blocks, which made good riding for trucks, bicycles, and autos, which were just coming along at that time. About 1904, there were only three houses on Southern Boulevard between 149th Street and Westchester Avenue"—a stretch of ten blocks.

Soon thereafter, with the arrival of the Interboro Rapid Transit line connecting the South Bronx to Manhattan and through it to Brooklyn, the pastoral years passed forever. By the start of World War I nearly all the old mansions of Hunts Point had been demolished. Thomas Hunt's imposing house was knocked down in 1906 and its site eventually taken over by a massive gas plant run by the Con Edison Company. In place of the country estates rose the occasional single-family frame Victorian house and row of brownstones. Mostly what arose, though, were block upon block of apartment buildings, extending further north as each new subway stop opened. Mass transit turned the Bronx into New York's first suburb, its first bedroom community. By the end of World War I, the great internal migration of New Yorkers had begun—a migration in some ways nearly as profound as the transatlantic migrations that had brought so many of them to the New World in the first place.

The first human wave to ride the subway out to the South Bronx was largely Jewish, refugees from the tenements of Manhattan's Lower East Side. Among them was a very young girl named Frances Sheer, whose family moved into a first-floor apartment at 952 Kelly Street at the start of the 1920s, two decades before the Powell family arrived there.

"I think it was the same apartment," Sheer says. (It wasn't; the Powells lived on the third floor of the four-story building.) "My family moved from the Lower East Side about 1917 or 1918. We moved in with my grandmother, then moved next door [on Kelly Street] to a larger apartment. It was beautiful—a seven-room apartment; the whole section on that side of the street were sixes and sevens. They were railroad, but not small. We had a Polish superintendent. George Raft's mother was superintendent of a larger apartment house across the street. Hunts Point still had many farms then. It was a lovely, intimate neighborhood. We remained friends for years and years after we had all moved away.

"When I went to junior high school in the 1930s, we had one black girl in the class—it was an all-girls school—and we had some Italians, who lived on the other side of Westchester Avenue. But it was a mostly Jewish neighborhood. They came from the Lower East Side, basically. They raised themselves by the bootstraps. My uncle had his office at 940 Kelly Street. He was a dentist by the age of nineteen—he'd completed college by then, he was that brilliant."

If the neighborhood was to remain a bootstrap one, a place where immigrant families struggled to raise themselves to the middle class, it was not to remain a mostly white or a mostly Jewish one for much longer.

Colin Powell, his sister Marilyn—older by nearly six years—and his parents, Luther Theophilus and Maud Ariel McKoy

Powell, were in the vanguard of the second great wave of migration to the South Bronx.

Both born in Jamaica, Luther and Maud Powell emigrated separately to the United States in the early 1920s, settling with cousins and extended family in the growing West Indian community in Harlem. There, the two met, married, found work in New York's garment district, and set up house in an apartment on Morningside Avenue across from Morningside Park in Harlem, where Powell and his sister were both born.

"They met at Pelham Bay Park on a picnic," Powell's sister, Marilyn Berns, now a schoolteacher in Orange County, California, says. "It was a little island. We thought it was very amusing."

"They came in the early nineteen-twenties," Powell said of his parents in a 1990 interview for *Washingtonian* magazine. "I've learned more about their early years in the United States in recent years. As my name has become a little more familiar around the countryside, people have said I remember that family. . . . People have sent me pictures of my father taken when he was a very young man in Connecticut. When he first arrived in the country, he was working up there as day labor. . . .

"In the case of my mother, my maternal grandmother left first. I'm not clear of the trail she took, but she went to Panama and worked for a while, and she went to Cuba and worked for a while. She was separated from her husband and had six or seven kids, and she finally made her way through Connecticut to New York City, bringing one daughter with her and leaving all her other children, four other daughters and three sons, back in Jamaica. . . . Ultimately a second daughter joined, but all of the other children remained in Jamaica. Whether she eventually planned to bring them all up or not, I don't know. I don't think so. She died in the late [nineteen-]forties. So the family remained separated with the two sisters in New York and all of the others in Jamaica. But although separated, it was as close a family as you could have because they traveled back and forth. The saying in New York is, 'I'm going home,' meaning I'm going back to Jamaica to see the others.

"My father's side was the same way. He came and his sister came, but they left all of their siblings back in Jamaica. But over the years I got to know all of them. The cousins then started to migrate back and forth as they left Jamaica to go get educated in England or educated in Canada or educated in the United States, so all of the cousins are extremely close, and we know each other."

Powell first visited Jamaica in 1961 at the age of twenty-four. "I finally decided that I had to see this place called 'home,'" he told a reporter for the Kingston, Jamaica, *Sunday Gleaner* Magazine. "I visited all my ancestral homes in Top Hill and Mandeville, Spur Tree and Kingston, and had an absolutely wonderful time. My grandparents were dead by then, but I saw where they were buried in Top Hill."

Still, as is common with families descended from slaves, the paper trail of ancestry dries up in a hurry. During a January, 1992, trip to Jamaica, Marilyn Berns says that she tried to dig into the family history.

"We can't go back more than two or three generations, and everything blocks up back there. Our maternal grandfather was the overseer on a [sugar] plantation. I don't have the dates. I'm relying on aunts. One is ninety; the other, in her eighties. Their memories are good, but they didn't pay a lot of attention. No one did back then. My mother died in nineteen eighty-four at the age of eighty-three and a half; she'd be ninety-one or ninety-two now. We're going back into the late eighteen hundreds.

"My father's side were from Saint Elizabeth, an area called Top Hill, a very rural area. They farmed. I went to visit the area and see the few people who are left up there. It's a very beautiful area scenically. Where my father's people came from is a very remote area, even right now. If you put yourself back in time, how remote it must have been back then. I don't think he came directly from there. I think he came from Christiana to New York City."

Eppie Edwards of the National Library of Jamaica says simply that "it is not likely that much would have been documented on earlier members of [Luther Powell's] family. Top Hill was populated then by peasant farmers for the most part, whose activities went unnoticed."

The British abolished the slave trade in all their colonies in 1807, more than half a century before the Civil War brought the trade in human chattel to a halt in the United States. In 1833 Jamaican slaves were emancipated—with compensation of nineteen pounds per slave awarded to their former planter-owners, and in 1838, after a five-year "apprenticeship," the slaves were effectively freed. Many left the lowland plantations and became small farmers in the hilly interior of the island, in areas such as Saint Elizabeth and Top Hill. Quite likely Luther Powell's lineage traces back to those early freed-man peasant farmers.

In New York, Luther Powell became a shipping clerk for a firm named Gaines in the garment district of Manhattan. He worked there for twenty-three years until Gaines went out of business; then he found similar work for a textile firm. Maud Powell worked for garment district firms as a seamstress.

"She did piecework at home," Colin Powell says in an interview with the author. "You did the work, and you cut off part of a tag that was on the garment, and that was your receipt—that meant you had done the work. My early memories are of watching her on Thursday night sitting at the kitchen table, bundling up all these little tags and putting rubber bands around them. That's how she got paid. She'd take them in the next morning, down to the garment district, and present them as evidence of what she had done the previous week."

His father, Powell says with a wry laugh, "was sort of in management whereas my mother was in labor. Here's this old man who was a shipping clerk, but I think we called him a foreman at one time—head of the shipping department. And there was always a little thing in the family that I wasn't that conscious of at the time that my mother was the laborer in the family and my father was the manager. My mother used to get even, though, because my father didn't finish high school and she did. Every now and then you would hear under her breath, never out loud, 'Him who never finished high school.'

"My parents were hard-working people," Colin Powell told *Parade* magazine reporter David Wallechinsky. "My father was gone all day, every day. He never came home before seven or eight at night. My mother came home tired, too."

Luther Powell served as a senior warden at Saint Margaret's Episcopal Church in the neighborhood—a legacy of his and Maud Powell's background in the high Anglican church in Jamaica. Colin Powell's childhood friend Tony Grant remembers Luther Powell as "always with a suit and tie and jacket on. Colin's parents were lovely people, religious people. They made sure Colin got his religious training." Occasionally, on the side, Luther Powell sold clothing out of his apartment.

The Powells' cousin, Jacqueline Lopez, a psychologist at New

York University, recalls buying her first dress suit from Luther Powell. "I guess I was about sixteen. 'Uncle' Luther sold me the very first suit I ever had." During the transaction, she recalls, "there was this little pale skinny kid hanging around in the background." It was her only memory of having seen her cousin Colin until they both attended a dinner at New York's Harvard Club in the late 1980s.

"I think probably it was at the end of the season," Marilyn Berns says of her father's side business. "They had extra garments. They would sell them out, heavily discounted . . . My father was a very much loved man, very outgoing and caring and compassionate. People just adored him."

Though other cousins who had emigrated from Jamaica to New York would go on to more prestigious jobs and greater wealth, Luther Powell remained a commanding figure in the extended family, Colin Powell says.

"He was only about five-three or five-four, a little man, but he was a patriarch because of his wisdom, because of his willingness to help anybody who needed help. He loved people. He would do anything to help them. He would drive my mother crazy helping people. At Christmas he would invite the garbagemen in, not only to tip them—you had to tip the garbagemen in New York in those days. My mother would be getting ready for Christmas dinner, and here were all the garbagemen in the kitchen, drinking with my father. To me it was wonderful. To her, it was 'him who never graduated from high school.' But the garbagemen would do anything for him. The mailmen, the garbagemen, anybody he ever knew—Luther was a soft touch. But it was for that reason people were always coming to him. When he said there was going to be a family party and you were invited to his house, you came to his house."

Alma Powell recalls a visit she and her husband made to the senior Powells: "One day I was in the kitchen, and the oil man came to fill up the tank. Luther came in. 'Here, make some coffee; the oil man's here.' And they'd sit down at the table and have a high old time. One day when [Colin and I] had moved out to [the northern Virginia suburb of] Burke, I looked out the window, and there's Colin leaning on his mailbox, just standing out there waiting to talk to whoever came by. And I thought, well, Luther, you're back!"

Luther Powell died in 1978 of cancer. By then his son was a

full colonel in the United States Army, a year away from his first star. By then, too, the Hunts Point area of the South Bronx that Luther Powell had moved his family to in 1940 was a burned-out ruin. Maud Powell would live to see her son become a general.

"When the Powells moved out of Harlem and came to the Bronx, they came to a better neighborhood," says Elias Karmon, an amateur historian of the area who opened his Hollywood Clothing store at 904 Prospect Avenue—several blocks from the Powell's apartment—in 1940. "It was still primarily Jewish. When I went into the clothing business, I had all Jewish names with a few Greek and Italian and a few blacks."

Eventually, Karmon says, Colin Powell became a customer of Hollywood Clothing. "I remember him, but I wonder if he remembers me. I think if I told him who I was and the store, he would acknowledge it. He was a young man, going to City College. . . . He was a busy fellow. I was always proud of anybody who went to college, and I remember talking to him. . . . I had letter cards for everyone who ever came in the store. Only a few years ago, I destroyed them. Now I feel sorry. Imagine, I had his history on the card—what he purchased, how he paid." That someone could see value in such a minor artifact is a testament to how far Colin Powell has come in the forty years since he shopped at Hollywood Clothing.

In the years during and just after World War II, Hunts Point was a safe place to live and work, Karmon says.

"I opened in the mornings as early as eight o'clock, and I would close at midnight—if I wasn't paying attention it would be twelve-thirty. We had women and men of all colors get off the trains, which stopped a block away, and walk home. They had checks in their pockets, and I would cash the checks. They'd walk home with that cash in their pockets, and nobody would attack anybody."

But change was coming. By the end of the 1940s and early 1950s, "the neighborhood might have been thirty to thirty-five percent black and Hispanic," says Barry Schweid, State Department correspondent for the Associated Press, who grew up in Hunts Point. "On my own block, weirdly enough, there was one apartment that was totally black. They were 'schoolteachers,' middle-class black folks. There were always two Irish and four Italians, but it was predominantly Jewish. Hunts Point was its own community. It had a hospital and a terrific library.''

In less than a decade the largely Jewish flavor of Hunts Point would simply disappear. The rising national prosperity in the decade after World War II provided the means for moving on for those with some access to the fast-filling pot of gold. New York's constantly expanding suburbs provided a place to go. What had been only two generations earlier a fringe, almost rural community found itself a decaying part of the inner city. "Everybody moved overnight," Schweid says. "I went into the army in 1954, came back in 1956, and everything was gone. The synagogues were closing up."

The Jews of Hunts Point, Elias Karmon remembers, "went to North Bronx, to Pelham Parkway, where I am now, to different areas; and a lot of them moved to Queens. If you had a couple more bucks, you would go to Westchester [County].''

Luther and Maud Powell moved away at the same time, following many of their Jewish neighbors. "My parents worked hard, and finally put aside a few dollars and bought a home of their own out in Queens . . . a little bungalow that they cherished so much for many years until they died," Powell told the *Sunday Gleaner* magazine of Kingston, Jamaica, in 1988.

By then, though, it must have seemed less a move than a preemptive escape. Just as the Powells were among the early blacks to leave Harlem for the relative comfort of Hunts Point—a trend that accelerated after the Harlem riots of 1943—so they were among the black families who could get out of the South Bronx before it went into free-fall.

"Somewhere in the early nineteen-forties to the early nineteen-fifties, the hue of the area began to darken," says John Redic, executive director of the Longwood Historic District Community Association, which includes Powell's old Kelly Street neighborhood. "It was done by Puerto Ricans and other persons of Spanish extraction moving in, along with the exceptional African-American who had acquired the money to afford to move in. As that happened, it upset the balance. Some of the more affluent persons ran further north—it was a very, very slow change. Over a period of time it was a trickle; then there was a mass exodus. By the nineteen-sixties, the area went from being almost exclusively Caucasian or persons of white complexion to just a few diehards."

Today, Redic estimates, the neighborhood is about three percent Caucasian, seventy-five percent Hispanic, and the rest African-American. But the percentages tell only a minor part of the story. As Hunts Point changed complexion, its economic base crumbled, and with that came a catalogue of nearly every ill that can befall an urban area, nearly all of them magnified to the breaking point.

The single-family brownstones and handsome turn-of-the-century Victorian frame houses scattered among the apartment buildings on Intervale and Westchester avenues and Southern Boulevard fell vacant and became unsellable. "They were gorgeous homes," says John Redic, whose historic district association now protects some of the surviving structures, "but the people moving in couldn't afford them. Arson became the way to get rid of the property. If you can't get your money, set it on fire and collect from the insurance companies. Whole blocks were decimated by that. We're talking about apartment buildings as well as private residences."

In the North Bronx, the vast Co-op City housing project opened in 1970 and "sucked up people from this neighborhood like a vacuum cleaner," says Getz Obstfeld, the former director of Banana Kelly, a social service and housing organization for the area. (The name comes from the "banana" shape of Kelly Street.) "You had a lot of vacancies. Owners weren't able to make money from their holdings." The solution was to become a familiar one in the South Bronx: "You had a lot of arson and abandonment," Obstfeld said.

Hunts Point residents who wanted to stay in the area found the doors to subsidized neighborhood housing closed to them as well, Elias Karmon recalls: "People who had their roots in the community couldn't get into the housing projects, any of them. That was a chronic complaint. I saw that. I was active at that time in the community. It was something I could never understand—why people from Puerto Rico or the South would rate quickly. If they had two little children, they could get two bedrooms. . . . People who wanted to get apartments through the housing authority began burning out their own apartments. They'd find themselves under the care of the Red Cross, and then they could get into the projects. It became an accepted way of doing things."

In the 1950s and '60s Hunts Point had been "the most crowded place in America," Getz Obstfeld says. "There were more people living here per square mile than anywhere else in the country—row upon row of five- and six-story buildings with immigrant families living doubled up in apartments."

By the end of the 1970s the Hunts Point neighborhood had one of the lowest, if not the lowest, per-capita incomes in the nation—statistics aren't kept by neighborhood—but it was no longer the nation's most crowded spot. The streetscape had become the familiar one seen by motorists on the Bruckner Expressway, which cuts through Hunts Point a half-dozen blocks from Powell's childhood home: a gap-toothed skyline where buildings had been burned out and demolished. From the ground, it was an urban war zone from which those who could had fled. In 1970, about 95,000 people lived in the area. By 1980, the population had fallen by almost two-thirds, to about 32,000—a clearing almost certainly of historical dimensions in urban America. It was as if some plague, some natural disaster had struck Hunts Point and the South Bronx. To that extent, the overpowering bleakness of *Fort Apache, the Bronx* is verisimilitude, but to some degree the movie was already dated when it first reached theaters in 1981. By then, the Fort Apache police station, which had gotten its nickname after being besieged by an all-night riot, was so surrounded by vacant, rubble-filled lots that it had been rechristened by some the Little House on the Prairie.

For Hunts Point, at least, it was a bottoming-out.

"Growing up in those days, you had to be a survivor," Obstfeld says. "The nineteen-eighties were really a time of rebirth, especially during the second half of the decade when the city decided to take the lead and pump billions of dollars into housing." Today, according to Obstfeld, there isn't a single vacant, city-owned building in the neighborhood surrounding Kelly Street that hasn't been rebuilt or isn't in the pipeline to be rebuilt. Much of the vacant land is being used for new single-family and two-family housing. Still, Obstfeld says, "It's a much more dangerous place than it was when Colin Powell was growing up. If parents want their kids to get ahead, they have to keep them inside. Kids who are going to make it out of here—to be successful—are fixed on school. After school, they go to the library. When they get out of there, they come home."

Izetta Skelton was living in one of those rehabilitated Kelly

Street apartment buildings when *Newsday* reporter Michael
Powell (no relation) interviewed her in September, 1989. Like
Luther and Maud Powell, Skelton had emigrated from the West
Indies in 1968 in search of prosperity—"a meat bone," she
said, "that turned out to be a shadow."

"The young ones," she said of today's children of Kelly
Street, "there are so many but they don't finish school. They
work at McDonalds or sell drugs and that's no way out." Still,
Skelton, who was working as a cleaning woman, is evidence of
why the immigrant dream is so abiding: at the time she was
interviewed, her three children were all in college.

In mid-April, 1991, a month and a half after Allied forces had
expelled Saddam Hussein's army from Kuwait, Colin Powell
returned to the South Bronx as one of the most celebrated military leaders in modern history, living proof of the dreams that
Izetta Skelton and other Hunts Point parents harbor for their
children. He began his visit with a tour of the last major defense
contractor left in New York City, the Loral Corporation Defense
Electronic Manufacturing plant in the Bronx, where radar-
warning systems used by U.S. aircraft during Operation Desert
Storm had been produced. During the visit, Loral executives
told Powell they were establishing a $6,000 annual scholarship
in his name so that a graduate of his high school, Morris High,
could attend his other alma mater, City College.

From there Powell went to the fortresslike Morris High School
at 166th Street and Boston Road, where he urged the students
to stay in school. "If you don't get that high-school diploma,"
Powell told them, "you're on your way to nowhere. You're on
your way to the dead end. In fact, if you don't get that high-
school diploma, you probably can't even get into my Army these
days. . . . Over ninety-seven percent of the G.I.'s who are serving have their high-school diploma." The reason the Army almost demands a diploma these days is simple, Powell went on.
It's proof that the person who earned it is "somebody who will
stick to the task given. Somebody who, growing in their life at
age fourteen, fifteen, sixteen, seventeen, when faced with a
challenge of hard work, of study, of commitment, of responsibility . . . met the challenge, stayed in high school, and got that
diploma. It shows that you can overcome obstacles."

Powell's visit to the school was his first since he had graduated nearly thirty-seven years earlier. "I remember this place," he told the students. "I remember . . . the route I used to take each day from my home on Kelly Street to school. I also remember, upon occasion, experiencing the feeling 'you can't make it.' But you can. When I was coming up, opportunities were limited. But now the opportunities are there to be anything you want to be. But wanting to be isn't enough, dreaming about it isn't enough. You've got to study for it, work for it, fight for it with all your heart, energy, and soul, so that nothing will be denied you."

Among those in the audience that day was then-eighteen-year-old Manuel Nunez, who had entered Morris High two years earlier after emigrating with his family from the Honduran capital of Tegucigalpa. In June, 1991, Nunez was named the first winner of the Colin L. Powell Scholarship.

"General Powell is someone to look up to and follow as a role model for all of us as minority students," Nunez wrote in his application essay. "By doing this we could realize that we are not limited in any way in this great country of ours because of our origin, color, or religion. He has proved to all of us that we can fulfill our educational goals. Anyone who says you can't change your future just isn't trying hard enough." In February, 1992, Morris High was able to inform the Loral Corporation that Nunez had achieved a perfect 4.0 average during his first semester at City College. It was a far better average than Powell achieved during his first semester there.

A kind of shrine to Colin Powell, a bulletin board filled with memorabilia of his high-school years and his subsequent career, was still on display in the principal's office at Morris High more than a year after his visit. "Many of the students here now have a sense of hope," assistant principal Gregory Hodge says.

That afternoon, Powell indulged in a time-honored right of heroes—throwing out the first pitch of the home season at the house that Ruth built in the Bronx, Yankee Stadium. The following evening at Manhattan's Waldorf-Astoria Hotel, in an address to the Association for a Better New York, Powell reflected on his visit, the beloved Army that had by then consumed thirty-three years of his life, and the lessons that could be taken from its performance in the Persian Gulf War. It was the sort of speech that makes political consultants weak in their knees when they think of the possibility—however faint—of someday having a

Candidate Powell to run. Were Powell ever to enter politics, it would be the very model of a stump speech, his short-course version of how to make America the place it once was, the place he seems fervently to believe it can be again.

During the war, Powell said, he had watched an episode of ABC-TV's "Prime Time Live" in which Sam Donaldson, on location in Saudi Arabia, interviewed some members of a tank company of the First Armored Division—part of the Army's VII Corps, which had just been flown in from Germany.

"First you see an Asian-American soldier," Powell said. "Then there's a white American sergeant who says a few words, and then a black soldier—an Afro-American—and then another white soldier, and then an old grizzled black sergeant who says a few words, and finally another white soldier who says he's from Texas. He concludes the little piece by saying that he's honored to be an American and honored to be in the United States Army. But it's the first black soldier who said something that was so significant to me.

"He looked like he was about nineteen years old. His language wasn't perfect but he was articulate. And he sat there, on a case of rations, and behind him you could see the other troops in his platoon standing there. You could see that they were white and they were black and that they were a family. Here's what that young soldier said: 'We've all been through the same training, and it instills confidence inside you and lets you know that no matter what it comes down to, you're around family. All of us are family. All these guys right here are my family.' And then you hear the grunts and shouts of his buddies. And you're familiar with what our troops today now say: 'Huu-ahh! Huu-ahh!' You've heard it on a thousand interviews. All of those young teenagers, my kids, bonded together as a family, knowing they were going to face danger, said 'Huu-ahh.'

"The bond in that family of soldiers, tankers awash in the middle of a sea of sand, was so strong that they would die for each other. That's what makes a hero. They'll die for each other, and they'll die for their duty. And every year your Armed Forces creates that kind of bonding among about three hundred thousand young men and women who come in and who leave. Young whites who go back to their homes all over this country having been family with young blacks. And young blacks who go back to their homes all over this country having been treated as an equal brother with their white colleagues.

"Look at those youngsters for a moment. You've seen them all over television. They're a cross-section of America. Notwithstanding the prewar pronouncements by so-called demographic experts, these young men and women come from all walks of American life. And they're clean, smart, dedicated, trained, motivated, responsible, reliable, self-confident, selfless, patriotic, drug-free, respectful, tolerant, and caring.

"But wait a minute: Aren't these supposed to be the clumsy, lazy, dumb, untrainable, drugged-up teenagers that aren't ready for the future? Only if you let them."

Powell went on to talk about the methods the armed forces has used to produce the soldiers, sailors, airmen, and marines he clearly is so proud of—everything from high expectations to tough discipline and standards to strict drug testing.

"I'm not going to get into the testing debate on whether it should be used more widely or not," he told the audience, "but in the Army and the other services it's used on a regular, random basis—so random and so regular that I have to stop and tell you a short story about something that happened two days after President Bush had nominated me to be Chairman of the Joint Chiefs of Staff.

"I had returned to my headquarters in Atlanta [where he was briefly head of Forces Command], and I was preparing to close down that office and get ready for my new responsibilities as Chairman. My secretary walked in—a charming southern lady of gentle birth—and she was flustered. And she said, 'A lieutenant is here.'

" 'What lieutenant?' I asked. She said, 'The company executive officer.' Everybody has to belong in a company somewhere in the Army so we can account for them. Even four-star generals have to be part of the company.

"So the company executive officer was there, and I asked, 'What does he want?' And being the gentle southern lady that she was, she could not bring herself to say. I suspect northern ladies might have had trouble [too]. But ultimately the lieutenant sort of appeared in the doorway and said my name had come up for random testing for drug abuse—a urinalysis. And the young lieutenant had his duty to do, and he didn't care if I was going to be the Chairman of the Joint Chiefs of Staff. My name had come up on the roster, and he was there with his kit and his rubber gloves. As you can see, I passed. That's the kind of approach you have to take to drugs.

"There's one other thing we do that's as important as all the rest of the actions I mentioned," Powell added. "We tell these young Americans that you give to us that we believe in them. We tell them we love them. We tell them we will not let them down or let them fail. They are now part of our family. And we tell them we are very, very proud of them."

Powell then went on to ask rhetorically if the experience of the Army is transferable to the civilian sector. "You bet your life it is," he answered, "and the transfer starts in school. It starts in schools such as Morris High School . . . and at thousands of other such schools across America. In our school, we must have high expectations for our children—parents *and* teachers must have them. We must *want* our children to learn. We must *want* our children to succeed.

"In our schools, we must have discipline and we must have high standards. To enforce that discipline and those high standards we must have a working system of rewards and punishments—a *working* system, not a paper system, and not a system simply to satisfy a bureaucracy. In our schools, what we teach our children must be meaningful; it must conform to the high standards we've set up; and our evaluation of their progress through these standards must be rigorous and demanding.

"In our schools, we must teach our children that alone it is difficult to accomplish things but that together, as a team, as a family, almost anything can be accomplished. The challenges are there to be overcome and not to become a burden to press you into the ground. And in our schools, we need to motivate our children, motivate them to be responsible and accountable for their actions. Eventually they'll learn to motivate themselves."

"I know schools can't be run like an infantry platoon," he concluded, "but it seems to me it was kind of like one when I went to school. But if we can work toward the standards I've just tried to describe to you briefly, I believe America would be well on the way to a twenty-first century full of hope, full of promise and a renewed sense of what matters in life. Like the young black soldier in the desert, we would come to know that we can depend on one another; we would come to know that 'all of us are family.' "

'Family" was a subject Powell would return to shortly after the Los Angeles riots that followed on the heels of the Rodney King verdict. In a May 4, 1992, speech at his wife's alma mater, predominantly black Fisk University in Nashville, Powell told the students: "We all have to live here together—Asian-Americans, African-Americans, all of us. Divided, fighting amongst ourselves, walking separate lines of diversity, we are as weak as newborn babies. Together, intertwining our many differences and diversities into a mosaic of strength, we will prevail over the darkness of racism. I want you to love one another. I want you to respect one another, see the best in each other, share each other's pain and joy." And, Powell added, "I want you to fight racism. I want you to rail against it. We have to make sure that it bleeds to death in this country once and for all."

During that same visit to New York Powell also drove through his old neighborhood on Kelly Street. "It was incredible for me to drive to all of those locations in the Bronx," he told the Association for a Better New York, "and to see the extreme difference in many of the places that I had walked as a child—underneath the Intervale Avenue station again. I went under that station that I had walked under so many, many days when I was late for school. And to see Kelly Street, where I spent so many years, suddenly rising up again out of the ashes. . . . Now it has apartments and people—people living for the future on Kelly Street."

He saw, too, the $7 million Kelly Street Park, adjacent to his old block, forged out of a tract of land that had been vacant and rubble-strewn as late as 1983. What he couldn't visit or even see except in the mind's eye was the apartment building he had grown up in, or the one across the street at 953 Kelly where his childhood friend Tony Grant lived, or the one down the street at 967 Kelly where another friend, Gene Norman, lived. Every one of them had been abandoned, burned out by drug dealers and users, and finally demolished in the great urban *blitzkrieg* that swept through Hunts Point.

CHAPTER 2

Hot Beans and Butter

For all its tortured history, for all the grim documentaries and movies and well-meaning reports that have ground it into the national consciousness and made it a byword for urban blight, there was something close to an idyllic period in the compacted history of Hunts Point and the South Bronx. For a span just shy of two decades, from the onset of World War II to the closing years of the Eisenhower administration, the area was a model of integration, an island of urban safety where family values still held. Before its economic base collapsed, before its small shopkeepers fled, before most of the people remaining there were those with nowhere else to go, Hunts Point was for some—though even then too few—an avenue out of poverty into the economic mainstream. It offered hope that the American experiment was still working. That was the Hunts Point that produced Colin Powell.

"What many people now call a slum was a tenement neighborhood and a neat place to grow up when I was a boy," Powell recalled in 1989 for the Hunts Point and Southern Boulevard *Observer*. "Our favorite pastime was making the walk. We would start at the corner of Kelly, walk up 163rd Street, around Southern Boulevard to Westchester and back down Westchester to Kelly Street. It was an exciting thing to do. Every block along 163rd had a repeating pattern to it. There was always a Jewish bakery, a Puerto Rican grocery, a Jewish candy store, a Chinese laundry, and other specialty stores.

"Southern Boulevard to us was downtown. It had three big movies and small and large stores containing almost every product you could want. As you went back down Westchester Avenue toward Kelly Street, there was a toy store at every corner. Across Westchester Avenue there was a wonderful street of food stores that had the most marvelous selection of fruits and vegetables, meats, candies, cheeses, and everything else you can imagine. The old Tiffany Theater was at the corner of Tiffany and Westchester. It was where we spent every Saturday morning watching B westerns and serials."

Southern Boulevard, Powell's childhood friend and across-the-street neighbor Tony Grant says, "was like the Rodeo Drive of the Bronx. It had all the stores. We'd look at them and wish we could own all those things."

It was "where everyone went," Barry Schweid remembers. "It was the magnet. You went there to pick up girls, to go to the movies. The Hunts Point Palace had big bands, dances, weddings. The first TVs coming in were put in the windows of the stores, and everyone would stand outside and watch them."

"You got your feet fluoroscoped for shoes at the StrideRite on Southern Boulevard," recalls Schweid's sister, Marlene Charnizon, who graduated from Morris High a year behind Powell. "You'd stick your feet in this machine, and you'd see your green feet, and now you're told you'll get cancer from having it done."

The Powells lived on the third story of an eight-family, four-story walk-up apartment building, in a row of four-story buildings along either side of Kelly Street—the height determined at least partially by the fact that city code didn't require elevators in such buildings.

"It was a large apartment, a four-bedroom," Marilyn Berns says. "My grandmother lived with us until I was a teenager; then she went back to Jamaica and stayed there. . . . It was sort of like living in a small town. Each neighborhood had its own character. A lot of relatives and family friends lived in that exact same area. It was at that time a very comfortable place to be brought up."

It was also a place of many tongues—"a multinational neighborhood," according to Tony Grant. "We had one of every kind. If you wanted to eat foreign food, you just found a friend to invite you to dinner. You could eat Italian, Irish, you name it.''

By the 1940s and '50s, Hunts Point had become a union center as well, Grant says. ''If you had a job there in the 1930s, you were fortunate. The start of unionism helped. It was a union neighborhood, a lower-middle-class union neighborhood, if you want to categorize it.'' And though Colin Powell has risen to international prominence through his service in two consecutive conservative Republican administrations, the small world he was raised in was staunchly Democratic.

''There's a park on Southern Boulevard,'' Barry Schweid says, ''although only a New Yorker would call it that. It's a concrete park with benches. The old-timers would stand there and argue about politics and politicians. It was a gathering place, a place for hot political debates.''

Almost every point of view could be heard in the park, except one—the Republican. In the politics of the South Bronx, Schweid says, ''the Republicans finished fifth. The Democrats would run away with everything—they'd get eighty-eight percent of the vote. Then came the liberals. I voted the liberal line in city politics because backing the Democrats meant you were backing the Tammany Hall machine [which had had a revival in 1945, following the reform administration of New York City mayor Fiorello LaGuardia]. For the real left-leaning, there was American Labor. Then came the Fusion Party; then, after that, the Republicans. Who would ever vote for them? Nobody had ever heard of them.''

In his reminiscence for the Hunts Point and Southern Boulevard *Observer*, Powell went on to list his favorite summer activities: stickball, kite-flying off the roofs ''using glass cord and razor tails,'' playing Sluggo, tossing marbles against a cigar box with various-size openings, and shooting checkers made of wax-filled bottle caps. ''You became a big guy when your parents finally got you a two-wheel bike,'' he wrote. ''A two-wheeler meant freedom. You could ride to Pelham Bay Park or over to Hunts Point to go careening down Bank Note Hill [named for the large American Bank Note Company plant, built in 1911, where stock certificates were engraved and printed until the factory finally closed in 1985]. And for a nickel the whole city was at your disposal by trolley or subway.''

And not only the city was accessible by public transport. Gene

Norman remembers that, in addition to flying kites and riding bikes, he and Powell would sometimes take a trolley car to the George Washington Bridge, hike across it, and spend the night camping in what were then the wild woods of New Jersey. In the 1990s, for someone negotiating the near endless approach ramps on the New Jersey side of the George Washington Bridge, it seems a daring act.

There were fights, too, although pale shadows of the violence and ethnic unrest that would sweep over the area in the decades to come. "In that part of New York City, and I think in a lot of the small neighborhoods in New York City, people got along," Powell told *Washingtonian* magazine. "It wasn't complete integration. I mean you essentially had family things to do. You never lost your cultural identity. It wasn't that much of a melting pot. But as far as us getting along together on the streets, we would kid each other, and there would be the usual epithets thrown back and forth from time to time, which sometimes would just be a joke and sometimes would be the basis of a real good fight. So the neighborhood was not without its tension, it was not without drugs, it was not without fighting, it was not without all of the temptations that exist in a city of that size."

As for his own fighting, Powell said that he was protected to an extent by the fact that he was a year or two younger than most of his friends on the block. "I was always sort of a kid. That had advantages and disadvantages. One of the advantages is they tended not to include me in the real troublesome stuff. I was on the outside of that."

Barry Schweid, half a decade older than Powell, recalls gang fights in the local burial ground, Hunt Cemetery: "There were ethnic divisions, but it wasn't black-white tension yet because there weren't that many blacks there. The Irish and Italian kids would go into the cemetery and beat each other up, and maybe the Jews would side with the Irish. But nobody ended up dead. By Powell's time it was beginning to get a little tense."

One element adding to the tension as the 1950s began was the influx of Puerto Ricans into Hunts Point. Novelist Ed Vega, who was born in the mountainous spine of Puerto Rico and would enter Morris High with Colin Powell in 1952, says that by high school two Puerto Rican gangs, the Lightnings and the Rockets, were operating in and around Kelly Street.

"I was friends with one of the Rockets, Peter Mercado, who

lived on Kelly,'' Vega says. ''Being in a gang meant that you defended a turf. It was basically then concerned for the safety of the girls—very macho kind of stuff. . . . People fought and they fought honorably, and once in a while, a horrible thing happened and there was a shooting or someone was stabbed. But it wasn't anything like this today. It was all very honorable.''

Mostly, though, the social center for Hunts Point boys in the 1940s and '50s was the apartment building stoop.

''I counted it up one day,'' says Tony Grant. ''We had approximately thirty-six games we could play, depending on how many guys were sitting on the stoop at the time. Football, baseball, stickball, basketball—we had teams for each one. There was also stoopball, punchball, hide-and-go-seek, and hot beans and butter. For that, you hid an object like a belt. The one who found it was permitted to beat everyone with the belt until they got back to base. Then he would go hide the belt, and it would start all over.''

Grant says that Powell was famous in the neighborhood for a game called ring-a-levio, an inner-city version of capture the flag. ''You chose up sides, maybe four to six on a side. One side ran, and the other side chased. When you caught someone, you put them in a den, an enclosed area of some kind. You could free the people who had been caught on your side by breaking into the den and yelling, 'Free all!' Guys had different ways of trying to break in. Some would be sneaky about it; some would try to negotiate for one or two people. Colin, if he saw someone had been caught, would come flying in with his body from half a block away and free them all.''

Everyone in the neighborhood, Grant says, was ''always in each other's home, and you always had forty or fifty babysitters looking out the window at you. They had no trouble telling your parents when you got out of line.''

It was among the neighborhood boys, too, that Colin Powell was given the modern pronunciation of his first name. The matter had been raised in the *Times of London* in February 1991— during the height of the Gulf War—by the newspaper's chief writer on linguistic affairs, Philip Howard. Powell, Howard told readers, ''pronounces [Colin] with a long *o*, so as to rhyme with bowling.'' The reasons, he speculated, are twofold: ''One is the American wish not to put up with elitist British pronunciations.

The other factor is American individuality and the wish to be different in names."

Several months later, in an April 26, 1991, letter to the *Times of London*, Powell corrected the matter himself. Far from anti-elitism or raw individuality, his pronunciation was derived from an Irish-American fighter pilot who had been killed while bombing a Japanese warship.

"My parents," Powell wrote, "were British subjects, and they named me Colin (KAH-lin). Being British, they knew very well how the name was supposed to be pronounced. But when I was a young boy, there was a famous American World War II hero whose name became very popular in the streets of New York City. He was Capt. Colin P. Kelly, Jr. He was called KOH-lin.

"My friends in the streets of the South Bronx, who heard Captain Kelly's name pronounced on the radio and by their parents and other adults, began to refer to me by the same pronunciation. So, I grew up with my friends saying KOH-lin and my family saying KAH-lin."

That Captain Kelly's last name was the same as the street KOH-lin Powell lived on must have made the New World pronunciation doubly tempting. Nor could it have hurt that from the earliest days that his childhood friends can remember, Powell was, in Gene Norman's words, "always in love with the Army. We grew up at the end of World War II. It was when we became aware of the world and of life."

"My first early memories are of World War II," Powell told *Washingtonian* magazine. "I was four years old when that war started and I was roughly nine years old when it ended. Then a few years later, at the age of thirteen, fourteen, the Korean War broke out, and when the Korean War ended I was graduating from high school. So for a large part of my elementary school days and a large part of my junior-high and high-school days the nation was at war."

Powell "liked the military—the discipline that went along with it," Tony Grant says. "We had our military games. He had a yellow German helmet that a relative had sent him. The ones with the foreign helmets were the bad guys. The good guys would give us three seconds to run, and they would catch us and play a tune on us. That started the seed. . . . The first time we met after thirty years, I told him that he was the only one that I knew without question what his career would be.''

As a boy growing up, Gene Norman says, Powell ''was light-hearted but not frivolous. He had a great sense of humor and still does, but he also has the ability to turn that off when there's a need to become very serious—and he's very serious, deadly serious, no pun intended. As a kid he was like that. When he needed to, when it was important, he could become very seri-ous. The other trait I see in a way as a continuum is that he was fiercely loyal. In those years we were the best of friends, like brothers. I could always count on his loyalty to take my side, and he could always count on mine. You couldn't come between us.''

Powell went to P.S. 39 elementary school, a few blocks down Kelly Street. ''I was in the slow class as a fourth-grader,'' he wrote in the November, 1991, *Guideposts* magazine. Indeed, his sister Marilyn Berns told a Los Angeles *Times* reporter that there were ''no sightings of greatness'' in those early years. ''I was the one who was always asking our mother to read street signs to me and spell words when she was taking me out for a walk. Colin could not have cared less. . . . I guess he was a late bloomer.'' In the great tradition of older sisters, she described her brother in those early years as a ''nuisance.'' Most members of the extended family remember him as simply mild-mannered and quiet.

''Colin was very, very nice; he was always pleasant,'' his older cousin Hugh Lopez recalls. ''I never knew him to say anything disparaging. But he's gotten much more eloquent. His father was very proud of him always, but he overshadowed Colin back then. He was such a lively, invigorating man.''

In 1949 Powell went on to junior high at P.S. 52—then an all-boys school—an expanded universe where he left no particular mark. ''It was a little bit of a tough place,'' Gene Norman, two years Powell's senior, recalls. ''For the first time it made us interact with people outside the neighborhood. It drew from a larger area, and it took a little bit to get acclimated.''

Walter Schwartz, who was Powell's classmate through junior high school, high school, and City College and would later be-come chief scientist for the Loral Defense Electronics Manufac-turing facility, remembers P.S. 52 as ''a dangerous place, a very ough place" without "the calming influence of the opposite sex. . . . There were fights in the halls; teachers got pushed against the wall. The shop teachers used to run around with boards to fend off the aggressors. The principal, it is more than rumored, walked around with a pistol. It was that kind of place."

Morris High, Schwartz says, didn't have that kind of feel. The school, he says, had "three dimensions. The commercial people went on to become secretaries, clerks. In [the] general [track] you were just surviving; you got through. The academic people went on to college, and most of those to City College." In the early and mid-1950s, Schwartz says, getting in to City College required a high-school average of 85, a mid-B. Those who went elsewhere—Columbia University, say, or Fordham—"did it by scholarship unless you had money. And if you were going to school at Morris High, you probably didn't have money."

New school district lines in the South Bronx, redrawn at the start of the decade, had brought into Morris many students who previously would have attended the mostly white and Jewish Monroe High School—the alma mater of Hall of Fame baseball player Hank Greenberg, whose fourteen-year Major League career had ended only a few years earlier in 1947. (Several generations later, modern baseball superstar Bobby Bonilla, who moved from the Pittsburgh Pirates to the New York Mets after the 1991 season, would grow up at 149th and Jackson streets, a Puerto Rican hero for the new population of the South Bronx.) For students such as Marlene Charnizon, who had grown up and gone to elementary and junior high school in the still mostly Jewish sections of Hunts Point and whose brother had attended Monroe High, coming to Morris "was a beginning of contact with black kids, not only with [Colin Powell]. I remember dancing with a black guy—he was teaching me to dance without holding on. . . . Somebody slashed my coat in my locker at Morris High School. There was that kind of vandalism. It wasn't prestigious, but overall it was great."

For those who lived more on the edge at the high school, there was no reward—either from the school or from other students—for their behavior. Novelist Ed Vega remembers being suspended from the school for a fight during his and Powell's tenth-grade year. "I hit someone with a metal tray. He touched my girl, and that was a little too much for me. I dumped the lunch on the floor and hit him with the tray. I cut his ear, and he punched me in the mouth. But, see, that kind of behavior was really frowned upon.''

Charnizon remembers Powell as ''an average, do-the-right-thing kind of guy.'' He was in the school's Service League; he had a brief fling at sports—until, he once told students at the high school, ''I discovered I wasn't very good at cross-country through Van Cortlandt Park, and I quit.'' By his own admission, he didn't set the world on fire academically. His C average stretched the admission criteria for City College. Mostly he seems to have stayed out of trouble. By the time he was in high school, that was becoming harder and harder to do in the South Bronx. Inner cities have a way of predicting where the next wave of bad news is going to come from, even if the nation often steadfastly refuses to hear it. For the young men and women of Hunts Point, the great divide of illegal drugs was arriving.

''The neighborhood in the fifties broke into two parts, the drug scene and the undrug scene,'' Tony Grant says. ''The friendship was still there between both groups, but guys like us just didn't bother with the drug scene. Some of our friends had died of overdoses. The rule then was that if you took marijuana, you became an addict. Then you moved on to heroin, and not being a scientist, you had a good chance of overdosing and dying on it. That started the separation between the two groups.''

''Drugs became increasingly difficult,'' Powell said in the *Washingtonian* interview. ''We knew about marijuana and we knew about heroin. It was commonly known that it was being used around the neighborhood. But for those of us who were a year or so behind the older kids, it wasn't anything we used. For those who were pretty secure in their family life, it wasn't something that was tolerated. But there were a lot of kids in that neighborhood who did not have that kind of support mechanism behind them and did succumb. We had drug overdose deaths back in the late forties and early fifties before it was a national tragedy. It was just something that happened in the inner city and the tenements. It was not a middle-class problem; it was not a problem for the broad population. But it was a problem back then.''

In his April 15, 1991, speech to the students at Morris High, Powell expanded on the subject. Drugs, he told them, ''isn't something that's just been discovered in the last couple of years.

We had lots of drugs in my neighborhood. On every street corner was some pothead or junkie who was trying to sell or deal or get others involved.

"I didn't do it. Never in my life, not even to experiment, not to try, not to see what it would be like, for two reasons. One, my parents would have killed me, but the second reason is that somewhere along the line I and a couple of other of my friends . . . we knew it was stupid. It was stupid. It was the most self-destructive thing you could do with the life that God and your parents had given to you."

Those who did do drugs, Powell went on to tell the students, "have paid the consequences." Of all the kids on Kelly Street, all the boys who sat on their stoops and waited for the next game of stickball or hot beans and butter or ring-a-levio, all the ones who took the walk down Southern Boulevard—of them all only three made it, Powell said: Gene Norman, who became Landmarks Commissioner of the City of New York and later president of the Harlem International Trade Center. Tony Grant, who would become corporation counsel for the city of White Plains, New York. And Colin Powell. The rest, Powell told the students, "went to jail, where they died, or they never were heard from again." As for himself, Powell told a 1990 interviewer, "it took me many years before I was able to reconnect with those kids who had been successful."

Why had he succeeded when so many others had failed? *Washingtonian* interviewer Kenneth Adelman asked. "I credit most of that to my family, to a very close family, a family that had expectations for the children of that family, for acquiring a fairly good education in the public-school system and having a desire to get off the block."

For all the pleasant memories Powell and his friends have of living on Kelly Street in those days, the final measure of success wasn't surviving on the block—it was getting off the block. "Getting to Kelly Street in the Depression was an accomplishment, I guess," Tony Grant says. "But people moved out of Kelly Street. No one moved in unless they had to."

At the age of seventeen Powell found summer work in a local soft-drink bottling plant. The pay, he wrote for the November, 1991, issue of *Guideposts* magazine, was "ninety cents an hour. I was thrilled. On my first day of work, having joined the ranks of other newly hired teenagers, I was full of enthusiasm. The bottling machine caught my eye, but only the white boys worked there. I was hired as a porter, and the foreman handed me a mop. I got to work. I mopped what seemed like acres of sticky, cola-stained floor.''

Rather than resent the work, Powell wrote, ''I decided to be the best mop wielder there ever was. Right to left, left to right. One day someone let fifty cases of cola crash to the cement, and brown sticky foam cascaded across the floor. It was almost more than I could bear. But I kept on mopping. Right to left, left to right.

''At summer's end the foreman said, 'You mop floors pretty good.' ''

'' 'You sure gave me enough opportunity to learn, sir,' I said.''

''Next summer he put me to work loading bottles on the filling machine. The third summer, I was deputy foreman.''

The moral Powell wrote for the religiously oriented magazine is ''that in whatever you do, someone is always watching.''

Powell also worked—for a longer time and for less pay per hour—at Sickser's baby furniture store on the corner of Westchester Avenue and Fox Street about two blocks from the Kelly Street apartment. Lou Kirschner's father-in-law had begun the business in 1913; Kirschner managed it from 1949 until he retired in 1972 and moved to Florida.

''It was a fairly large store—three stories,'' Kirschner says. ''We sold cribs, carriages, and in the Christmas season we took in a big line of toys, that type of thing. We happened to need some help in the store, and he was going someplace—just walking past. We didn't know him, but we asked him to give us a hand. He was a very good worker, worked very nicely, and we asked him to stay on. . . . It was mostly setting up merchandise, cribs, that sort of thing. Part of it was menial, loading and unloading trucks, sending shipments out. Around Christmas we had to put together toys for the display. I knew his mother and father. They came into the store once or twice. I don't remember too much of them but very fine people from what I remember. We kept very long hours in those days, working around the clock practically, eighty or ninety hours a week. He was getting half a dollar or seventy-five cents an hour, working twelve, fourteen, fifteen hours a week. He did his job, very pleasant, very nice.

Whatever he was supposed to do, he did, and very respectful at all times.''

Among the side benefits of the work was a short, basic course in Yiddish. ''Almost no customers were speaking it by then,'' Kirschner says, ''but my father-in-law had been from the old times. We used it some in the store, and he picked it up from us.''

Powell, Kirschner says, worked part-time for about six years at Sickser's, through high school and into early college. ''One day I noticed he happened to come in a green uniform. I said, 'What's that for?' He said, 'Well, I joined the ROTC,' and the rest is history—big history. . . . We always had people working for us, local kids, but nobody of that stature.''

More than thirty years later Kirschner was watching a news show on TV when he saw his one-time store employee standing beside Ronald Reagan. ''I knew him right away as soon as I saw him.'' It was, Kirschner says, his first inkling of Powell's rise in the world. Soon thereafter he wrote Powell a letter. ''He knew my wife very well—she was in the store at the time—and I let him know she had passed away. And he sent me back a beautiful letter; he mentioned people who worked in the store at the time. So I wrote him and asked him for an appointment.''

The first appointment—set for Powell's Pentagon office—had to be canceled, but a second date was set.

''It was just before the Gulf War,'' Kirschner says. ''I thought he wouldn't be able to keep it—he was so busy, but he met with me. The door opened, and he grabs me around just like the old times. . . . He had a menorah in his office that he got from [Israeli Prime Minister Yitzhak] Shamir. He posed with me with the menorah. When I left, I said, 'Colin, when you're in the White House, will you grant me an appointment?' He just laughed and pushed me aside.''

The visit, Kirschner adds, ''was such a gracious thing. I'll never forget it the rest of my life.'' It seems to have been vintage Powell. He has an almost boundless facility for remembering and acknowledging in big and small ways the people he met on his way up the ladder.

Much has been made of Powell's facility with Yiddish—no magazine profile of him would be complete without mentioning it—and of his affinity generally for the Jewish roots of his Hunts Point neighborhood. Certainly he is able to salt his conversation with expressions from the ancient language: "We kibitz back and forth," Kenneth Duberstein says. "He understands Yiddish. He calls me up on the phone and we talk a little Yiddish." Powell's linguistic talent can even bring stars to the eyes of political planners. Tony Coelho, the former House Majority whip and leading fundraiser for the Democratic party and now a Manhattan investment banker, says that the fact that Powell is an African-American and speaks Yiddish would make him an ideal candidate for the governorship or a Senate seat from New York State, where Powell, as an active-duty military officer, maintains his voting residence. (Mario Cuomo's term as governor expires in January, 1995. Republican Senator Alfonse D'Amato next stands for election in November, 1992, halfway through Powell's second term as Chairman of the Joint Chiefs of Staff; Democratic Senator Daniel Patrick Moynihan is up for reelection in 1994.)

"The black and Jewish population [of New York] would love him," Coelho says. "If he decided to run for governor as a Democrat he'd win easily and immediately become a contender for the top of the national ticket in 1996. He stops Jesse [Jackson]; he stops [Virginia governor Douglas] Wilder. You've got a genuine hero who just happens to be black. If he runs as a Republican and wins—and I think he could—he becomes creditable as a vice-presidential candidate in 1996."

At the least, Coelho suggests half-kiddingly, once Powell's second term as Chairman is through, George Bush could find other work for Secretary of Defense Dick Cheney and move Powell into his job. "You'd have the first Yiddish-speaking cabinet member, and you would have a general cutting defense."

"Yiddish-speaking" may, in fact, stretch the point. Those familiar with the language who know Powell suggest he's comfortable with some phrases but not ready to address the nation or even the cabinet in Yiddish.

But that's a quibble. Certainly, too, Powell is comfortable with the practices of the Jewish religion: He spent Passover dinner in 1991 with Democratic Rep. Stephen Solarz of New York and Solarz's wife, Nina. But as is often the case with Powell, it's less a matter of what he knows—the raw volume of his learning—than his ability to get the most out of his knowledge, to use it in the most advantageous setting and to the most effective end. When he was working at the Pentagon in the Carter administration, Powell was jokingly known as "the black Jew," according to Vice Adm. John A. Baldwin, who worked with him then. "When it seemed appropriate for the moment in dealing with Jewish civilian officials at the Pentagon," Baldwin told Saul Friedman of New York's *Newsday*, "Powell sprinkled his language with Yiddish." The same chameleonlike linguistic talent was evident when Powell, who speaks in public with no trace of race or region in his voice, was dealing with blacks, according to Baldwin. "[I could] always tell when Powell was speaking to a black person on the telephone because his accent suddenly changed." In other words, Colin Powell knows how to be a politician—which is not a complaint.

In many ways, Colin Powell's education has been less a matter of school learning than of lessons accumulated from experience—from the inner city, Vietnam, his service in the Pentagon and the Reagan and Bush White Houses. From having lived on the streets of the South Bronx, his boyhood friend Gene Norman says, Powell "recognizes the problems African-Americans like the two of us face. I'm sure he believes hard work is important because hard work certainly got him much if not all of what he has attained, but he also thinks there's a level of unfairness— that the playing field has to be leveled off."

From that same neighborhood, his friend and fellow New Yorker Kenneth Duberstein says, Powell also carried away "street smarts"—the kind of tough, intense survival course in human nature that is offered free of tuition in the inner city.

"He understands people," Duberstein says. "He understands what motivates people, what they like and don't like. He has something that makes his nose twitch if things don't smell exactly right, if the aroma is wrong. He knows that on the streets of the South Bronx they fight not only with fists and knives but with loaded guns. If you want to succeed, you have to work your way through the maze of personalities, motivations, histories. When you play punchball, you measure your success by how many sewers you can hit with the ball. You have to keep things in narrow bounds, and you have to be strategic in where you hit the ball. And all the time there are cars driving down the street. When you do that, you learn what matters in the world, and Colin Powell was a two-and-a-half-sewer man."

Duberstein does acknowledge that "two-and-a-half-sewer man" stretches the metaphor to a breaking point, and perhaps reality as well: Powell lays no claims to having been a gifted athlete as a youngster, at punchball or any other sport. Just as critical to explaining Powell, Duberstein says, are two Yiddish words: *chutzpah* and *seykhl*: "He's savvy, he's street smart, he's got *chutzpah*. But he's got *seykhl* as well."

As commonly used, *chutzpah* implies gall, nerve, brazenness, even effrontery. But as Leo Rosten points out in *The Joys of Yiddish*, *chutzpah* is really a word almost untranslatable into English; the classic example of *chutzpah*, Rosten noted, is someone who kills his father and mother, then throws himself on the mercy of the court, claiming he's an orphan. The *Modern English-Yiddish Yiddish-English Dictionary*, edited by Uriel Weinreich, defines *seykhl* simply as common sense, though that's probably putting it mildly.

In addition to street smarts, to *chutzpah* and *seykhl*, Powell also had a family—immediate and extended—that had no intention of letting him fail. It seems to have been a priceless asset.

CHAPTER 3

"You Got to Go in Engineering; That's Where the Money Is, Man."

The columnist Jimmy Breslin was perhaps stretching a point for effect when he wrote in the March 3, 1991, issue of *Newsday* that Colin Powell "is part of what is at the very least one of the most prominent families in the city of New York." In a city of Rockefellers, Sulzbergers, Tisches, Guggenheims, and Fricks—a city of great and long family traditions in commerce, finance, the arts, medicine, and publishing—the title "most prominent" is hard won. But he was not stretching the point terribly far. Between roughly 1913 and 1923, a remarkable clan emigrated from the mountainous interior of Jamaica to New York City.

"The success story in terms of the American dream has been realized by so many of those related to Colin," says his cousin James L. Watson. Watson himself is one example. His father came to New York in 1913 or 1914 and found work as an elevator operator, while his mother worked as a maid. A decade later the senior Watson became the first black graduate of New York Law School, and in 1930 he became the first black judge—an elected position—in the city and in New York state. James Watson himself, wounded in Italy during World War II, became a senior judge on the United States Customs Court of International Trade. His sister Grace would become a reading specialist for the U.S. Department of Education. Another sister, Barbara, now deceased, was the U.S. ambassador to Malaysia in 1980-81 and the first woman to be named an assistant secretary of state, in her case of consular affairs.

Richard Lopez, from another side of the family that is Ja maican on its paternal side and Trinidadian on its maternal side (James Watson is James Lopez Watson), was one of America' earliest black aerospace engineers and the chief designer fo many years at Republic Aircraft. Jacqueline Lopez is a psy chologist at New York University. Delores Lopez Lowery is a biochemist with the National Institutes of Health in Washington D.C. Another cousin, J. Bruce Llewellyn, is among the nation' wealthiest black men—founder of the One Hundred Black Men service and philanthropic organization, owner of WKBW-TV in Buffalo, and co-owner with former professional basketball sta Julius "Dr. J" Erving of a Coca-Cola bottling plant in Phila delphia. Llewellyn was also the first black to head the Federa Overseas Private Investment Corporation. Yet another cousin Dorothy Cropper, became a New York State judge in the Su preme Court of Claims. Still another, Arthur Lewis, served a U.S. ambassador to Sierra Leone. The list goes on to include prominent engineers in Kingston, Jamaica, and Toronto schoolteachers, and, of course, Colin Powell himself, who would be not only the first black Chairman of the Joint Chiefs of Staf but also the youngest and in some ways the latest blooming o all his illustrious family.

"I was not one of the burning lights of this extended family," Powell says. "The ones they had all the expectations for were some of my cousins—the Watson side and the Meikle side, the Lopezes and Llewellyns. My two closest cousins from Jamaica Vernon and Roy Meikle, my first cousins, went to Oxford and McGill. What more could you do than send a son to Oxford' They were both going to be engineers. The one who went to McGill [Vernon Meikle] is my age—we're contemporaries; w were born the same year to two sisters." [Here Powell makes a face to indicate that his mother's sister had gotten the better o the deal.] "The other one who went to Oxford was a coupl years older; he was closer to my sister's age. So you had Ro going to Oxford, Vernon going to McGill. The Lopez family doing well. My cousin Bruce [Llewellyn], the most successfu member of the family, got out of the Army and went to medica school, went to law school, kept going to different schools tryin to figure out what to do, and after all the schooling ended up opening a liquor store in Harlem. But then that was just a step ping stone to great things. He bought out a supermarket chain and one thing led to another. And so you had all that—my sister going away to school in Buffalo—and here's Colin who's sitting around fiddling with this Army stuff and kind of bouncing his way through life."

Yet because Powell was not a burning light of the extended family, perhaps he felt he had more time to attain the rank the older family members seem to have expected of the younger generation. A military career, after all, rewards the careful planner, the long-distance runner.

Eventually the Watson clan became wealthy enough to acquire an abiding symbol of East Coast upper-crust prosperity—a summer home on Martha's Vineyard, at Minks Meadow, on the West Chop overlooking Vineyard Haven Harbor. Bruce Llewellyn would acquire his own Martha's Vineyard home as well on the East Chop overlooking the beach at Oak Bluffs, where prominent New England blacks and such celebrities as Paul Robeson, Ethel Waters, Adam Clayton Powell and the composer Henry T. Burleigh began vacationing in the 1920s and '30s. Not only in black society but in American society as a whole, summer property in Martha's Vineyard is proof of having "arrived."

"I think we counted up forty-seven [undergraduate and graduate] degrees among all the known relatives," James Watson says. "It all starts in Christiana—in the center, the mountainous part of Jamaica," he adds, making it sound like a fairy tale, which in some ways it is. Like any good fairy tale, the Powell-Watson-Llewellyn-Lopez story also has a moral.

It was Watson's parents whom Luther Powell first came to live with when he arrived in Harlem. Precisely who is related to whom in the clan and in what ways gets foggy—some "cousins" may be later generations of intimate friends from Jamaica—but as Watson recalls the familial connection, Luther was a cousin of his aunt and uncle, the parents of J. Bruce Llewellyn. By then, Harlem was in the throes of its Renaissance, the celebration of black accomplishments in the arts and music that took root in W. E. B. Du Bois's *Crisis* and Charles S. Johnson's *Opportunity* and that counted among its leaders the Philadelphia-born writer and philosopher Alain Locke and the Jamaican-born poet Charles McKay. The New York of the 1920s was also the home to another Jamaican-born black, Marcus Garvey, the self-appointed provisional president of the Empire of Africa and an early exponent of black separateness and the Black is Beautiful movement. Garvey's United Negro Improvement Association grew to as many as half a million members before Garvey was jailed for fraud in 1925, in connection with a steamship line with which he was going to transport American black colonists to Africa.

Simultaneously New York, and especially Harlem, was receiving large numbers of Jamaicans and other immigrants from the British West Indies. Prior to 1900, West Indian immigration to the United States had amounted to little more than a trickle. Then in the first ten years of the new century, about 30,000 West Indians emigrated. More than 60,000 came over the next ten years, and another 40,000 during the early part of the 1920s. In the first six months of 1924 alone 10,600 people emigrated from the West Indies, and then one of those periodic bouts of xenophobia swept over American immigration policy and the curtain rang down. As of July 1, 1924, no more black West Indians were to be accepted into the United States, except for immediate family members of those already here. Not until the 1960s would the strictures be lifted. Had Luther and Maud Powell waited another several years to try to emigrate, their offspring, whomever each might have married, almost certainly would have grown up in Jamaica.

A half century later, spurred on by the political unrest in Jamaica that attended the socialist administration of Prime Minister Michael Manley, a new generation of Powell's extended family were to repeat in a different venue what the generation of Powell's parents had done in New York.

"A large number of the family members—my family who had stayed in Jamaica left [in the mid-1970s] and went to Miami," Powell told *Washingtonian* magazine. "They have now done in the last fifteen years in Miami exactly that which they had done in New York fifty years ago. I now have whole neighborhoods of relatives in Miami who have totally left the West Indies, brought what assets they had, and they have built entirely new lives. . . . They have built homes, they have businesses, and they have been very successful."

Among the Miami immigrants are two of the three surviving sisters of Powell's mother, both in their eighties.

What the sudden reversal of immigration policy in the summer of 1924 couldn't stop, though, was the drive to succeed of the black West Indians already in this country.

"I've sat and talked with West Indians all through those islands," says Caribbean historian Bonham Richardson of the Virginia State University and Polytechnic Institute. "I've heard people tell me stories about their families and in-laws and what they've done once they got here. It's very impressive, and they're not embellishing it for a white North American. It's a remarkable bit of U.S. society."

In a sense, the success of Colin Powell and his extended family is only a magnification of the success of the transported culture they emerged from. At the very least, their accomplishments have to be seen against that backdrop, for the Watson and Powell and Lopez and Llewellyn story is not just another story of immigrants finding success in the New World. It is a far rarer tale: one of immigrants whose ancestors had once been chattel making that success. Virtually all American blacks are descended from slaves—whatever the nationality of the masters who bought and sold them. Whether their ancestors were taken off the slave ships when they first stopped in the Caribbean or remained on board until the ships reached the United States, slavery is their common heritage. By most statistical measures, though, to be descended from West Indian slaves, as Powell and his cousins are, is not the same as being a black descended from the slaves of the American South. The distinction is critical, for while Powell seems acutely aware of the experience of blacks generally, he himself is the product of and was definitively shaped by a very singular strain of the African-American experience.

"As early as 1901," Thomas Sowell writes in *Ethnic America*, "West Indians owned twenty percent of all black businesses in Manhattan, although they were only ten percent of the black population there. American Negroes called them 'black Jews' "—the same nickname Powell would later acquire at the Pentagon for his familiarity with Yiddish.

In the decades to come the advantage of black West Indians over black Americans would continue to grow. (Sowell confines the term "West Indians" to people from the islands of Jamaica, Barbados, Trinidad, and other parts of the British West Indies.) By 1969, Sowell notes, West Indian incomes in New York City were twenty-eight percent higher than the incomes of other city blacks and fifty-two percent higher than black incomes nationally. West Indian blacks also had an unemployment rate below the national average. "As of 1970," Sowell writes, "the highest-ranking blacks in New York's police department were all West Indians, as were all black federal judges in the city. For many years, successive borough presidents of Manhattan were all West Indians," even though collectively West Indians were too few in New York to exercise any bloc-voting power. Malcolm X, former congresswoman Shirley Chisholm, actor Sidney Poitier, entertainer Harry Belafonte, psychologist Kenneth B. Clark, Sowell notes, are all celebrated American blacks of West Indian heritage. To that list Colin Powell's name can now be added—Sowell's book was published in 1981. In terms of contemporary celebrity, the list is, perhaps, notable for its absence of black American athletes.

Sowell also cites studies from the 1930s, '40s and '50s of social and behavioral determinants of economic advancement that favor West Indian immigrants over American blacks. "West Indians were much more frugal, hard-working, and entrepreneurial. Their children worked harder and outperformed native black children in school. West Indians in the United States had lower fertility rates and lower crime rates than either black or white Americans."

Jamaican-born economist Ransford Palmer of Howard University has localized the study to immigrants from his own island. "The income data from the 1980 census—I haven't looked at the 1990 census yet—suggests quite strongly that the Jamaicans have done extremely well," he says. "In many cases they've done as well as whites in this country. In fact, when you look at second-generation Jamaicans—those who were born in this country—their median income was higher than that of native white Americans."

What explains the discrepancies in groups that are both descended from slavery? Sowell argues that perhaps the most distinguishing factor is the difference in the conditions of slavery that prevailed on the British-owned islands and in the American South—most notably and perhaps most ironically the fact that the treatment of island slaves was generally even harsher than the treatment of slaves kept on the plantations of the South.

"The cost of raising slaves in the West Indies was considered higher than the cost of importing replacements from Africa,'' Sowell writes, ''and the slaves were treated accordingly,''—with predictable results. Infant mortality among island slaves was several times higher than it was among American slaves. On one large Jamaican plantation, historian John Hope Franklin notes in *From Slavery to Freedom*, more than half of all children died in infancy. Those who survived infancy on Jamaica also died on the average far younger. In the 130 years up to 1820, 800,000 slaves were imported to Jamaica alone—more than were imported into the United States during the entire history of American slavery. Yet by 1820 the black population of Jamaica was less than 400,000. (James A. Michener notes in his novel *Caribbean* that by the mid-1830s the Jamaican population had grown to 450,000 citizens, precisely 753 of whom were enfranchised with the vote.) Forty years later, by contrast, the U.S. black population stood at about 5 million.

Interrelated with the cruel treatment of West Indian slaves, Sowell writes, was the fact that ownership of the vast sugar plantations they worked was largely absentee. ''Complete control was in the hands of local white attorneys and overseers, whose financial incentives were to maximize current production (on which they received a percentage) at all costs, without regard to the long-run cost in terms of worn-out slaves or worn-out land.'' Many of the attorneys, overseers, and managers in Jamaica were of Scottish origin, Caribbean historian Alan L. Karras notes, which may explain the Scottish ''Colin'' of Colin Powell. Furthermore, while U.S. plantation owners tended to hire married overseers to mitigate the sexual exploitation of female slaves, their sexual exploitation by white men on the islands was ''more systematic, pervasive, and even commercial,'' Sowell writes. Inevitably a *de facto* caste system developed in the West Indies that favored those blacks with the lightest skin—the visible evidence of white genetic stock.

Yet, Sowell argues, it was the very absence of paternalism in the West Indies that may account for the relative prosperity of the islands' black American immigrants. ''Unlike slaves in the United States, who were issued food rations and were often fed from the common kitchen, West Indian slaves were assigned land and time to raise their own food. They sold surplus food in the market to buy amenities for themselves. In short, West Indian Negroes had centuries of experience in taking care of themselves in a significant part of their lives, even under slavery, as well as experience with buying and selling. . . . They had the kind of incentives and experience common in a market economy but denied American slaves for two centuries.''

West Indian slaves, too, were freed a generation earlier than U.S. slaves. They emerged into a culture in which they were the overwhelming majority, even if they were poverty-driven, and under the tutelage of the British, who if they were cruel imperial taskmasters at least were experienced in colonial administration. Eventually, from sheer force of numbers, the emancipated slaves would be integrated into the lower rungs of the civil service. Schools, too, were established on Jamaica in 1811, more than a century and a half after the British had taken possession but decades before the first stumbling attempts to educate American blacks systematically.

The cumulative result, says Howard University's Ransford Palmer, is that Jamaican and other West Indian blacks ''grew up with a certain special sense of their own self.'' For years, that special sense tended to keep West Indians in the United States apart from native American blacks even when they lived in the same neighborhoods. West Indian immigrants socialized with one another and married among their fellow islanders. Powell once told a reporter for a Kingston, Jamaica, newspaper that his 1962 marriage to Alma Powell—''an American from Birmingham, Alabama''—had ''caused a bit of a scandal in the family. . . . The feeling then was that you had to marry somebody from home, and, of course, home was Jamaica.'' Eventually, Powell said, ''[my wife] was like a daughter to my mother. A great love affair developed between my wife, my mother, and my aunts, but not before they had picked her apart, had examined her closely and had determined that she would be all right for me.''

Alma Powell says that she first met her husband's full extended family at a New Year's Eve party thrown by Luther Powell: ''There was no better spot to be looked over than that.'' ''Among those who paid particular attention,'' she says, was Luther Powell's sister. ''All night long, every time I turned around, here she was. I'd turn around, and there she is at my shoulder. All night long. She never said anything; she just looked. I'd smile and go on about my business, and soon I'd turn around and she was still there. She never quit looking me over, and now she says"—here Mrs. Powell falls into a West Indian accent—" 'But I picked you out, you know.' " A Lithuanian Jew marrying, say, a Spanish Catholic could expect much the same scrutiny.

"It took, I think, the civil rights movement to bring [West Indian blacks and southern blacks] together," Ransford Palmer says. "There was a commonality of purpose there. That was the major integrating force." But a sense of separateness continues to linger today, according to Ed Vega, the Puerto Rican-born novelist who attended Morris High with Powell. "I hear lots of my black friends talk about it. There's a significant difference in the way West Indians are viewed by native African-Americans. They're considered arrogant, overachieving, hoity-toity."

Thomas Sowell's analysis of the debilitating effects of plantation paternalism in the American South, it should be noted, is in keeping with his widely expressed views on what he considers the similar effects of the contemporary welfare system. (Like Charles Murray, the author of *Losing Ground*, with whom he shares much common intellectual ground, Sowell has been a favorite theoretician of Republican conservatives.) Colin Powell's own analysis of the difference between West Indian immigrants and native African-Americans, expressed in a 1990 interview, stresses the effect of the British influence on the islands.

"We have different roots," he said in the *Washingtonian* interview. "We have a different cultural system, a different intensity in religious systems. . . . Most of the West Indians who came up from that time period [the 1910s and '20s, when his parents emigrated] and who came up particularly from Jamaica were Anglicans, High Anglicans; a strong Anglican statement [was] built into us. We all were High Episcopalians, the higher the better; the higher an Episcopalian you could be the more you were like the mother church, the Church of England."

American and West Indian blacks all have a "slave past," Powell said. "The blacks in the West Indies were also brought from Africa, and they intermixed with Indian cultures that existed in the West Indies. But they came up under a British system where slavery was abolished [earlier], and then there was a responsibility taken on the part of the British masters to provide education and to create a sort of civil-service culture that made them more than just indentured people and more than just slaves. That didn't exist in the United States. . . . [American blacks] were systematically deprived of every opportunity of the culture, of the ability to be educated, of any suggestion that they could be anything other than second-class people to be trod upon. They were oppressed in this country, totally oppressed. Then the Civil War came, and there was a great flurry, and then in the Reconstruction period they lost again.

"Lincoln freed the slaves, but it was Martin Luther King who freed the whites and freed the American people. . . . The real civil war was fought in the nineteen-sixties—as important a battle as was fought in the eighteen-sixties—to free Americans from segregation."

Later in the interview, Powell returned to the point: Martin Luther King, he said, "freed the nation."

Many of the West Indians who emigrated to the United States were "people who were in their own countries a little better than the common laborer," says historian Bonham Richardson. "They were clerks, petty managers, that sort of thing. When they got to the States they were like everyone else with dark skin. Articles with headlines like 'Stoop to Conquer' were common in the West Indian papers then. The stories would say, Look, when you come to the States you're going to be treated like hell; you'll be abused, people will call you names, but there are jobs."

And with the worldwide collapse of the sugar market in the years after World War I, jobs were the issue. There's an irregular feature on the black-oriented TV comedy "In Living Color" that pokes fun at Jamaican immigrants: Everyone in the family is holding down multiple jobs; the household is chaotic as people run from one workplace to another. In fact, the satire contains more than an element of truth.

"The major factor behind the success of Jamaicans in the United States was their dedication and diligence at achieving what they came to achieve," Ransford Palmer says. "There was a certain singlemindedness. They came to improve their economic condition—very few have been political refugees—and they have dedicated a great part of their lives in this country to achieving some measure of economic well being. . . . They also came with a sense that their children ought to do better than they did. There's a tendency for them to make great sacrifices on behalf of their children.''

For the early emigrants of Colin Powell's extended family, ''the idea was that in the United States the streets were paved with gold—you could get rich,'' says his cousin Jacqueline Lopez. The Lopez-Watson-Llewellyn-Powell clan was not necessarily middle class in Jamaica, Lopez says, ''but their values were definitely middle class''—chief among them ''an emphasis on education.''

''Education,'' she says, ''was one of their highest possible attainments. It was stressed. That group of Jamaicans was totally hooked and sold on education. I'm sure the British system had something to do with it. Education was compulsory and very good. I had the experience of going to Jamaica. My father was forever returning and thinking he would relocate. When I was ten we went down there—my sister and I. I had been in fourth grade in New York, but I was put in kindergarten to learn the times tables. I learned them in a hurry, too, partially because they believed in corporal punishment. There was someone going around with a ruler. My mother had to go and set them straight: We were American children; we were not used to corporal punishment.''

All of the family that arrived in Harlem from Jamaica in the 1910s and '20s came ''with good fundamental education, early childhood education,'' James Watson says. ''Then they came and took advantage of the educational opportunities here and the opportunities to advance themselves as far as they could.'' The most significant factor in the success of the extended family ''was the values we were brought up with: the family, the work ethic, and the necessity of pursuing an education. There was none of this stuff about when I finish high school I'm going to take a sabbatical. It was what colleges are you applying to and where am I going to get the money.''

''Until the day [my parents] died,'' Colin Powell told *Parade* magazine reporter David Wallechinsky, ''I was never able to convince them that it would never be possible for me to do better than they did in providing their children with values and goals. It wasn't a matter of spending a great deal of time with my parents discussing things. We didn't sit down at night like the Brady Bunch and review the work of the day. It was just the way they lived their lives. That's what children get from their parents:

what they see. Not lectures or speeches. Children watch the way their parents live their lives. If they like what they see, if it makes sense to them, they will live their lives that way, too. If the parents' values seem correct and relevant, the children will follow those values.''

As with the rest of the clan, the chief value the senior Powells transmitted to their children was the necessity of learning. ''Our parents had these expectations that were kind of passed along to us,'' Marilyn Berns told the Los Angeles *Times*. ''It was expected that we went to high school and after that we would go to college. They made us feel that education was the way to pull yourself up. Education was the key to success.''

A higher education, Powell says in an interview with the author, also satisfied the acute sense of status that permeated his own and his extended family. ''Jamaicans are an extremely inbred, close-knit kind of family,'' he says. ''They love life, love each other, take care of one another. Everybody lives for their children; everybody knows everybody else's business. And there's a great deal of status consciousness within West Indian families and Jamaican families, especially between those who have a little bit of education and those who don-don't, between those who are light-skinned and those who are dark-skinned, between those who had British and Scottish relatives and those who didn't. My father came from a little lower down in the Jamaican hierarchy—the economic and cultural and social hierarchy—than my mother did. So he married a little above himself but not a whole lot—I mean, we're not talking about Kennedys. But it was a source of great amusement. They would jab one another all the time about how well someone had done in the family. And that's why it meant so much to them to have children who had gone to college. Everything was sacrificed for the children.''

Marilyn Berns describes her mother as ''very pragmatic, very down to earth, very practical.'' And Mrs. Powell—perhaps mindful of the status already bestowed on the Meikle cousin who was studying engineering at Oxford, perhaps thinking it was the last status link needed for a young man who already had light skin and a Scottish name—was to give her only son practical advice when it came time to pursue a higher education and a career. Her advice, as Powell recalled it for the Sunday Gleaner magazine of Kingston, Jamaica: "You got to go in engineering; that's where the money is, man." As a good son and future good soldier, Colin Powell tried to obey. But it was one order he could not follow.

CHAPTER 4

Pershing Rifles

"I cannot translate to people what it means to say that the Chairman of the Joint Chiefs of Staff went to City College," Barry Schweid says. "You went to City College to play basketball, maybe. They had the championship team in my time, two blacks and three Jews—the ones who were caught in the scandal. But it was absolutely a prole school. And, my God, Army! You were either a socialist or a liberal Democrat."

In the 1949–50 collegiate basketball season, City College of New York—CCNY—accomplished the unequaled feat of winning both the National Collegiate Athletic Association championship and the championship of the National Invitational Tournament, then nearly equal in stature to the NCAA title. It was to be the last gasp of glory for the team. The next year the school's basketball program was one of several caught up in a bribery and point-shaving scandal from which it never recovered. Banned by New York's Board of Higher Education from playing in any arena not supervised by educational authorities, the Beavers—the renowned City College team playing the city game—faded from the headlines. That left the college only its singular spot in the history of higher education and its impressive alumni list.

By practice and design, City College was, indeed, the school of the proletariat. By 1846, New York City had more than half a million residents and only two colleges, with 247 pupils enrolled. The next year, urged on by Board of Education president

Townsend Harris, New York City voters were asked to approve funding for a "Free Academy" to provide higher education for the children of the working class. Despite what the college's official history describes as "editorials that appeared almost daily in Col. James Watson Webb's *Morning Courier and Enquirer*, [maintaining] that a Free Academy would be 'onerous to the city finances, injurious to institutions of learning already established,' and a cause for 'strife among different classes and religious sects,' " voters approved the funding measure by a six-to-one majority. (In a nice twist of history, Colonel Webb's son, Alexander Stewart Webb, would become City College's second president.) A little over a year later, on New Year's Day, 1849, the new Free Academy opened at a site then considered "far uptown"—Twenty-third Street and Lexington Avenue, three dozen blocks downtown from what is now the southern tip of Central Park. At opening ceremonies president Horace Webster described the school's mission thus: "The experiment to be tried, whether the children of the people—the children of the whole people—can be educated; and whether an institution of learning of the highest grade can be successfully controlled by the popular will, not by the privileged few."

At CCNY "the children of the whole people" flourished. Colin Powell was in his junior year at Morris High when Dr. Jonas Salk (City College Class of 1934) announced the first successful tests in humans of his vaccine against poliomyelitis; by the time Powell was entering his sophomore year at the college, the Salk vaccine was being administered worldwide and the scourge of polio was practically eradicated. By the time Powell was a college senior Felix Frankfurter (Class of 1902) was nearing the end of his seventeenth year as a Justice of the United States Supreme Court, and the financier and counselor to presidents Bernard Baruch (Class of 1889) was nearing the end of his eighth decade. (Frankfurter and Baruch would die within four months of each other in 1965.) Other distinguished City College alumni include playwright Paddy Chayevsky, sociologist Nathan Glazer, author Lewis Mumford, novelist Bernard Malamud, philosopher Sidney Hook, labor leader A. Philip Randolph, actor Edward G. Robinson, lyricist Ira Gershwin, former New York *Times* editor A. M. Rosenthal, New York City mayors Abraham Beame and Edward Koch, Bronx politician and former Congressman Herman Badillo, longtime United

States Senator from New York and New York City Mayor Robert
Wagner, Jr., novelist and social critic Upton Sinclair, and TV
newsmen Bernard and Marvin Kalb. The eight Nobel Prizes
won by its graduates place City College first among all public
institutions in the nation for alumni who have been so honored.
It also ranks fourth nationally among all institutions, public and
private, in the number of graduates who have gone on to earn
doctorates. If the tenement neighborhoods of New York have
been the most traveled highway out of immigrant poverty in
America, City College has been the final passageway for many,
many of them. The list of famous graduates put out by the
school's public-relations office now includes two other names:
Colin Powell and the man Powell calls his "rich" cousin, Bruce
Llewellyn.

For Powell, who graduated from high school at the end of the
first semester of his senior year and entered CCNY still two
months short of his seventeenth birthday, it couldn't have been
a less auspicious start. Of all those on the college's roster of
notable alumni, it is unlikely that any had a less distinguished
undergraduate academic record than Powell.

"He was ready intellectually," his sister Marilyn Berns told
the Los Angeles *Times*, "but I worried about him socially. Sixteen is awfully young for anyone to start college."

"My odyssey began on a winter's day in February, 1954, when
I entered City College at sixteen and a half—having just been
graduated from Morris High School on Boston Road in the
Bronx," Powell wrote for the City College alumni magazine. "I
went to college for a single reason: My parents expected it. I don't
recall having had any great urge to get a higher education. I
don't even remember consciously thinking the matter through."

Powell wrote that he applied to two colleges, New York University, in Manhattan's Greenwich Village, and City College,
by then centered at its present campus, which stretches from
131st to 141st streets along Convent Avenue on Saint Nicholas
Heights in Harlem. "Notwithstanding my rather mediocre high
school grades I was accepted at both institutions. Making the
final decision was tough, but one I was able to come to grips
with readily—NYU cost $750 a year; CCNY cost $10. That was
the end of that. So, on that cold morning, I took the bus across
the 155th Street bridge, rode up the hill, got off, met Raymond

the Bagelman—a fixture on campus—and began my career as a CCNY student.''

Powell's first semester, from February through June of 1954, was relatively successful. He managed a B average in the School of Engineering, a traditionally strong program at the college. (As of the 1991-92 academic year, CCNY had more black and Hispanic students enrolled in engineering than any other school in the nation, despite being only the nation's 168th-largest institution of higher education.) That summer Powell enrolled in a mechanical drawing course to beef up his technical skills for the engineering program—and met his academic Waterloo.

"One hot afternoon," he wrote, "the instructor asked me to visualize a cone intersecting a plane in space. It was at that point that I decided to drop out of engineering; it was the worst summer I had ever spent."

Powell would graduate from City College in four and a half years—he never recovered the semester lost in engineering. Along the way, he wrote for the CCNY alumni magazine, "as an incidental dividend I received a B.S. degree in geology for mastering the rock formations under Manhattan." Along the way, he told *Washingtonian* magazine, he also discovered that he had other academic weaknesses besides not being able to visualize a cone intersecting a plane in space: "I discovered I was . . . not pretty good in physics, calculus, geology, history, languages, or any of the other [courses]."

What Powell discovered he was "pretty good" at was the Reserve Officers Training Corps—ROTC: "There I was with this menu laid out before me by the City College of New York, and you tend to go in those directions that seem to be successful for you. In my case it was the ROTC program. I really don't know if I would have finished college if it had not been for the ROTC program."

Nor is it likely that Powell would have been able to get his degree at the end of four and a half years without the officer training program. As it was, he wrote for his alumni magazine, he graduated "with an average that barely crept above C." The only way it did creep above a C, he went on, was "four straight years of A in ROTC, which, thank goodness, counted on your academic record."

History is full of examples of future intellectuals who barely squeaked through college, of corporate heads who spent more time in the pool hall than the university library. To that end, Powell's collegiate academic record "should not be seen as diagnostic," John Ranelagh wrote in the National Review, in a highly favorable profile shortly after the victory in the Gulf. Powell, his friends say, learns what he needs to learn when he needs to learn it. "Colin watches a lot of TV. He sees all kinds of talk shows," says Kenneth Adelman, "but he does read books, which is nice and somewhat unusual in his circle. I can't imagine his reading Paul Johnson or the people from the Iowa Creative Writers Workshop. He has an operational turn of mind. His reading is more focused on what he needs to know."

If Powell has thus far left behind no sweeping governmental or military philosophies, the reason may simply be that thus far none have been called for in the positions he has occupied. His friend Harlan Ullman of the Center for Naval Analysis says that Powell has the "flexibility—and I use that in a nice way—to be able to expand his capacity as necessary. He balances that with pragmatic judgment. For example, when he was working for Reagan as National Security Adviser, I think Colin was not prepared to come up with a Henry Kissinger-like strategic view of the world. It would have been a waste of time. There was no Richard Nixon to talk about a Nixon Doctrine with."

Powell does get credit for understanding what one high-ranking Pentagon official—someone who has worked closely with him—calls "the simple things" that no academic course on government can teach: "He understands how executive, political, and military power are wielded in Washington." In the nation's capital, no understanding is more important than that, nor is any harder to arrive at. As disappointed scholars are forever finding when they try to bring fresh thinking to Washington, it is a city that thrives far less on raw intellect than on the ability to get things done. Bringing new ideas to Washington, scholar Richard Pipes once noted, "is like trying to have a good time in town with a ten-thousand-dollar bill." You can't break the bill to buy the first drink. At the time, Pipes was on his way back to Harvard after a frustrating stretch as director of Eastern Europe and Soviet affairs with the National Security Council during the early years of the Reagan administration.

"I've often said in the jobs I've had, spare me geniuses," Powell's mentor Frank Carlucci adds. "Judgment doesn't always accompany genius."

Powell also deserves credit for simple candor: "I had not done particularly well in college," he once told the *Washingtonian*. "My wife and children wish I would stop saying that, but it's true."

Within the ROTC program at CCNY there was a group known as the Pershing Rifles—a fraternity of sorts—and there it was that Powell found a campus family. The group became his true collegiate home.

"The Pershing Rifles," he wrote for his alumni magazine, "were the ones who walked around with a little whipped cord on their shoulders, suggesting that they were a little more serious than the average ROTC cadet and possibly that they had made some sort of tentative commitment to military service as a career. That appealed to me."

Powell joined the ROTC program in the fall of his freshman year, "immediately pledged Pershing Rifles and spent the next four years concentrating on ROTC, spending most of my time on Pershing Rifles activities and tolerating the academic demands of the college as best I could," he wrote.

Membership in ROTC was far from uncommon in the early and mid-1950s, even at a school for the proletariat. Military training had a long and honorable history at City College. In World War II the Army Specialized Training Program there had been the largest in the nation, and by Powell's time the college's ROTC unit was the second-largest voluntary one in the country. What was unusual about Powell was the intensity he brought to military training, says Walter Schwartz, who had been a schoolmate of Powell's since junior high and was a member of the ROTC program, but not the Pershing Rifles, at City College. "I took it, as did a majority of people, as a necessity but also a lark. I thought I was destined to be drafted at any rate. As a contrast to that, his attitude was that he took it very seriously." By the mid-1950s attitudes also had shifted enough that "a military career was not viewed as a very popular or terribly attractive field to aim for" at CCNY, Powell wrote.

For the large contingent of CCNY students who had no interest in the armed forces—the "proles" of "the whole people"— the stern military demeanor of the Pershing Rifles seemed, at best, somewhat outmoded. "Those of us who were English literature majors kind of thought [Powell] was square," says Marlene Charnizon, who was a year behind him at both Morris High and CCNY. "We looked at these people like, who are they, what are they doing? I learned about dangling earrings at City College, about the Village. I wanted to leave home."

But for Powell, his sister Marilyn Berns told the Los Angeles *Times*, ROTC and the Pershing Rifles "happened to be the perfect niche for him. I think he liked the fact that it was structured. He came from a very structured family with rules and order. . . . It gave him security." In the *Washingtonian* interview Powell also talked about "the sense of order that [ROTC] brought to your life."

In the Pershing Rifles, Powell also seems to have learned something about himself that was more important than coming to grips with his deficiencies in mechanical drawing and calculus. He seems to have learned that the tall, pale, skinny kid whom his older cousins remember hanging quietly and pleasantly on the fringe of family gatherings was a natural leader. Perhaps he had to escape the gregarious, naturally attractive shadow of his father to find it out. Powell suggests that it was more a matter of simply finding a setting he could shine in, among people who could appreciate his talents.

"I never felt that I was under [my father's] domination, that I suddenly was out of it," Powell says. "It was really my first experience away from the family, my first experience with a different kind of family. Growing up on Kelly Street, I had a few close friends, but there wasn't anything big there. I wasn't a great athlete or a great stickball player; I wasn't a great kite flyer. So there was nothing really for me to demonstrate my ability in. Then I went to school for the first six months in college, and that was kind of a bummer. Then I met this group, and they were guys a lot like me, and I enjoyed it."

To his fellow Pershing Riflemen "there was no question whatsoever that Powell was going to make the service a career," says John Marchisotto, now an executive with the Loral Corporation. "Even back then he had the stamina. He had that bearing. Even in the cadets he was very stern, very disciplined, very military-oriented. But he had a good personality, too; he was one of the guys." By the time he graduated, Powell would be the group's leader—its company commander—as well as a cadet colonel of the larger ROTC.

Although its members called the Pershing Rifles a fraternity, the group had no traditional fraternity house—"You're talking CCNY in the city of New York," Marchisotto says; "Columbia, Fordham, that's where the fraternity houses were." Headquarters was an office in the student center at Finley Hall, named for a former president of the college who would later become editor of the New York *Times*. The official work of the Rifles was to be a drill team, but for Powell and many of the other members, the group became a social organization as well, a nucleus of friends on and off campus.

"We were living at each other's houses," Powell told the *Washingtonian*. "There was sort of a moveable feast around the city of New York as we went to parties and we all grew up together." His parents, he said, "liked the young men I was associated with, my buddies, the guys I hung around with. They were all good kids—nobody was a troublemaker—and they loved all of those young men."

The group, says Sheldon Zwimbler, was "a melting pot. . . . Probably earlier it had been mostly Jewish, but by the 1950s it was Italian, Irish, black. It was a rainbow concept. I don't think anybody ever discussed religion or ethnicity or race. Pershing Rifles taught you to live in a realm where race didn't matter."

For some of the members, the Rifles also functioned as a kind of informal counseling service. Just as ROTC had helped Powell stay in school, so he helped some of his fellow fraternity members stay on, according to Marchisotto. "He was very receptive as far as people were concerned, very people-oriented. Whenever he could, if it was within his power on a pow-wow basis, he would really try to keep people in school, see what he could do to assist."

Zwimbler, who joined the fraternity in Powell's senior year, recalls the first time he met the future Chairman of the Joint Chiefs of Staff: "He was dressed in regular slacks and wearing a Pershing Rifles sweater, and he was over six feet tall and very regular. And I thought this is the kind of person I want to have as a friend. He had a very commanding presence."

In the Pershing Rifles, Colin Powell also seems to have found his own first exemplar outside of his family: Ronnie Brooks, who would precede Powell as company commander of the Rifles.

"Ronnie was a very great influence," Powell says. "Ronnie

was two years older than me and sort of became my PR [Pershing Rifles] brother. He was another black kid, an American black, but he understood West Indians. He was a hard driver; I mean, Ronnie *was* a driver. I never thought about it for many years, but Ronnie was really my role model in those years. He was the son of a preacher—Baptist churches in Harlem—and Ronnie and I ran together constantly for a couple of years. And I essentially followed Ronnie in every position in the Pershing Rifles. Whatever he did I did two years later, so Ronnie had enormous influence on me. Ronnie was a hell of a lot smarter than me but was also able to do all this Army stuff.''

It was only after college that the two lives took separate turns, Powell says: ''Ronnie was as gung-ho as I was. At least everybody thought he was, but he was not. Ronnie went active duty for six months, I guess it was, and then went off to Brown [University] to do his masters and doctoral work in chemistry. He graduated, and I thought the world was his in those days—a young black with a Ph.D. in chemistry. He then married a West Indian, of all things, from British Guyana. For a while, he and she were going to go off to Africa and help the natives learn chemistry or something, but they suddenly discovered what the bliss of married life was all about. They moved to Schenectady, New York, and he spent his whole life working for General Electric.''

Just about the time Powell became Chairman of the Joint Chiefs of Staff, in October 1989, Ronnie Brooks died of a sudden, massive heart attack. Powell was among those who delivered eulogies at the funeral service.

In his junior year, Powell became rush chairman of the Pershing Rifles, in charge of recruiting new members. Zwimbler, now a financial consultant on Long Island, was one of the twenty-one young men Powell initiated into the group that year. Another of the twenty-one was Tony Mavroudis, for whom Powell, in turn, would come to serve as a definitive life example.

''Tony,'' Marchisotto says, ''was one helluva guy. He was like Colin, very military-oriented. Basically he was going to make a career out of the service, too.''

''Tony lived near me in Queens [where his parents moved in 1956],'' Powell says. ''He was one of the craziest guys I ever met. I loved him dearly, loved him like a brother. He was smart, he was sharp, he was a Greek—raw, coarse, but a hell of a

soldier. I was his role model just as Ronnie had been mine. . . .
Tony just latched on to me. We ran around together and dated
together. We learned about girls together. We were either driving his father's car or my father's car, and we succeeded in
destroying both of them during the course of our college careers.
I lived in his house and called his parents mom and dad, and he
lived in my house and called my parents mom and dad. He
followed me into the Army two years later and he was doing
everything I was doing. He went to Vietnam after I did, and
then for a while we were both at Benning together. I wasn't
going back to Vietnam right away; I was going to Leavenworth.
And Tony volunteered to go back to Vietnam. He said, 'I got to
go, I got to go.' He said, 'The only reason you're not going with
me is Alma and the babies.' And I said, 'I'm going to go in due
course, Tony.' ''

During that second tour in Vietnam, in 1967, Tony Mavroudis
was killed—he was one of three Pershing Rifles members from
Powell's time at CCNY to be killed in combat in Southeast Asia.

"The day I attended Tony's funeral," Sheldon Zwimbler says,
"I came home that evening and turned on the TV, and there
was this documentary made by the Army. It was called 'Blood,
Sweat, and Mud.' It said we're all here in Vietnam, trying to
win this war—black blood, Spanish blood, it didn't matter. I
was watching it, and there was this voice, and I said, 'That's
Tony.' My wife said, 'You're crazy. How can you tell that?' But
when you've been in school with someone for four years you
recognize his voice. When the film ended, the credits came up
and, sure enough, it said, 'This film was narrated by Tony Mavroudis, who was killed five days after it was made.' ''

Nearly a quarter of a century later, in October, 1990, Powell
took Gen. Mikhail Moiseyev—then his counterpart as Chief of
the Armed Forces of the Soviet Union—to see Mavroudis's name
inscribed on the black marble wall of the Vietnam Veterans
Memorial. The following Memorial Day, Powell described the
moment in a speech at the site:

"I didn't bring him directly here to this Wall. He wasn't ready
for it. I had to show him other things first. I had to show him
what America was really about, what we really stood for. I had
him look into the very crucible where America's values were
fired."

Powell took Moiseyev first to the Jefferson Memorial to show him Thomas Jefferson's words carved into those memorial walls: "his nation-building words about our Constitution, his freedom-loving words about the abomination of slavery, his God-given words about religion, his ageless words from the Declaration of Independence." From there the two went on to the Lincoln Memorial to read more words: from the Gettysburg Address and especially from Abraham Lincoln's Second Inaugural Address—words, Powell told the audience, that "mean so much to me. . . . 'With malice toward none; with charity for all; with firmness in the right, as God gives us to see the right, let us strive on to finish the work we are in; to bind up the nation's wounds; to care for him who shall have borne the battle, and for his widow and orphan.' "

Then, Powell said, "We were ready to visit the Wall. As we walked, I wasn't exactly sure how to describe to him what he was to see next. I knew my own feelings were wrapped up in this beautiful monument, and I knew I wanted to communicate some of those feelings to General Moiseyev. But I wasn't sure how to do it.

"As we approached the monument my thoughts began to form. I looked at the people gathered around. I noticed how heavily worn the pathways are—as if centuries rather than a few years have trod these walkways. And I felt the emotional power of this place begin to affect me as it always does. And I looked at General Moiseyev, and I could see it was touching him as well. So I took him to one of the stands, and I showed him how we look up the name of a fallen comrade and how we locate that name on the Wall.

"Together, we looked up the name of Maj. Tony Mavroudis. Tony and I went to college together. We grew up together in the streets of New York. We were pals together. We became infantrymen together. And in 1967, on his second tour, Tony was killed. And we found his name in the book; we moved to Panel 28 East and we found his name on the Wall. It was an emotional moment, and not just for me.

"General Moiseyev was moved as well. Staring at this black marble immensity of grief and pain, disappearing into the earth in both directions, he told me, a fellow soldier, that monuments such as this were what he wanted also—for the veterans of Afghanistan and also for their Great Patriotic War, World War II, where they suffered over twenty million casualties, many unknown. And he was moved by the exquisite detail of this Wall. The painstaking effort to recognize every friend who fell or was lost. The meticulous attention to keeping everything in balance, everything proportional. The powerful, powerful effort to remember.

"I told him Americans do remember. I told him that this Wall will never be complete until the fate of every name is known. I told him we would never rest until everyone—every Vietnam P.O.W. and M.I.A.—is accounted for. And I pointed out to General Moiseyev the three soldiers, the ones who watch the Wall. From their position in the trees there, they search—for the names of friends or perhaps their own names. They pay homage to their buddies and they guard the Wall. They symbolize the eternal vigilance of America's warriors, of America's armed forces.

"I believe that as a fellow soldier, General Moiseyev understood. He reached out gently and touched the Wall. And I believe he understood."

The Vietnam Veterans Memorial speech was doubly revelatory of Powell. He seems to have a soft spot for tales of Soviet valor and suffering in time of war. At a dinner in Geneva in 1987 hosted by Secretary of State George Shultz, Powell, who was then National Security Adviser, asked Marshall Sergey Akhromeyev if he was the last of the Soviet Union's World War II officers still serving in its military. He was, Akhromeyev replied, indeed, "the last of the Mohicans." The marshall, who then was Chief of the Armed Forces and later apparently would commit suicide after the failed coup attempt against Mikhail Gorbachev in the summer of 1991, went on to tell something of his war experiences. He had joined the army at the age of seventeen, he said, on the eve of the war, and been stationed sixty kilometers outside Leningrad with orders to stay put and defend the road against the Germans. For eighteen months, through two winters in which temperatures plunged to fifty below zero, Akhromeyev did what he was told. "I never went inside a building during those eighteen months," he told the dinner guests. ". . . We were told to stay there. We stayed there." Powell was "visibly moved by the story; it was a magic moment," says Kenneth Adelman, who was at the dinner. (Adelman recounts the story in greater detail in his book, *The Great Universal Embrace.*)

Powell's Memorial Day speech at the Vietnam Veterans Memorial Wall also suggests his unabashed love of the sentimental, his willingness in his public addresses to reach broadly for the heartstring. In his "60 Minutes" interview with Powell, correspondent Ed Bradley asked, "Do you ever think that kids, that adults would perceive you as corny? Do you ever feel that you sound corny?"

"Yeah," Powell answered, "I sometimes think that I'm probably sounding a little too corny, a little too preachy. But then I realize that all I'm talking about are values, values that I was raised with, that you were probably raised with, that are traditional American values. . . . Even if it is corny, it's still valuable to hear. It's good stuff."

Vietnam was to prove the end of the Pershing Rifles at City College. More than a decade after Powell had graduated from the school—and after he had served two tours in Vietnam—the ROTC program folded its tent, as it did on so many other campuses, in the face of student protests against the Vietnam War. The social unrest of the Vietnam era and the rapidly shifting demographics of New York also dramatically changed the face of the college.

The CCNY Colin Powell attended was mostly a white school and a rigorous one. The Open Admissions policy instituted in 1970 required the college, in effect, to accept anyone who had graduated from a New York City high school with an average of 80 or higher or who had ranked in the top half of his or her class. Increasingly, too, the school, which had been founded to serve "the whole people" of New York, became the college of New York's new wave of immigrants, its next generation of "the whole people." By the start of the 1990s its student body was largely black and Hispanic—over half the students today were born abroad and are living somewhere in New York City. In the face of the extraordinary fiscal pressures placed on governments everywhere, the college is not the virtually free institution it was when Powell was a student. CCNY cost him $10 a year to attend. For the 1991–92 academic year, tuition was $1,850, up nearly fifty percent from the previous year.

But CCNY is still the college of the proletariat and the political left. When the name of Gen. Colin L. Powell, Chairman of the Joint Chiefs of Staff and Class of 1958, was mentioned at the college's 1990 graduation ceremonies—he was to have received an honorary degree but was unable to attend—it was booed loudly. Powell had assumed the chairmanship in October of the previous year, in time to help direct the U.S. invasion of Panama and the seizing of Manuel Noriega. "No school with as many Hispanics as City College should be honoring him," one student told New York *Times* reporter Joseph P. Fried.

Colin Powell stands in the center of the back row in the class photo of the 1958 graduates of City College's advanced ROTC program. A newly commissioned second lieutenant, he is one of two blacks among the twenty-one budding officers. He stands at attention, lips closed, but a faint smile seems to be playing over them, as if he were amused. Perhaps he is merely swallowing some private joke, but just perhaps he is thinking of his family—the immediate and extended family that was always part of his life—and their befuddlement at this strange calling he had chosen for himself.

"What was most important was—and this was expected of me by my parents—that I had a job, even if it was in the military," Powell wrote for his alumni magazine. "In those days, you see, you went to school for the purpose of making yourself employable. Today, I have several children who don't think that the end of college is necessarily the beginning of a productive work life. But we're sorting it out, each child at a time."

"For me," Powell wrote for the CCNY alumni magazine, the military "was a route out, a route up. For minority youth back in the mid- and late 1950s there were not that many avenues out. It was still a time when your possibilities were limited by your religious background or your racial heritage. . . . I was told, 'If you do everything well and keep your nose clean for twenty years, we'll make you a lieutenant colonel.' That was my goal."

Still, he wrote in *Guideposts* magazine, the military was not exactly what the transplanted Jamaican contingent had in mind for him. "Some folks in my family wondered: 'Cousin Johnny went into law, cousin Cecilia is studying medicine, and here Colin, of all things, is going into the Army. He isn't in trouble or anything?' "

As for his own parents, Powell told the *Washingtonian*, "they figured . . . he's going to get drafted anyway, so let him go in as an officer. He'll be in three years; he'll get a nice job with the city; he'll get a pension; it will all be okay. But then I didn't get out, and that confused them. Then when the three years were up, I still showed no signs of leaving. And then in my fourth year, I was sent to Vietnam, a place they had never heard of. And it was all very strange and curious.''

CHAPTER 5

Buffalo Soldiers

"So General Colin Powell was born in Harlem, to British citizens, Jamaican, working-class immigrant parents," a reader wrote in a letter to the editor of a British newspaper, the *Independent*, which had profiled Powell. "His good fortune that they took the New York rather than the Southampton boat. If they had, he might have made sergeant, that is, providing he did not try for a Guards regiment."

The letter may say less about the still-limited opportunities for blacks in the British military, especially in the most traditional units, than it does about the nature of any highly successful career and life, which require combinations of talent, ambition, determination, and to a certain extent timing—opportunity. Had Colin Powell joined the Army a dozen years earlier than he did, he probably would not have been housed with white soldiers, much less commanded them. Had he joined even eight years earlier, during the build-up of the Korean War, he would have been entering an armed forces integrated in word but not in deed. And had the effective integration of the services come, say, a dozen years later than it did, he would have been too far along his career path, even had he chosen the military, to take advantage of it. As it was, though, Powell joined the Army at precisely the moment when it was changing from one of the most rigidly segregated elements of American society to one of the most adamantly integrated. His military career stands as testament to the speed with which that transition was accomplished.

Retired Air Force Gen. Benjamin O. Davis, Jr., the first black graduate of West Point in the twentieth century and the son of the first black to achieve the rank of general officer, says that he did not "in any way in my lifetime" expect to see an African-American Chairman of the Joint Chiefs of Staff. "Yet," Davis says, "when it happened—and when I found out about his background—there was no surprise at all, except that it took some courage on the part of the [Bush] administration to make the appointment. . . . The greatest significance is that a black man could have had the background that enabled the administration to appoint him. That, I think, is the most remarkable part of the whole thing."

African-Americans, of course, have taken part in every war the nation has fought. Sixteen black soldiers and another five black sailors received the Congressional Medal of Honor for their valor during the Civil War, in which more than 33,000 black men were killed and nearly 180,000 black soldiers fought for the Union—and other blacks for the Confederacy. Seven more black fighting men received the Medal of Honor during the Spanish-American War. A runaway slave named Crispus Attucks, as every schoolchild learns, was the first person, black or white, to die in the Boston Massacre of 1770, which heralded the coming of the Revolutionary War. Blacks fought on Lake Erie with Capt. Oliver Perry in the War of 1812; others, a few, fought in the Mexican War. The so-called Buffalo Soldiers, the Ninth and Tenth U.S. Cavalry Regiments formed in 1867 out of black soldiers who had fought in the Civil War, battled the Cheyenne, who gave them their nickname, and later the Utes, Apache, and Sioux. They fought, too, in the Spanish-American War, both world wars, and the Korean conflict. In World War I, nearly 2.3 million blacks registered for the draft, and 367,000 were called to duty. The all-black 369th Infantry fought for 191 straight days through Champagne and Minaucourt and became the first Allied unit to reach the Rhine River. The all-black 370th fought one of the last battles of the war, capturing a German wagon train and its crews a half hour after the Armistice had gone into effect, John Hope Franklin notes in his history of black Americans, *From Slavery to Freedom.* A quarter century later, some 700,000 blacks served in nearly all the theaters of World

War II, many as messmen and in other menial capacities. At Pearl Harbor on December 7, 1941, in one of the most famed incidents of the war, black messman Dorie Miller manned a machine gun on the deck of the USS *Arizona* and, with no previous experience with the gun and in the face of withering aerial fire, shot down four Japanese planes. Gen. Davis himself was part of what became known as the Tuskegee Airmen, pilots who trained at the all-black Tuskegee Army Air Field, next to Tuskegee Institute in Alabama. Davis commanded the 99th Pursuit Squadron and, later, the 332d Fighter Group, both of which were highly decorated for action in North Africa and the southern European theater.

Powell's spacious Pentagon office is a kind of art-gallery monument to the contributions of black soldiers. Over the sofa at the far end of the room from his desk hangs a painting of Henry Ossian Flipper, the first black graduate of West Point, leading Buffalo Soldiers on a cavalry patrol on the Great Plains. Along the window wall is a portrait of another Buffalo Soldier. Further along the wall, over the standing desk where Powell often works, yet another painting shows an all-black Civil War regiment preparing to charge. In the anteroom to the office hangs a poster from *Glory*, the Civil War movie about the all-black 54th Regiment of Massachusetts and starring Matthew Broderick, Morgan Freeman, and Denzel Washington. Powell takes an obvious pride in the art—he points it out to visitors; he stands ready to give details. That the art is drawn from the segregated history of the military may be mere happenstance, but Powell does not seem at all inclined to forget what the flip-side of these all-black fighting units represents: that to be part of the American war machine was not, for blacks, to be integrated into American military life. More and more, it is a subject Powell takes on directly in his public speeches.

John Hope Franklin records an almost endless stream of insults, race-baiting, and open hostility in the nation's military camps and the southern cities where so many of the camps were located. At Camp Greene, near Charlotte, North Carolina, five YMCA buildings were set up during World War I for the white soldiers training there, but none for the ten thousand black trainees. At Camp Lee, near Petersburg, Virginia, white soldiers prevented black soldiers from attending a prayer meeting. The worst of the incidents—one of the bloodiest moments in the whole history of America's war between the races—occurred in August of 1917 in Houston when men of the all-black 24th Infantry got into a riot with white locals. "After much goading and many insults by the white citizens," Franklin writes, "the black soldiers were disarmed when it was feared they would use their weapons in defending themselves. Refusing to be outdone, the soldiers seized arms and killed seventeen whites. With only a slight pretense of a trial, thirteen Negro soldiers were hanged for murder and mutiny [and] forty-one were imprisoned for life." During World War II, a white bus driver in Durham, North Carolina, killed a black soldier with whom he had been arguing and was found not guilty by a jury of his peers. In Kentucky, three black WACS were beaten by local policemen for refusing to vacate promptly the train station's whites-only waiting room. Nor, Franklin notes, were any Congressional Medals of Honor awarded to black soldiers in either world war. Nor, for that matter, was Henry Ossian Flipper immune from the military's racism. In July, 1881, the West Point graduate was stationed at Fort Davis in western Texas as the only black officer with the Buffalo Soldiers. There he was set up by fellow white officers on an embezzlement charge. Found innocent by a military court, he was nonetheless given a dishonorable discharge for conduct unbecoming an officer and a gentleman. It is almost certainly the only time that a dishonorably discharged soldier has been so prominently featured in the office art of a chairman of the Joint Chiefs of Staff, and beyond almost any doubt, Powell means to make a point by it. He is not a haphazard man.

"My own experience with the military was not happy in the nineteen-twenties, thirties, and forties," General Davis says. "The reason was that the people making up the armed forces were really prejudiced human beings."

Davis cites a survey made in 1925: "This study done by the Army War College, where presumably the best and brightest officers went to school, was done by not one but by a succession of classes. And this study found that blacks were superstitious, not intelligent and not courageous, and that they generally should not be mixed with white people because of these types of deficiencies."

Seventeen years later, a report by the Chairman of the General Board to the Secretary of the Navy on the subject of "Enlistment of men of colored race in other than messman branch" used different logic to arrive at the same conclusion: "Men on-board ship live in particularly close association; in their messes, one man sits beside another; their hammocks or bunks are close together; in their common tasks they work side by side; and in particular tasks such as those of a gun's crew, they form a closely knit, highly coordinated team. How many white men would choose, of their own accord, that their closest associates in sleeping quarters, at mess, and in a gun's crew should be of another race? How many would accept such conditions, if required to do so, without resentment and just as a matter of course? The General Board believes that the answer is 'Few, if any.'"

The report goes on to say, "If Negroes are recruited for general service, it can be said at once that few will obtain advancement to petty officer. With every desire to be fair, officers and leading petty officers in general will not recommend Negroes for promotion to positions of authority over white men." In October, 1989, the Chief of Naval Operations would find himself a supporting player on the Joint Chiefs of Staff to a black soldier who was five years old when the General Board report was issued: Gen. Colin L. Powell.

On July 26, 1948, President Harry S Truman signed Executive Order 9981, decreeing that the U.S. Armed Forces should henceforth provide equal treatment and opportunity for all servicemen, regardless of race, and with that a tradition of military segregation that was as old as the nation came officially to an end. It took a surprise visit from George Marshall to Korea to bring it effectively to an end, according to Ret. Gen. Mike Lynch, who was present at the time.

"In Korea," Lynch says, "there was all this anti-black business. It was kind of token integration. We said we were doing it, but we really weren't. We said the black wasn't worth a damn and damned him with faint praise at the same time. We said they could be worth a damn as soldiers only if they had white officers in charge.

"George Marshall was the secretary of defense then and on in years and not in the best condition. I happened to be [Gen. Matthew] Ridgway's flying aide. One morning, unannounced, I found that I was to fly a very high-ranking VIP. There weren't many above Ridgway. We had to put plates on the airplane to indicate the rank, and they said, 'Put on five stars.' I said it had to be [Gen. Douglas] MacArthur—but he was fighting for his political life in Congress—or [Gen. Omar] Bradley or Marshall. By then I had flown all the brass; I was never mesmerized by them."

The surprise brass did turn out to be George Catlett Marshall, Chief of Staff of the Army during World War II, architect of the Marshall plan as Secretary of State from 1947 to 1949, and Secretary of Defense under Harry Truman from 1951 to 1952.

"When VIPs go overseas," Lynch continues, "they carry what we used to call horseholders with them—these aides who run around like the world is going to come to an end if anything goes wrong. I was trying to get Marshall buckled into the aircraft when his horseholder comes over to me and says, 'Now watch your landing. The old man is brittle.' I said to myself, as if I don't have enough problems—we had two-hundred-foot ceilings, rain, and wind. I got into the cockpit, closed it, and was just getting ready to crank up when I heard this chuckle. Marshall had these steely gray eyes, and they had the biggest twinkle I ever saw. 'I may be brittle,' he said, 'but I'm not deaf.' "

Lynch flew George Marshall out of Seoul to meet Matthew Ridgway, who was then heading the U.S. 8th Army and would soon become Allied Commander for the Far East, at a small airstrip that had been cleared just behind the front lines. At the end of the meeting, Lynch says, "there was a conversation between the two of them. Marshall said, 'Let's finish this black thing. Let's integrate blacks in the fullest sense and not put them in separate units anymore.' If you wanted to ask for when a Colin Powell could then become Chairman of the Joint Chiefs of Staff, it was at that very brief moment. This was in April of 1951."

Years later, rummaging through the George Catlett Marshall files at Virginia Military Institute—from which Marshall had graduated in 1901—Lynch would find an entry in Marshall's log for a spontaneous trip to South Korea and "this one small memo about finishing the integration of the armed forces." Among the groups first integrated by Marshall and Ridgway's intervention: the Ninth and Tenth Cavalry Regiments—the Buffalo Soldiers.

Although Colin Powell serves as a kind of final proof that the integration of the American armed forces is real and enduring—

as of May, 1992, seven percent of the Army's general officers, for example, are African-Americans, a higher percentage than can be found in the top management of any other sector of American society—blacks are not entirely without ambivalence toward Powell, in large part because many blacks remain ambivalent about the military and its mission. As noted earlier, Powell split openly—and to his great pain—with the Congressional Black Caucus over the ultimate use of military force in the Gulf. In an opinion article that appeared in the December 22, 1991, Washington *Post*, Colbert I. King, a black editorial writer for the newspaper, used the 1942 Navy General Board report on blacks and the military to take Powell to task for not moving against even harsher discrimination within the armed forces against gays. In fact, as King notes, Department of Defense Directive 1332.14 of January, 1982, does bear an uncanny resemblance to the General Board report issued almost forty years to the day earlier: "The presence of [homosexuals] adversely affects the ability of the Military Services to maintain discipline, good order and morals; to foster mutual trust and confidence among servicemembers . . . to facilitate assignment and worldwide deployment of servicemembers who frequently must live and work under close conditions affording minimal privacy."

When Powell was invited in November, 1990, to be honorary grand marshall of the January 21, 1991, King Week parade in Atlanta—celebrating the birthday of Martin Luther King, Jr.—Rev. Joseph Lowery, president of the Southern Christian Leadership Conference, protested, saying the invitation was at odds with King's ideology of non-violence. A month before the parade, Powell quietly excused himself from the grand marshall's duties. As Howard University political scientist Ronald Walters told a Boston *Globe* reporter after the Gulf War, "People want to say, 'Great, [Powell] has been successful in his role,' but they aren't sure that they like what he has done."

There is a feeling among some blacks that Powell is, in effect, somehow guilty by association with his service in the Reagan and Bush administrations. In 1988, when Powell was Ronald Reagan's National Security Adviser, Jesse Jackson told Lou Cannon of the Washington *Post* that Powell "will not attain hero status from the masses of black people because Reagan has been so indifferent, so insensitive to blacks. But,'' Jackson added, ''there is an appreciation of the predicament of his job.''

The relationship between Jackson and Powell—perhaps the two best-known black Americans outside of the sports and arts-and-entertainment worlds—is a difficult one to parse. According to the Washington *Post*'s Lou Cannon, Powell once cut off an interviewer who was questioning him about Jackson by saying, ''You're trying to get me to criticize him, and I won't.'' For his part Jackson talks about Powell in terms oblique enough to leave more than enough room for interpretation: ''In an era of imagery, [Powell] has outstanding imagery,'' Jackson said in an interview with the author. ''It means there's an assumption he can command the armed forces in time of crisis, that he can lead the country. During the most visible war we ever fought, he was the most visible leader, around whom was no scandal. Because he commands forces black, white, and brown, he is perceived to be fair.'' There is also, Jackson says later, ''the perception that he makes independent judgments.'' Asked to explain further what ''perceived'' and ''perception'' mean in this context, Jackson says, ''I know of no reality that is different from the perception.'' On the whole, it's a statement that begs for deconstruction. One senses in it a glimmer that Jackson considers Powell a possible political rival.

Jackson does say that a report in the September 10, 1990, *People* magazine, which asserts that Powell had performed a rare double-duty during the 1988 presidential campaign—simultaneously serving as informal adviser to both George Bush and Jackson on defense and foreign policy—is wrong: ''We have got to know each other,'' Jackson says, ''and I respect him. When I ask him questions about unclassified stuff, he gives me frank answers,'' but, he adds, ''no,'' Powell never served as an unofficial adviser to his campaign. Fred Francis, the veteran NBC defense correspondent who has been covering Powell closely for a number of years, says flatly that Powell and Jackson have ''no relationship. None.''

Although it is not specifically a criticism of Powell, some blacks argue that his very success serves ironically as a validation of continuing discrimination against African-Americans. ''America loves black heroes. We love black exceptionalism,'' Roger Wilkins, the civil-rights leader and professor of history at George Mason University, said on an April, 1991, showing of

PBS's "Frontline." "America loves to have black heroes because it tells America that we're fair and that the doors are open. And for those people who want to believe that the doors are open and we have a level playing field, you can look at Colin Powell and Michael Jordan as Exhibit A and say, 'Well, you see, those people from the ghettoes, if they'd just pull up their socks and stop going to bed at the age of fifteen, they, too, would be fine.' "

Powell himself agrees there is validity in that. "A lot of white people salve their consciences by saying, 'Well, look, we've got a Colin Powell, and he's not a basketball player. They can do it.' And so they cop out. I try to compensate for that by my own public remarks about . . . how hard it was to be a black when I was coming along. I can't go so far as to become the leader of the civil-rights movement in my position, but I never leave any doubt in anyone's mind that there's a lot more to be done. The other way I compensate for that is—however many white people use me as a cover for their conscience, I assume at least ten times as many black people are gaining some inspiration from me."

Again, though it is no specific criticism, even open Powell admirers such as Clarence Page, the conservative black commentator and columnist for the Chicago *Tribune*, say that the extraordinarily favorable attention Powell drew during and after the Gulf War was at least partially tied to race: "In reality," Page says, "if Powell were white, history would say Schwarzkopf would be the one everyone would be talking about. He was in the field commanding. Powell was way back in the rear. But because of race and history, Powell was the one everyone was looking at."

What almost no one accuses Powell of doing is using his race for his own advancement or of forgetting that he is, in fact, a black American.

"The doors are open to him everywhere," Roger Wilkins told the Boston *Globe*'s Michael Frisby. "He has access to power that excludes ninety-nine percent of us. There are some African-Americans who, when that happens, conclude they are just far better than those people from where they came and are really much more like the white people who have this power. The fact that this man is not like that speaks to his character."

In a February, 1991, speech to a group of black airmen, Powell said, "Many interviewers, when they come to talk to me, think they're being progressive by not mentioning in their stories any longer that I'm black. I tell them, 'Don't stop now. If I shot somebody, you'd have mentioned it. Fifty-three years you've been saying it. Don't stop now.' "

Washington attorney John Kester was special assistant to Secretary of Defense Harold Brown in the Carter administration when he chose Powell to be his military assistant. "He has never been one of the professional minority types who try to make a big deal of their racial background," Kester says, "but he's clearly always maintained a sense of loyalty to where he has come from. He's always been decent to little people. He could be very tough and tell people what they were supposed to do, but he dealt well with people of any station."

It is perhaps among those black people "of any station"— and especially those with memories long enough to include the days of the segregated armed forces—that Powell's accomplishments mean the most. It is to that group, too, that Powell seems to make the greatest effort to reach out and with whom he feels the greatest emotional attachment.

Simeon Booker, the Washington editor of *Ebony* magazine, recalls an incident in November of 1988 when Powell, who had only days before been named National Security Adviser, was scheduled to address the women's auxiliary of the James Reese Europe American Legion post, Washington's oldest black patriotic organization. "The luncheon was being held out at the Howard Inn, on the edge of the Howard University campus," Booker says, "and all of a sudden the snows came up. He was speaking to some black war widows, and it was snowing like hell. I never expected him to come, but he did. He told them, 'You don't understand. I had to show up for my people. I owe them that much.' " The drive, normally about fifteen minutes from the White House, took almost two hours.

Vernon Jordan tells of accompanying Powell to Fort McPherson, Georgia, in April of 1989 for Powell's swearing-in ceremony as head of the Armed Forces Command—a post he was to hold for only five months before being named Chairman of the Joint Chiefs of Staff.

"I went down there because for years my mother ran the officers club at Fort McPherson," Jordan says. "I went and took her to that ceremony. She sat there and wept because she remembers when before World War II a black soldier was a piece of shit. To sit there and see my friend Colin Powell sworn in as the commander-in-chief of that operation was for her a very significant moment. It probably meant more to her than it did to Colin."

Later Powell happened to be in Atlanta when an eighty-second birthday party was being thrown for Jordan's mother. "And he came," Jordan says. "He came out of tribute to her and to family. He likes family. You don't see that on TV—the warmth that he generates."

In an interview with the author, Powell tells the story of revisiting an aged barber at Fort Leavenworth in 1981, thirteen years after he had been there as a student at the Army Command and General Staff College.

"His name was Old Sarge," Powell says. "He died recently. I vaguely remembered where the barber shop was from my days as a student. I couldn't believe it would still be there. Well, lo and behold, I kind of dead-navigated my way, and there it was right on the corner. So I got out—it was a little hole in the wall, a typical little small community black barber shop, and I went in. There was nobody there except the barber. I said hello and sat down, and there were photographs of black generals on the wall. . . . So I got in the chair, he started cutting my hair, and he said, 'Sign the book.' And he had this 1959 diary which he had been using to get people to sign for many, many years. And so I wrote on the blank page—it was like a guest book—'Good to be back in Leavenworth. Nice to see your barber shop's still open. Warm regards,' and so on. And then sitting there getting my hair cut, when I could still read without my glasses, I started to flip the pages back and saw all these black officers that had been at Leavenworth that had written in it. There was Roscoe Robinson, Julius Becton [both retired Army generals], all these guys from the past, giants. I kept going back and back and then suddenly I came to 1968: 'Colin Powell, Major.' I'd forgotten. This guy, an old Buffalo Soldier, had been keeping track of all of us in his own little way. I fell in love with the guy, and that kind of got me going on the whole Buffalo Soldier thing.''

Among those Powell has been able to enlist in his effort to increase public awareness of the Buffalo Soldiers is Lynne Cheney, chairman of the National Endowment for the Humanities and wife of Powell's civilian boss, Defense Secretary Dick Cheney. ''We started talking about Buffalo Soldiers,'' Mrs. Cheney says, ''and he told me about how he had been jogging through the fort at Leavenworth and found only a back alley that was in any way a commemoration. I subsequently went to the [National Endowment for the Arts] and to Reader's Digest, and between us we were able to make a very substantial contribution to Buffalo Soldiers. I believe it was $30,000 from NEH and $20,000 from NEA, and Reader's Digest matched it. You had about $150,000. They're going to put into place a program for interpreting, for telling the history of the soldiers, as well as a monument.''

As planned, the Fort Leavenworth monument will include a bronze sculpture of an equestrian Buffalo Soldier with a natural pond behind him and a reflecting pool in front of him beneath a waterfall. Powell keeps brochures for the public-private fundraising effort in his Pentagon desk drawer and is only too happy to hand them out. Contributors of $25,000 or more receive a two-foot replica of the monument.

''It is difficult to accuse him of being a white man's black man,'' John Lichfield wrote in a profile for the *Independent*. ''The story is told of an elderly waiter at a White House dinner who almost dropped his tray when a large hand settled on his shoulder and a voice boomed: 'How're you doing, brother?' It was Powell.''

That Colin Powell is acutely aware of the segregated past of the Army that has been his home for more than thirty years, that he feels a debt to the black men and women who served in those armed forces, was never more evident than in August of 1991 when he addressed the twentieth annual national convention of the Tuskegee Airmen in Detroit.

''At Tuskegee, surrounded by some of the most vicious racism in America, the best and the brightest of their time set their individual and collective minds to what, even in retrospect, seemed an incredibly impossible task,'' Powell told the surviving airmen and their guests. ''The men—and women—at Tuskegee didn't just need to master aviation and military skills and the support of their husbands in time of war. They had to do it while much of the power of the United States Army tried to stifle the entire enterprise. While the civilians who surrounded them wasted no opportunity to express their hatred. While some of the very people who were teaching them their new aviation skills believed without question in their ultimate failure. And while the general feelings of the people in America were at best those of neglect and at worst violent disagreement with the whole idea.

''But these were not ordinary men and women at Tuskegee,'' Powell went on. ''If there is one thing about the history of the Tuskegee Airmen that is as unmistakable as the silhouette of a P-51, it is the fact that *these were not ordinary people* [Powell's emphasis]. They were *extra*ordinary men and women. Like Jackie Robinson, they stood above the crowd. They brooked no opposition to their goals, accepted no shortcuts, and took solace in the fact that they were paving the way for the future. Courage. Character. Determination. Drive. Devotion to duty. Love of America despite her imperfections. These are the things that made up their character, that gave it strength, that gave it resilience and pointed the way to the future.

''It was on this road to the future, paved with the sacrifice and blood of black patriots—especially the airmen—it was on this road that I traveled to become the first black Chairman of the Joint Chiefs of Staff. I never forget for a day, or for an hour, or for a minute, that I climbed to my position on the backs of the courageous African-American men and women who went before me.

''Any one of the airmen here could have been chairman, decades ago; at least six of them told me that tonight. But the opportunity fell to me because I came along at the right time, because you had paved the way, because you had given me inspiration by being the wind beneath my wings. So today I am chairman because of you and I do it for you. I will never forget where I came from and I thank you.''

As Powell spoke the last two sentences, his voice hitched and faltered. He was clearly overwhelmed by emotion. Powell ended shortly thereafter with the closing lines of a poem, "These Are Our Finest," written about the Tuskegee Airmen. (The poet, Pittsburgh journalist John H. Young III, had washed out of the Tuskegee Airmen flyer course and become, instead, an instructor in the program.)

> *Heroes? Men are heroes . . . these are*
> *　more than men.*
> *They are the valiant, the brave, the*
> *　"black boy" tried and true.*
> *They are the exploited, the expendable*
> *　. . . the birds with clipped wings.*
> *They are the noble, the greatest . . . these*
> *　are our finest.*
> *Hats off to the men who tried. Hats off*
> *　to the men who cried.*
> *Hats off to the men who died.*

"Ladies and gentlemen, our hats are off to the Tuskegee Airmen and to the brave black soldiers who went before them. And our hats are off to today's soldiers, sailors, airmen, marines, and coast guardsmen—black and white—who are your proud successors and who learned from the example of the Tuskegee Airmen how to be true American patriots. Hats off to all Americans who love their country and who will not rest until the dream is realized and the wind is beneath all our wings."

It is quintessential Powell oratory.

"Growing up on Kelly Street, particularly on Kelly Street in the Bronx, everybody was a 'minority,' " Powell wrote for the CCNY alumni magazine. "I didn't know what a 'majority' was. You were either black, Puerto Rican, Jewish, or of some strange European extraction."

At age nineteen, after his sophomore year at CCNY, he did a summer training session at Fort Bragg, North Carolina: "My father saw me off. He wasn't sure I would ever return from this adventure in the South." It was only when he arrived at Fayetteville, North Carolina, Powell told the Washington *Post*'s Lou Cannon, "that I had brought home to me in stunning clarity the way things were in other parts of the United States.''

Two years later, a newly commissioned second lieutenant, Powell was told to report to Fort Benning, Georgia—near Columbus, in the far western part of the state along the Alabama border—and there, he wrote for his alumni magazine, ''I came to understand the nature of bias.''

CHAPTER 6

Romping, Stomping Youngsters

"I was sitting in my room," Ret. Maj. Gen. William Roosma recalls of his and Powell's introduction to basic training at Fort Benning, Georgia. "I think we arrived about two days early. Here I was just out of the military academy. I was sitting on my bunk waiting for someone to tell me to do something. That's what you do if you've been to the military academy.

"Colin Powell had moved in down the hallway. He ducked his head in and said, 'What are you doing? Let's go somewhere.' I said, 'Can we?' He said, 'Sure.' . . . As I recall, we went to the club and had a few drinks. It was great. It was my first day officially in the Army, and he was the first guy I met."

"Great," though, can be a relative term when it's applied to basic training and the Ranger and Airborne courses that followed, all crammed into less than five intense months and spread over terrain that ranged from nasty to mean. "There were three phases," Ret. Lt. Col. William McCaffrey, now a Detroit insurance executive, recalls. "The first was at Fort Benning—combat training, hand-to-hand, rope climbing, all the physical skills. Then they took us up on the divide, where there are mountains between Tennessee and Georgia—wherever [the movie] *Thunder Road* was. We used to run into all the stills back there. We had to wear red bandanas to identify us so they would know we weren't revenuers. Then at Eglin

[Air Force Base] we were on the verge of the northern swamps of Florida. You could go for miles without seeing another person; I'm sure there hasn't been another person there since we came by. There were snakes all over the place, but we were just too tired to worry about them. We walked and they got out of the way. The greater danger was snapping turtles; they could bite right through a boot.''

Because they were the two tallest members of their unit, Powell and McCaffrey got the dubious honor of carrying the company machine guns on exercises. "It was brutal," McCaffrey says. "The Ranger course was designed to test your endurance—long patrols, nights in the swamps—and when you're lugging a machine gun waist-deep in the water, it's trying. The one thing that's always stayed in my mind is that people would sometimes offer to take the machine gun from you and give you a rifle in exchange. This one evening I recall no one was helping either of us, and at some ungodly hour in the morning, two or three, somebody finally offered to take the machine gun from Colin and give him his rifle in exchange. A little while later, we're walking along, and he turns around and takes my machine gun and gives me the rifle that he had been given. I'll never forget that.''

It was at Fort Benning, Powell wrote for his college alumni magazine, that he first "saw what is referred to as a White Anglo-Saxon Protestant.'' It was also at Fort Benning that he first came face-to-face with what were then the crown princes of the Army—its West Point graduates, the corps within the corps from which the service had been crafting its leadership since 1802.

"From our point of view, there was an advantage [to having gone to West Point],'' Roosma says. "We were probably more grounded in some of the military aspects. On the other hand, on the social side, the ROTC people might have had the advantage. But once you broke the ice, the associations developed not on college lines but on who wanted to be friends.''

In fact, says Ret. Gen. Mike Lynch, Powell's City College and ROTC background—the social advantage of *not* having attended West Point—may be critical factors in Powell's success. "When you take an individual—and I don't care who it is—the most formative years in shaping his personality and views occur roughly between the ages of eighteen and twenty-two. When you take that guy out of society and put him in an elitist environment like West Point and Annapolis, his only perspective is going to be that. When you're on a college campus in a civilian community, you learn to use the values of the society itself as a basis for your conduct on the battle-field.

"Powell had that advantage, and being black, he had it even more so. He couldn't get away from those values. His formative years were very different from his West Point contemporaries and subordinates. He couldn't turn white in those situations where being black puts extra pressure on you, and from that he learned tolerance and sensitivity to the issues. . . . I look back on the guys who were in my view the great commanders—and [Gen. Matthew] Ridgway is a good example of this. The one trait that dominated was compassion. Ridgway was being judged by people who viewed compassion as a weakness. In a way it's the same thing with Powell. People look at him and they say, 'Well, he has one weakness; he's not hardhearted.' But in an army that doesn't have the rigid discipline it once had—an army, let me say, that doesn't rely on discipline to get the job done but rather relies on rationality—that's the only guy who in the end is going to contribute."

Colin Powell also entered the armed forces at a time when the important career-building and career-making distinctions between a ROTC and a service academy education were just beginning to erode. Any military officer's career is a winnowing process. Many are called to be second lieutenants; few of those—even those who want to make the military a life's work—are chosen to be general officers. And to be constantly advanced in rank in the military is vital. Unlike many sectors of civilian life where someone passed over for promotion can be shunted off to a branch office or a dead-end vice-presidency, the military is an up-or-out proposition. On June 9, 1958, when Powell received his commission as a second lieutenant in the United States Army, the decided edge in rising to a brigadier general's star was a West Point degree. It was an edge that began with the newly minted commission itself: service academy graduates and graduates of officer candidate schools got regular commissions, a badge of being a professional soldier. ROTC graduates such as Powell received reserve commissions, an indication they were passing through the Army on their way to other careers. If they decided to make the service their life's work, they had to apply for a regular commission. When Powell reached the rank of major on May 24, 1966—the first barrier of any real significance that he had passed—the pendulum had begun to swing in the other direction. By the time he received his first star, temporarily on the first of June, 1979, and permanently on January 22, 1982, the edge was all but erased. By the time he was serving his second tour as Chairman of the Joint Chiefs of Staff, even the distinction between the two commissions was headed for extinction—as were, perhaps, the service academies themselves, at least as they have long functioned.

"It used to be that going to West Point was some advantage, as it should have been; it's the nation's academy," says one retired general and West Point graduate. "About the time I was selected to general—in the mid-nineteen-sixties—it was about a fifty-fifty thing, with probably a slight edge to the West Pointers. Now it's gone the other way."

As of 1997, ROTC and military graduates will enter the services and begin the quest for a general's star on an equal footing: both will receive reserve commissions initially and then compete for regular ones. The law, pushed hard in the Senate by Sam Nunn, was budget-driven—academy graduates cost an average of about $200,000 each for their education, or more than $2.6 billion for the 13,000-plus students enrolled at any given time in the three major academies—but the practical effect, the same retired general says, is to threaten the very existence of the academies. "The selection process to general plays itself into the central question of what in fact is the role of West Point," he says. "Do you really want to pay that much money to produce a second lieutenant artillery officer?"

David Evans—a retired Navy officer and the defense correspondent for the Chicago *Tribune*—has suggested that the academies may, in time, become military graduate schools of sorts—places where new officers who have taken their undergraduate degrees from civilian colleges and universities would come for a concentrated one-year course on warfare.

* * *

If the Fort Benning that Colin Powell arrived at in June of his twenty-first year was a meritocracy, a place where performance counted more than pedigree or race—and if the Army itself was more and more becoming a meritocracy in larger ways—off base in western Georgia in 1958 for a young black officer was another story. William McCaffrey, Powell's fellow machine-gun hauler, recalled one example for *Newsday*.

"There was a string of bars outside the place, and when we tried to go in, they wouldn't serve us because Powell was black. We just kept telling the bartender this guy is a Ranger just like us, but we got into some kind of fight. We went back a second night, and things got really ugly. The third time he just went off by himself, and we found him later at that same bar. He'd gone in and talked to the guy, and they'd given him a beer and told him to go sit in a corner and leave them alone. It's incredible to believe, to even put in perspective after all these years, that a man who is now Chairman of the Joint Chiefs of Staff, a possible vice-president, was denied service in my lifetime," McCaffrey adds.

"Unfortunately, that was the tenor of the times," says William Roosma. "It was so difficult. We were all cut out of the same cloth, doing the same things. On the post itself, there were so many clubs, so many outlets that it was never noticeable. It was only when someone would say, 'Let's go down here [off base],' and he'd say, 'Well, I'm busy. I can't go with you,' to avoid embarrassing us. That's when it was really tough for us to take . . . There were a couple of times we wanted to go and clean the bar out. And we were capable of it—we were romping, stomping youngsters. One time I had to be restrained, held back. Here was a good friend put on the spot, and you don't let that happen to friends. But guys like Colin Powell wouldn't let us get into trouble for that. Another one of my black friends there said, 'It's bigger than us. I appreciate what you want to do, but it's just bigger than us.' Those guys were truly great friends."

Without any special effort or intent to do so, Roosma says, Powell simply stood out in the crowd of new second lieutenants at Fort Benning. "Sometimes when things got going a little tough, Colin Powell was the one that would rise above it. He always had a smile, a sense of humor to bring things back in perspective again. That's been one of the marks that's carried through for him. One of the things that struck you was his maturity, even at a very young age. He had a sense of confidence about himself that was like an aura. He truly had so much self-confidence. When you're that young, it's an incredible thing to have.''

Powell and Roosma would eventually reconnect professionally, at the Pentagon in the mid-1980s when Powell was serving as the military assistant to the Secretary of Defense and Roosma held a similar position with the Secretary of the Army. The experience, Roosma says, ''just solidified my initial impression'' of nearly thirty years earlier. ''Even then, from the very beginning, it was obvious. He just had an innate gift for leadership. You have those instincts: here was someone who was going to rise rapidly. As I look back, that's the only person who came to me, who struck me so vividly.''

And, Roosma adds, for all its physical rigors the Infantry Officers Basic Course at Fort Benning was a blast: ''We were fired up; we were all young second lieutenants, all eager to get out in the field. There was a lot of teamwork, a lot of team effort. We were,'' he repeats, ''romping, stomping youngsters.''

Powell's first field assignment—the second item in a military resumé that would grow to thirty-four entries and include three continents, seven U.S. forts, the White House West Wing, and nearly every ring of the Pentagon—was as a platoon leader with Company B, Second Armored Rifle Battalion, Forty-eighth Infantry, with the United States Army in Germany. Powell arrived in October of 1958, four years and ten months after Secretary of State John Foster Dulles had first enunciated the policy of ''instant, massive retaliation'' against a direct Soviet attack ''at times and places of our own choosing''; almost two years after Soviet troops and tanks had rolled into Budapest and crushed the revolt there; and long after there was any real hope, except in the dreamiest diplomatic circles, that the two post-World War II superpowers could find any sort of meaningful common ground. Powell was stationed for much of that time in Gelnhausen, near the border of the Hessen and Bavarian states, on the Kinzia River, less than fifty miles from the East German border, where—so military doctrine held—the ground war between East and West was most likely to begin. Over the next twenty-four months he would shuttle between the Second Armored Rifle Battalion and the Third Armored Division. He would also find a good friend and what seems to be his first rabbi.

"Colin and I were thicker than thieves," says retired Col. Keith Bissell. "It was hard to tell who was thick and who was the thief. I was a bit more senior than he was. When I assumed command of the company, he was my mortar platoon leader but only for a short time. This was the time of Khrushchev. I was scheduled to come home to the Eighty-second Airborne, but that didn't happen. They held me there. We got to know each other socially and at company grade. Some of the time he was off in the field doing certain things and I was off doing other things. We were in the ballgames, or we'd sit there and throw a beer back in the club—just things young lieutenants do. I remember the times he was in the field and on the alerts, guarding the artillery pieces. I'd bring the food and pay out to him in the cold and misery, and he was always pleasant. Nothing bothered him. He always had a smile. He was just a very good friend.

"And," Bissell says, "I can always remember the Christmas Eve we went to church. . . . We were at a party that night. It was cold, snowy. I guess we were feeling a bit homesick. I said, 'I normally go to the Episcopal church on Christmas Eve.' " Powell, who had been raised in the Episcopal church in the South Bronx, said, " 'I'll go with you.' We drove from Gelnhausen to Frankfurt. In those days it was a good hour-, hour-fifteen-minute drive. Now it's pretty much a four-lane road between the two."

Powell's first rabbi in the military—one of those critical senior officers who can help guide a career through the bureaucratic advancement labyrinth of the services—appears to have been Ret. Col. Raymond "Red" Barrett.

"I was executive officer of the battalion he went to," Barrett says. "I was there from 1957 to 1960. That was the Third Armored Division, Germany. He was great at that time. There's no question. He was an outstanding officer. His sense of responsibility—he had that from the word go. And a cheerful disposition—he was never dead serious, even under adverse conditions he'd find something humorous. He was an all-around guy, not just rifle platoon but heavy mortar. He was a real goer, a real doer.''

Keith Bissell says, ''We got our asses kicked regularly by Red Barrett, just for being young platoon leaders, for not following through on various things. That was typical in the Army. But Colonel Barrett was a mentor. We all came to admire him greatly. He watched over all our activities and he shaped our careers, a lot of careers. He was in the Pentagon later on, where he was able to do that. He was in career management at that time—chief of this or that or whatever— and he was very interested in all of us. He didn't single out anyone, but he was very interested in all of us. . . . I think without a doubt he had a great deal to do with where Colin is today.''

''If you're really lucky as a young man,'' says Ret. Col. David Hackworth, ''you impress a major or colonel who goes to the office of personnel directorate at the Pentagon—that was called the career branch. If you've got a patron there, he's making sure you get the right school, the right assignments.''

Other patrons, mentors, and rabbis would follow, more powerful ones both in and out of the military—Powell seems to attract them—but it is wholly typical of him that Powell has not forgotten the one who seems to have started everything rolling. He is a man attentive to details large and small, human as well as strategic.

''All these young lieutenants, Mrs. Barrett kind of mothered them around a bit,'' Colonel Barrett says of his wife. ''And Colin's never forgotten us, regardless of how far along he went. When my son was in the desert [during the Persian Gulf War], Colin somehow managed to get down to his unit and somehow managed to call his mother and say he was fine. For a man as busy as he was, I thought that was goddamn kind. I can't say enough good about him.''

Since Powell has been Chairman of the Joint Chiefs of Staff, he and his wife Alma have hosted a very large annual New Year's reception, in accordance with an old military tradition. Among those asked every year have been the Barretts. ''I feel rather flattered to be invited,'' Barrett says. ''I don't have anything to offer.''

If he has ''nothing to offer,'' as he says, Barrett nonetheless offers a spirited Army-style defense when asked about one of the few complaints about Powell—that he is a political general, a soldier who has risen to the top more by keeping a finger out to the always complex winds that direct a top Washington career than by leading troops into battle: "That," Barrett says, "is bullshit. It's a bunch of goddamn pissant Navy types, probably. They figure if you don't come out of a goddamn aircraft carrier, you ain't worth crap. I'm glad he's where he is because he won't compromise. That's a misstatement: he won't compromise on the *important* things. Like he says, 'I won't have a hollow force; I'll quit before I do.' And he means it."

Nearly twenty-six years after he was rotated out of Germany, Powell would return as a three-star general to command the Army's V Corps, headquartered in Frankfurt—the front-line command in the more than thirty-year face-off across Europe between the U.S.-led NATO forces and the Soviet Union.

"For a lieutenant general, that was the absolute plum," says Ret. Col. William Abernathy. "It was a command for one thing, and it was in Europe where possibly the biggest threat to security was. It just required great capability and must have brought great personal satisfaction."

Like all of Powell's field commands in the later years of his military career, it was also notable for its brevity—barely six months in this case, from June to December of 1986, before he was called back to Washington to be the deputy assistant to National Security Adviser Frank Carlucci. Six years later the Soviet Union had collapsed as a political entity; the two Germanys had become one; and Combat Command B of the Third Armored Division, where Powell and Keith Bissell had been "thicker than thieves," was deactivated, victim of a world order changing more rapidly than almost anyone could imagine. The deactivation, Bissell says, "made me cry a bit."

Keith Bissell would go on to become a civilian employee at Fort Benning. In 1986, as Powell was leaving Washington to assume his command in Germany, "he came through [Fort Benning] for the infantry commanders conference," Bissell says. "I left my card and wrote on the back, 'If you have a minute, give me a shout.' He always knew I was in my office

early. I got a call from Colin, and he came in about seven
A.M. . . . He hasn't forgotten the people he grew up with.
That tells you a lot right there.''

Powell's next stop, by now a first lieutenant, was at Fort
Devens, Massachusetts, where he would be stationed from
December, 1960, until September, 1962. It was there that
what would become a familiar pattern with Powell first be-
came evident: being jumped over senior officers, just as
George Bush would finally jump him over more than thirty
senior officers to make him Chairman of the Joint Chiefs of
Staff.

"I was operation officer for the brigade, and he was in
another unit," William Abernathy says. "He was liaison officer to our headquarters and he was very impressive in that
capacity. He carried information back and forth between the
headquarters on positions of the units and what was going on
with them.

"Later on, I became a commander of an infantry battalion,
and he was in the battalion. It was a new organization, and
he was one of the officers. Shortly after it was activated, there
was an opening for the job of adjutant, and I put him in that
position. Normally, the organization chart called for a captain, preferably a senior one, but I put him in there as a
twenty-four-year-old lieutenant because he had a very impressive performance up until that time.

"He hadn't had any experience in that kind of position
before, but within a week you would have thought he'd been
doing it all his life. There are eleven functions that go with
that job—it's a son of a gun. It has to do with maintaining
the strength of the units, the records, the assignment of personnel, the discipline, law and order, morale, awards and
decorations—I can't remember all of them anymore, but it
requires an intricate knowledge of army regulations, which
he knew extremely well. . . . We had a very warm relationship. He was easy to deal with in his position. We conferred
many times during the day and particularly late in the afternoon for planning the next day and beyond. He had a perception very rapidly of what his job entailed and how it
affected me personally and how it affected the soldiers. And
he had a good feeling, a perceptive feeling for the troops—

he was an excellent adviser on matters relating to the troops. I had great confidence in him from the start. He showed not only a perception of his job, but a very keen sense of humor to go with that. That certainly helped.''

Over the years that followed, Abernathy says, ''I wrote him a couple of times when he got particular jobs. I would write him to the effect that when the chips are down in the military service and they had to have somebody to bail them out of trouble, they always call in the first team, and that he always seemed to be a part of it.''

At Fort Devens, too, Colin Powell seems to have found his vocation for good, if he had ever had any real doubt about it. Along the way he also fell in love, although it seems to have taken a war to get him to the altar. Powell and Alma Vivian Johnson—then an audiologist with the Boston Guild for the Hard of Hearing and a graduate student at Emerson College in Boston—met on a blind date. For Alma Johnson it was not a good way to begin a romance. ''I was not happy about it,'' Mrs. Powell remembers. ''My roommate had done this, and I said, 'I don't go out on blind dates and I definitely don't go out with soldiers. How do I know what's walking in that door?' I tease [Colin] and say that if I had been living in Birmingham [Alabama] in my father's house, he never would have gotten in the front door. My mother used to call people like that 'traveling salesmen'—'Why do you want to date a traveling salesman?' '' As Mrs. Powell remembers the first date, her future husband took her to ''a little nightclub on Massachusetts Avenue [in Boston]. We were married eight months later.'' The only thing that gave her pause about her future husband, Alma Powell once told Lou Cannon of the Washington *Post*, was ''when I asked him when he was going to get out of the Army, he said he intended to make it a career. Everyone else I knew in the Army had the days and minutes of their remaining service counted.''

By the summer of 1962 the terms of a career in the Army were about to change for Powell's immediate generation of officers. While Americans had been staring eastward across the Atlantic Ocean, mesmerized by a potential ground war with the Soviet Union across the battlefields of Europe—and a potentially far more devastating nuclear confrontation beyond that—the nation was slowly sliding into war in Asia for

he third time in a little more than two decades. Beginning
n 1961, a search had gone out across the Army for officers
o serve as military advisers to the Army of the Republic of
Vietnam. In July of 1962 Powell got orders to do just that.
'I was an infantry officer. I was stationed at Fort Devens,
Massachusetts,'' Powell told the *Washingtonian*. ''I was
hinking of getting married, or at least I was going very steady
with a young lady, and suddenly I got orders saying, 'You are
going to Vietnam.' ''

Powell said that the first thing he and several other officers
who had gotten similar orders did was to look Vietnam ''up
on a map and make sure we knew where it was. You have to
emember, this was the very early stages. I was going in with
he second group of advisers as it was building up to the
ifteen-thousand level, and sure, as an infantryman, it was
erribly exciting. I couldn't wait to drive in and tell my girl-
riend that I was going to Vietnam. That caused a bit of a
roblem, but I was very excited about going. It was what
nfantry officers should want to do. So I not only had no
eservations about it, I was looking forward to it. I was
wenty-four years old or something. It was hot stuff.''

In an interview with the author, Powell recalled the ''bit
of a problem'' he got into when he told Alma Johnson he
was headed to Vietnam: ''I said to my girlfriend, 'I'm going
o war!' And she said, 'Oh.' So I said, 'You'll write, won't
you?' and she said, 'No.' So I married her. We got married
hree weeks later,'' on August 25, 1962.

Mrs. Powell calls her husband's memory ''roughly accu-
ate.'' ''I said, 'No, I'm not going to tell you I'll be here
when you get back or that I will be writing. I'm too old to
do this.' I was twenty-four years old, an old maid by the
standards of those days. 'You go on, kid, go ahead; I'll go
ind somebody else.' . . . He went away and thought about
hat a little bit, and he came back the next weekend and said,
'Okay, let's get married. Call your folks. We'll do it in two
weeks.' It was my father's birthday. Here I'm calling to tell
him I'm marrying somebody he's never seen before. I'm doing it in two weeks, the week after next—'Do whatever you
want to. I'll buy the dresses.' That was it.''

''[Colin] just came in one Friday afternoon and wanted to
know if he could have three days off,'' William Abernathy

recalls. "I said, 'Well, yes.' He said, 'Well, I want to get married.' It was just like that."

"When we hit this impasse about how she wasn't going to write to this soldier boy," Powell went on, elaborating, "I said, 'Well, let's get married.' She said, 'Are you asking me?' And I said, 'Yeah.' So she called her mother in Birmingham and said we were getting married. Her parents weren't surprised and neither were mine. They knew we were serious. So a full-sized wedding was planned in Birmingham. It was hell getting my parents there. They said, 'We're not going to Birmingham. You're crazy. Have a happy life.' My mother was willing, but my father had *no* desire to go south. But my beloved sister and my brother-in-law [Norman Berns]—my brother-in-law is white—said, 'We're going. Colin's getting married, we're going.' So Mother and Dad decided they better go, 'since if they lynch Norm, we all ought to be there.' . . . We got married on a Saturday, spent the night in Birmingham, flew back to Boston on a Sunday, and I was at work Monday."

The fact that Alma Powell's parents weren't surprised by their daughter's desire to marry Colin Powell does not, however, mean that they were uniformly overjoyed by the match. "Somebody told me," Mrs. Powell recalls, "that after the wedding that day [my father] said, 'My whole life, I've been trying to get away from those West Indians, and now my daughter is marrying one.' I don't know why he was trying to get away from West Indians."

In October, 1962, the newlyweds moved to Fort Bragg, North Carolina, where Powell took a six-week training course at the Army's Special Warfare Center. In December he shipped out for Southeast Asia, and his new wife—by then pregnant—moved in with her parents in Birmingham. "I remember him talking to his mother's next-door neighbors, explaining to them the domino theory—a very impassioned speech about why this was necessary because they were very skeptical. I was amazed at how few people knew what it was really about," Mrs. Powell says about her husband in the weeks before his departure. In Birmingham not long afterward, Mrs. Powell recalls, she was talking "with a very prominent citizen in town, well read, well educated, a writer

imself, and he said to me, 'Are you going to join your hus-
and once the baby is born?' "

In effect, Colin and Alma Powell had gone to the separate
ronts of the two wars America would wage in the 1960s.
'owell was leading a combat unit near the North Vietnamese
order when his son was born. Like many soldiers at war, he
vouldn't find out he was a father until more than two weeks
after the fact. Meanwhile, Alma Powell was holed up in a
ity being torn apart by racial violence—"I probably saw
nore action than he did," she says.

CHAPTER 7

Walk on Water

Army slang has various terms for them—walk-on-water guys, fast-burners; the young officers who are singled out early in their careers for the long march to the top ranks. Powell's selection as an adviser to the Army of the Republic of Vietnam was the first clear sign that he was one of them, says Col. David Hackworth, the most decorated American soldier from that war and now a contributing editor to *Newsweek*.

"When they asked for volunteers in 1961," Hackworth says, "to me, the writing was on the wall: Go to Vietnam. I was very important to get that experience. Those young first lieutenants and captains who went to Vietnam in 1962 were all walk-on-water types—they only picked water-walkers. They wanted to give them battle experience so that later, when they were three- and four-star generals, they at least would have some combat experience. . . . We sent them to Vietnam so they would be ready for the real war we were going to fight with the Soviets. They went in lieu of old guys with a lot of combat experience who were abrasive and tough. We sent green guys who had nothing under their pistol belts. We lost that war to prepare for the war we were going to fight with the Soviets."

Although it received scant attention in the press, the U.S. military effort in South Vietnam was in its seventh year when Colin Powell arrived in Saigon in December of 1962. With the final fall of the French army at Dienbienphu on May 7

1954, to Gen. Vo Nguyen Giap and his Viet Minh forces and the subsequent Geneva Accords agreed to on July 21 of that year, the former French colonial state of Indochina had been divided into a communist-dominated Democratic Republic of Vietnam in the north and the Republic of Vietnam in the south—a coalition of non-communist groups headed by president Ngo Dinh Diem. (French Indochina had also included Laos and Cambodia.) Almost immediately after the accords were reached, the U.S. Military Assistance Advisory Group, to which Powell would eventually report, was formed to extend American military aid to strengthen the Diem regime and to forestall civil war in the south among numerous armed factions, religious and political, none of them wholly reconciled to Ngo Dinh Diem. At least for the time being, that part of the operation worked—Diem managed to put together a working government. Then, Jeffrey Clarke of the U.S. Army Center of Military History writes in *Advice and Support: The Final Years, 1965-73*, the three- to four-hundred-man U.S. advisory group "went to work creating a national army." It would prove the work of ages.

"Much had to be done," Clarke writes. "Although thousands of Vietnamese had served in French military units, few had had any leadership or staff experience, and fewer still had received any technical training." As the decade drew to a close the Army of the Republic of South Vietnam—ARVN, as it became known—had grown to a 150,000-man force but one pointed mostly in the wrong direction. Its primary mission, Clarke continues, "was to repel a North Vietnamese army invasion across the demilitarized zone that separated North and South Vietnam. Diem and his American advisers thus organized and trained the new army for a Korean-style conflict, rather than for the unconventional guerrilla style of warfare that had characterized the earlier Franco-Viet Minh struggle." By then, too, the fragile coalition that supported Diem was beginning to come apart at the seams. "In 1960 an internal insurgency that had been simmering unnoticed for several years suddenly began to boil over throughout the length and breadth of the country," Clarke writes. "With but limited assistance from the North, the southern communists had managed to rebuild their political organization and openly challenge the government of Saigon. Diem's new state, once regarded as a model bulwark against communism, began to totter, and the elaborate military machine constructed by the American advisers seemed incapable of dealing with the new situation. The second Indochina war had begun.''

A year later, on the twentieth anniversary of the Japanese attack on Pearl Harbor, Diem wrote American president John F. Kennedy: "In the course of the last few months, the Communist assault on my people has achieved high ferocity. In October they caused more than 1,800 incidents of violence and more than 2,000 casualties. They have struck occasionally in battalion strength, and they are continually augmenting their forces by infiltration from the North.''

"Mr. President,'' Diem went on, "my people and I are mindful of the great assistance which the United States has given us. . . . But Vietnam is not a great power and the forces of international Communism now arrayed against us are more than we can meet with the resources at hand. We must have further assistance from the United States if we are to win the war now being waged against us.''

A week later, on December 14, 1961, Kennedy replied: "We shall promptly increase our assistance to your defense effort. . . . I have already given the orders to get these programs underway.'' Colin Powell would be part of Kennedy's response—an escalation to fifteen thousand U.S. troops in South Vietnam—but the work when Powell arrived was much what it had been for the relative handful there a half a decade earlier: to create a national army. Whether it was water-walking work or not, it was a job to which Powell seems to have been particularly well suited. In a sense, too, it both foreshadowed his future success in the complicated corridors of the White House and the Pentagon and groomed him for that later task.

"The idea was to get some kind of backbone into the above-quality units of the Vietnamese military so that there would be something to look up to, something that would enhance professionalism in the rest of the military,'' says military historian Shelby Stanton, who at the time was training South Vietnamese Rangers at a school in Thailand.

To have been selected for the job, Stanton says, "means that you're considered among your peers above average in endurance and toughness, but you have to have more than a undamental knowledge of patrolling, infantry tactics, and how to set up weapons. You also have to be able to work with people. [Gen. George] Patton is a very good example of the sort of person who wasn't right for the work. He was a brilliant soldier, but he couldn't get along with people.

"It takes a very political person. You need the utmost consideration in knowing when to apply pressure because it's another culture. It's a very difficult type of interpersonal relationship. There's a Hollywood myth that the Army never puts the right people in the right place. It gets perpetuated by a lot of bad experiences people have in the military, especially in the enlisted ranks. But when the military had an excess of good officers as they did in the early days of Vietnam, before they had to pull a lot of American troops over here, you would find that they really did sort of tag people as far as assignments went. The fact that certain people would be slotted for certain assignments went to the fact that they had not only outstanding attributes but personalities that befit the job. . . . At the same time, the work would have further molded Powell as he molded the troops."

President Diem had divided South Vietnam into three—and later four—"corps tactical zones," or military administrative units, each headed by its own corps commander who was responsible for maintaining internal security within his region as well as planning tactical operations against the enemy. Powell would spend nearly all his time in his initial Vietnam tour with the First Infantry Division of the South Vietnamese army in I Corps, the northernmost of the regions, stretching from the demilitarized zone (DMZ) that separated the two Vietnams some two hundred miles south along the coast of the South China Sea and including the air base at Da Nang and the ancient imperial Vietnamese capital at Hue.

The ARVN First Infantry "was the crack South Vietnamese division, stationed up along the DMZ, just south of it," says historian Vincent Demma of the U.S. Army Center of Military History. (Demma's *Advice and Support: The Middle Years, 1961-65* will complete the center's trilogy on the Vietnam war.) "Generally speaking, the division was deployed through the two most northern provinces of South Vietnam. It was focused on defense of the DMZ and the major port cities of both North and South Vietnam."

"We were on operations in the jungle for six months," says another U.S. adviser whose work paralleled Powell's in I Corps. "Basically they were search operations for the Viet cong, attempts not to give them any stable areas to operate from. Most of our operations were on the coast, but they ranged as far west as the Laotian border. Our role was to advise the Vietnamese infantry and their artillery on how to conduct operations and how to maintain their equipment as well as in tactical operations. Many of these companies had been formed by mass conscription; they didn't go through any basic training. One of the things we were able to do was get them to return from the field and run through a training cycle. We put them through rifle marksmanship, physical fitness, small-unit tactical operations, that type of thing. . . . We saw each other from time to time," he says of Powell. "He was a basic infantry soldier, very capable, sort of one of the guys."

Simultaneous with the expansion of U.S. military advisers in Vietnam came a build-up of Army Special Forces, the Green Berets, whose early mission was to develop paramilitary groups loyal to Diem in the remote parts of the nation where little or no government authority was exercised. (The Montagnard tribesmen of the central Vietnamese highlands would become the most notable example of the Special Forces effort.) Ret. Col. Joseph Schwar, now an IBM account executive in suburban Washington, was with the Special Forces in I Corps in 1963.

"I think I was one of the first people who had been attracted by John Kennedy's drive to increase the Special Forces capability of the country," Schwar says. "That's why I found myself there. I remember I was stationed at Fort Bragg with the Special Forces unit when the Powells showed up to go through the advisers' training. They stayed with us in the fall of 1962. That was the time of the Cuban missile crisis. The Special Forces I was part of was alerted and actually deployed. Colin had to help my family get through that trial. Then he went to Vietnam, and I was able to help his wife with that."

Schwar followed Colin Powell to South Vietnam several months later. Some time after that, Schwar was commanding a Special Forces detachment at Khe Sanh, in the west of I

Corps toward the Laotian border, when news reached him that Secretary of Defense Robert McNamara had declared the war was over. (Such reports were far from uncommon; in May, 1962, McNamara had made his first visit to South Vietnam. "He looked at the figures and concluded optimistically after only forty-eight hours in the country that 'every quantitative measurement . . . shows that we are winning the war," Stanley Karnow writes in *Vietnam: A History*.) When Schwar heard the news, he called Powell, who was then advising an ARVN unit at Quang Tri, about twenty-five miles away near the coast. "Colin said, 'You tell Mr. McNamara to come and see where I am, because someone is shooting at me.' " Getting shot at during that first Vietnam tour, Powell says, was more common than not.

Powell arrived in South Vietnam in December of 1962, first in Saigon where he was processed in, then on to the U.S. air base at Da Nang and to Hue, the imperial capital of Vietnam where the First ARVN division had its headquarters. At Hue he stored his foot locker and shipped out to the A Shau Valley near the Laotian border—his base for most of the tour of duty.

"From A Shau," Powell says, "we would go out for weeks and months at a time and just live in the jungle, looking for Vietcong. It was a needle in a haystack at that time. They could find us more easily than we could find them. We were getting ambushed every morning."

The ARVN troops Powell served with, he says, "were good soldiers. They were fairly well led by the officers at that time. . . . My counterpart was a Captain Hieu, and he was quite a competent soldier, a good man. After working with us for a few months, he transferred out and another guy came in who wasn't as good, but then I left. Over the years, I lost track of Hieu, but after the collapse I assumed he had either died somewhere or gone to jail."

One of Capt. Vo Cong Hieu's family members would escape from Vietnam after the end of the war—a boat person named Mrs. Thuyet Do who sailed off into the South China Sea and eventually settled in New Hope, Minnesota, about fifteen miles from Minneapolis-St. Paul. But Captain—later Colonel—Hieu would not be so fortunate. With the final defeat of the Army of the Republic of Vietnam, Hieu had been

taken prisoner and spent nearly thirteen years in a "reedu
cation" camp before being released in 1988. A year later i
the fall of 1989, not long after he had been named Chairma
of the Joint Chiefs of Staff, Powell received a letter addresse
to him at the Pentagon. When he opened it, a photograph fel
out that showed a grass hut in the A Shau Valley with si:
small Montagnard children in the foreground. Behind then
were himself and Captain Hieu—Powell had the identica
photo in his personal album. Accompanying it was a lette
from Hieu, asking for help in leaving his homeland, and by
then Powell was in a position to do something about it. H
enlisted Gen. Jack Vessey and Richard Armitage, both ex
perienced hands in dealing with the Vietnamese governmen
in Hanoi, in the enterprise. Two years later, Hieu, his wife
and many of his children and grandchildren were reunite
with Thuyet Do in Minnesota. The two—Powell and Hieu—
met for the first time in nearly three decades in November o
1991 before Powell delivered a speech in Minneapolis. "
saw him in a hotel lobby," Powell says. "He was standing
there, looking forlorn. He'd only been here about two week:
and he was freezing to death."

Col. Frederick Smullen, Powell's public-affairs officer, re
calls the reunion. For security reasons, he says, "We walke
in the side door of the hotel, and as we walked in, Colone
Hieu turned around. He was all dressed up in the best outfi
he could muster for the event—a coat, tie, and trousers tha
didn't quite match. He got this big grin on his face, and he
and the chairman walked to one another and embraced. I
was a poignant moment, a special moment in time."

Powell was also in the A Shau Valley when his son Michae
was born. Learning that he was a father would involve on
of those classic snafus for which the Army is so famous. "
was in the jungle [when it happened]," Powell recalls, "an
Alma and I had arranged a signal for when he's born—there
wasn't even Red Cross in those days. I said, 'Write on the
letter *Baby Letter*.' And everybody at the base camp at Hue
had been told to look for the letter that says *Baby Letter*
'When the letter comes,' I said, 'open it up and radio it to
me. *Don't* wait to send it.' And you know, military fashion
it gets to Hue, and nobody notices so I've got to wait for it
to get delivered to me. Meanwhile, another letter has come

in and gets to me first from my mother. It gets thrown out of an airplane that was looking for us in the jungle, and they drop this package of stuff with some letters. And it was a letter from my mother which went on chattily telling me about this aunt and that aunt and this cousin and that cousin and 'Dad and I are fine' and 'Love, Mother—Oh, by the way, we're absolutely delighted about the baby.' And that's how I found out I had a child. She never did say what it was. So then we had this ancient radio you had to crank and hang a wire through the jungle [to use], a sort of strange AM radio. And we radioed the base camp and said, 'Look in the god-damn mailbox!' And sure enough there was the letter—oh yeah!—and that's when I learned Mike had been born.''

On a patrol through a rice paddy near the Laotian border, Powell was wounded when he stepped into a booby-trap rigged with a sharpened punji stick, which pierced his left instep and came out the top of his foot. Shipped back to the division headquarters at Hue for treatment, Powell returned to the field a few weeks later. By then, as spring turned into summer, 1963, a temporary paralysis was settling over the war effort and the South Vietnamese government, and Ngo Dinh Diem had become ever more certainly a marked man.

''There came a period when nearly all the army divisions became involved in the political situation in South Vietnam,'' Vincent Demma says. ''Each division commander was jockeying for position in whatever faction he thought could prevail. By and large, the war stopped. They were devoting their attention to the maneuvering in Saigon from May of 1963 on, when Diem's position became less tenable. There was also a tacit policy that Diem wanted to avoid incurring casualties among his major combat units, and this also dampened whatever enthusiasm there might have been to fight.'' Another complicating factor, Demma says, was that ''no one really knew how the Buddhists, who were very strong in I Corps, in the northern region, were going to react.''

In Hue on May 8, 1963, the Diem government—pro-Catholic in a nation where four out of five people professed themselves Buddhists—had forbidden Buddhists to fly their own flag in recognition of the 2,587th anniversary of the Buddha. When Buddhists demonstrated by the thousands, government forces had fired into the crowd, killing nine of the protesters. Two months later on June 11, when no apology from the incident materialized from the Diem camp, "an aged Buddhist priest, Thich Quang Duc, sat down at a major intersection [in Saigon], poured gasoline on himself, took the cross-legged Buddha posture and struck a match," David Halberstam wrote in the September 11, 1963, New York *Times*. "He burned to death without moving and without saying a word." The photograph of the incident showing a stoic, shaven head engulfed in flames was for many Americans the first image of the Vietnam War to be engraved in their conscience. And with that the Buddhist protest against Diem and the U.S. presence in Vietnam began in earnest. Particularly in I Corps, Demma says, the ARVN divisions "became essentially garrison units. I'm sure it must have been a very frustrating period. The war came to a virtual halt." Stymied by President Diem's inability to deal with the mounting Buddhist protest and frustrated generally by the progress of the war effort, the American backing of Diem and his regime came to a virtual halt as well.

At four-thirty in the afternoon, local time, on November 1, 1963, Diem telephoned U.S. Ambassador to South Vietnam Henry Cabot Lodge—who three years earlier had been Richard Nixon's vice-presidential running mate—to tell him that yet another effort was underway to overthrow him. "Some units have made a rebellion," Diem said, "and I want to know what is the attitude of the United States."

"I do not feel well enough informed to be able to tell you," Lodge answered. "I have heard the shooting but am not acquainted with all the facts. Also, it is four-thirty A.M. in Washington, and the U.S. government cannot possibly have a view."

"But you must have some general ideas," Diem persisted. "After all, I am a chief of state. I have tried to do my duty. I want to do now what duty and good sense require. I believe in duty above all."

"You have certainly done your duty," Lodge responded. ". . . No one can take away from you the credit for all you have done."

A little more than fourteen hours later, on the morning of November 2, as they were being transported in an armored personnel carrier from a French church in Saigon's Chinese district to meet with the rebel generals, Diem and his younger brother and chief political adviser, Ngo Dinh Nhu, were shot at point-blank range and then repeatedly stabbed.

Powell was in Saigon either the day of the assassinations or the following day, he can't remember which—"I could see all the damage," he says. For Henry Cabot Lodge, Stanley Karnow writes, the death of Diem and his brother was the key element in bringing the war to an expeditious and successful end: "Elated and unrepentant, Lodge invited the insurgent generals to his office to congratulate them on their victory, which was his triumph as well. A few days later, he cabled Kennedy: 'The prospects now are for a shorter war.' " As with so many other calculations involving Southeast Asia, that one was wrong, too: it would be more than ten years and 58,000 American dead before the last U.S. troops would leave South Vietnam.

Gen. Maxwell Taylor, who was serving as Chairman of the Joint Chiefs of Staff in 1963, recalled that when John Kennedy heard of Diem's murder, he "rushed from the room with a look of shock and dismay on his face," Karnow writes. Three weeks later, Kennedy himself would be murdered.

Nearly three decades later, in an interview for *Washingtonian* magazine, Powell would express doubts about whether the United States "had a clear political objective during the entire thirteen years of the Vietnam War," but that was in the future. At the time, he says in an interview with the author, the war "had a coherency. We all were very supportive of it. We all thought it made sense. We got great briefing on the way in; I'd gone to school at Fort Bragg for six weeks and heard all about counterinsurgency. You've got to remember, young captains of infantry—I'd been a captain about three months by that time—we don't worry about such things. Just tell us what the job is. There's sufficient excitement about the mission to believe that whatever you're doing is right. I thought it was right, and I still think now it was right at the time. When I came back from there, though, after walking around that place for a year and seeing time, space, and terrain factors, I remember . . . saying to somebody at the time, 'It'll take a half-million people to succeed.' " A half-million soldiers is almost exactly what the height of the U.S. involvement entailed—Powell was back in Vietnam by then. But even that wouldn't prove enough.

Shortly after Kennedy's assassination on November 23, 1963, Powell flew from Saigon back to the United States, to the other American war of the sixties, one that in the isolation of the A Shau Valley he had only barely realized was going on. "Things were troubling when I left," he says, "but I don't have recollection of its being as bad as I subsequently learned it was. All I got was letters. That was the only means of communication. I didn't see any other Americans except every second week when the Marine helicopter pilots would bring food. So I really didn't know." In fact, his wife, newborn son, and especially his in-laws had been near the center of America's war between the races.

"My family was living in Birmingham in 1963 when Bull Connor and his damn dogs were running up and down the street," Powell once told the Washington *Post*. "I was in Vietnam while my father-in-law was guarding the house with a shotgun . . . so I completely identified with the [civil rights] struggle. Because of my position and the things I was doing in my career, in my life, I didn't have a chance to participate in that struggle in any active way. I did it my own way by my own example and by helping other people who were coming along as best I could, but you better believe that I identified with that struggle and continue to identify with that struggle."

Alma Powell was pregnant with Michael on April 12, 1963—living with her parents in Birmingham, Alabama—when Martin Luther King, Jr., was arrested by Birmingham police chief Eugene T. "Bull" Connor for leading a protest march on City Hall. (King would write his famous "Letter from Birmingham Jail" during the week he spent in prison.) Three weeks later, on May 3, Connor turned police dogs and high-pressure firehoses on a thousand black children demonstrating at the Sixteenth Street Baptist Church. Four months later, four young girls were killed when the same church was bombed—and two young black men killed in the ensuing rioting. Five days earlier, on September 10, 1963, the schools of Birmingham had been integrated with the help of the Alabama National Guard, called out by President Kennedy.

Alma Powell's father and uncle were the principals of the two black high schools in the city. For both of them, she says, it was an especially trying time.

"While they wanted change," Mrs. Powell says, "they were of another generation—don't go to the streets—and they had a very hard time. They had to deal with this at school because the demonstrators would go to the high schools to take the children out and go demonstrate. My father felt that the parents had sent their children to the school—as long as they were there, they were under his care, and he was not going to let them go. So there were many heated confrontations. It was a very hard time for both of them. I can remember my uncle saying, 'The children, why do they have to use the children?' . . . The parents of those children were very philosophical; they'd send them off to school in the morning with a toothbrush in their pocket and an extra sandwich for when they got arrested. I don't know that I could have done it."

Mrs. Powell had been raised in the Congregational church. Her paternal grandfather had been a master carpenter in Ohio, near the campus of Oberlin College, a Congregational school and the first integrated college in America. Her father had grown up on the campus of then all-black Talladega College sixty miles east of Birmingham, and her mother, who had been head of the black Girl Scouts in Birmingham, had become a national official of the Congregational church shortly before mayhem broke out in Birmingham. But, Mrs. Powell says, she knew the Sixteenth Street Baptist church well: "That very bathroom those little girls were in, we used to hang out there, too. Right this moment, I can smell it—the wet-concrete smell. That particular day [of the bombing], my mother, my aunt, and I had gone to [the Congregational] church. My uncle called from downtown and said, 'A bomb just went off. I don't know where. Don't come through town, go the back way home.' So I did. . . . I stopped for a stop sign, and a black man said to me, 'You better get out of here. You're too fair to be here.' "

The Johnsons, Alma Powell's parents, lived outside of town, but that didn't insulate them from the violence. "One day I went out to put some diapers on the line," Mrs. Powell recalls, "and I heard gunshots. And I was concerned because it was time for my parents to come home from work. What had happened was that [the black family who lived up the road] was turning into their driveway, and as they turned, a car came by—sped by and shot at them." Another time, Mrs. Powell recalls, she and her father had put her infant son Michael in a basement-like recess of the house just below the ground while they stood watch. "[My father] gave me a gun, and he had one, and he said, 'Anything that comes up that driveway, you shoot first and ask questions later.' And so you lived with that kind of thing."

Alma and Colin Powell would spend the next three-and-a-half years back where his military career began—at Fort Benning, Georgia. On base, he was another soldier with a son and, soon, a daughter. He had won a Purple Heart for walking into the punji-stick trap, and he had a year of Vietnam under his pistol belt. Off base, he was still a black man in a South that was dragging itself—and being dragged—toward change.

Shortly after he returned from Vietnam, Powell tried to order a hamburger at a restaurant called Buck's Barbeque in nearby Columbus. The waitress—a "nice lady," he told *Ebony* magazine—asked him if he was an African student. "No," Powell answered. "A Puerto Rican?" "No." "You're Negro," she said. "That's right." "Well, I can't bring out a hamburger. You'll have to go to the back door"—where blacks traditionally came in to place their orders. "I wasn't even trying to do a sit-in," Powell said. "All I wanted was a hamburger." Five months later, after the Civil Rights Bill of 1964 had been enacted—forbidding among other things segregation in places of public accommodation—"I went back to the restaurant and got my hamburger." Three decades later, the road that Buck's sits on would be named Martin Luther King, Jr. Avenue; Birmingham, Alabama, where King was imprisoned, would have a black mayor; and the man who had to go to Buck's back door for a burger would be a confidant of presidents and prime ministers.

"There are no more major civil rights laws to be passed," Powell told *Parade* magazine reporter David Wallechinsky two months before he was named Chairman of the Joint Chiefs of Staff. "What we are dealing with now is changing of hearts, changing of perspective and of minds. We need to start to erase the cultural filter with respect for minorities. One of the most flattering things said about me the last couple of years is that I am a role model. That's a heck of a responsibility. Hopefully, I can be a role model for young blacks coming up, for all young Americans, one that says: 'Here's a guy that, even though he is black and his hair is kinky, has been rather successful. He's done a good job.' So next time I see a black man who I might be able to help, maybe he has that kind of ability and can do a good job.''

Powell began his second stint at Fort Benning as a test officer with the United States Army Infantry Board—from November of 1963 to June of 1964 and again from May of 1965 until February of 1966.

"The Infantry Board is no longer," says Al Garland, editor of *Infantry* magazine, published at Fort Benning, and an instructor at the fort from 1966 through 1968. "It went out of existence last year after seventy years. It was the official test agency for the user of infantry-type equipment. There was also a test agency for the quartermaster corps—they'd test socks, raincoats, that kind of thing. The infantry board performed what were called user tests as opposed to developmental tests, the engineering tests that were always done by some lab. The rifle, the pistol, whatever, would come down to the infantry board, and the board would run them through a series of well-defined tests—for accuracy, for mobility. Can this thing be jumped on the back of a paratrooper? The three major criteria were RAM—reliability, availability, and maintainability. Could this thing do what the engineering requirements said it should do? Industry has a way of producing items and saying it will do anything.''

In between his time on the Infantry Board, from August, 1964, to May, 1965, Powell was a student in the Infantry Officer Advanced Course. Structured to produce company commanders, and a basic step for any infantry officer's career, the course was—if Powell's required monograph is any evidence—dry going. Its title: "Distribution of the Light-weight Radio Transmitter AN/PRT 4 and Radio Receiver AN/PRR9 (Squad Radio Sets) Within the Rifle Company, Infantry Battalion, Infantry Battalion (Mech) and Airborne Infantry Battalion." Powell concludes that both the then-new transmitter and the receiver are superior to their predecessors. A year after he completed the course, Powell—who had been made a captain on June 2, 1962—became Major Powell. "Four years from captain to major is pretty fast," Garland says. "There's one of two things happening. Either he was selected below the zone"—that is, after a briefer time as captain than the average—"or it could have been because of the expansion of the Army. But those were the early days in Vietnam. I would think he was below the zone. That promotion to major would indicate that he's a comer."

By 1966, the signs that Powell was a comer—a water-walker—had been mounting for some time. Just as important, the indifferent college student seemed to have found his subject material.

"At Fort Benning in 1964 there were four hundred captains of the various combat arms going to school and covering the same material," says Ret. Col. James Garvey. "We were broken into two classes, two groups of two hundred each. . . . The course was not intense. You could make it intense if you wanted to, but it wasn't a gentleman's course either. It was sort of a mix. They just gave us a hell of a lot of stuff to do that wasn't relevant to what we were studying. Finally they let up on us and let us go back to what we were supposed to be doing.

"Basically everybody there had either just come back from Vietnam or was going there. I hate to use the words 'devil-may-care attitude,' but there was a lot of bravado that existed. I wouldn't say we were enthusiastic about [Vietnam], but that was our profession. I'd been in the Army at that point in time for eleven years. I'd spent probably six years of it going to school to prepare me to go to battle, so maybe a lot of the bravado was a little bit of fear, too. The guys who had been there and survived were glad to be home."

Powell "wasn't a spring bud," Ret. Col. Kenneth Montgomery recalled for the Washington *Post*. "[He wasn't] the one who always wanted to jump up and answer the questions or, when the rest of us wanted to get out of class, would ask a question."

"He was gung-ho," Garvey says, "but he wasn't the outward gung-ho type. What I mean is that he was very professional; he instilled a sense of discipline and confidence in the

people he communicated with. I mean, there's no doubt in my mind the guy was fearless, but you've got the rah-rah guys and then you've got the guys who are just very professional and you know how the hell they are going to react. He was one of those guys; you knew you didn't have to worry about him. He worked hard to do well because he was committed at that point in his career to staying in the military. I look back on it, and I think there was a guy who set a goal for himself and who didn't deviate from it and didn't compromise himself to get where he got.''

In many ways it was an extraordinary group that took the Infantry Officer Advanced Course at Fort Benning in the latter part of 1964 and early 1965: Powell, who would become Chairman of the Joint Chiefs of Staff; Thomas Griffin, a retired three-star general who would become chief of staff of the Allied Forces/Southern Europe; Gen. Howard Graves, who eventually would become commandant at West Point; and a one-time all-American running back and *Sports Illustrated* poster boy from the United States Military Academy at West Point—and later unsuccessful Senate candidate from New Jersey—Gen. Peter Dawkins.

''Colin,'' James Garvey says, ''stuck out in that group. He came across as, number one, a very intelligent individual, very articulate. He had a charisma about him. When I say charisma, he didn't need to speak loud for people to listen. He's a very handsome guy—his stature alone attracts attention. He was one of the guys you look back on. I remember commenting to my wife then that that guy is going to go far. . . . To be a leader among two hundred captains is very, very difficult.''

Powell and Pete Dawkins, who had gone from winning the Heisman Trophy in 1958 to becoming a Rhodes scholar before starting on active duty, worked at the Pentagon together in the early 1980s. By then, there was no question that Powell had mastered at least one side of the political-military complex: ''I would meet him in his office,'' Dawkins told the Washington *Post*'s Jacqueline Trescott, ''and I would feel I had just been to the schoolmaster. He displayed the kind of virtuoso mastery of the political complexities of the Pentagon that is rare.''

James Garvey remembers seeing Powell on television in

January of 1991, during the aerial assault on Iraq, telling a group of reporters, "Trust me. Trust me." "He'd say 'Trust me,' and knowing the guy, I don't care what he would have said, I believed him."

Joseph Schwar, who had been in Vietnam with Powell in 1963, had a similar experience as he was walking through Dulles International Airport. "When he said, 'Trust me,' I said, 'Damn right. I know I can trust you.' And as I looked around, people were nodding and saying, 'If he says it, I can believe it.' "

In February of 1966 Powell was pulled off the Army Infantry Board, which he had returned to after his advanced infantry course, and assigned to be an instructor at Fort Benning's Army Infantry School, where he had been a student only nine months earlier. "By then," Al Garland says, "Benning was expanding tenfold. They were getting a huge officer-candidate program started, much as they did during the Korean War and World War II. You had a lot of advanced courses coming in. . . . An instructor is considered a step above the [infantry] board. It's another mark on his record. He gets transferred to be a hot-shot instructor, and it's a feather in his cap."

The students, Powell says, were fresh batches out of Officers Candidate School, and teaching them required some creativity. . . "They'd come back in on a Friday morning after an all-night combat patrol," Powell recalls. "They'd be allowed to shower, get a hot lunch, and then for that Friday afternoon they had to get all these dogged mandatory subjects that they had to have, and the doggedest of them all was how to fill out a unit-readiness report. And I got that every Friday afternoon. You haven't lived until you've had two hundred guys who are going to be second lieutenants tomorrow who have been up five straight days and nights, have just had a shower and a hot lunch, and they're in an air-conditioned room on a hot summer afternoon at Fort Benning—you have not lived. I never had to make presentations like I had to make at that time. I did anything. I threw rubber chickens at the class—I did it. I'm ashamed of it, but they could fill out a unit-readiness report."

Ret. Col. Ben Willis, who was to serve under Powell six

years later in Korea, was a student of his in 1966. ''He was a great teacher,'' Willis says. ''He stands six-two or six-three; he was lean as a rail then and cut a fine military figure. He'd stand up on that stage, and he was a good-looking soldier back then. He didn't have that little paunch that he has now.''

A year and a half later, in August of 1967, Powell became a student again, this time at the United States Army Command and General Staff College at Fort Leavenworth, Kansas. For Powell, it was a far bigger feather in his cap, as well as perhaps a first clear indication that a lifetime career in the military was his for the taking. The school also would broaden him and give him a sense of the totality of the Army, not just the infantry.

''Advanced courses are taught other places, but those are intended for infantry officers only,'' Al Garland says. ''Ninety-five to ninety-eight percent of all officers go there. But for Leavenworth, it's highly selective. All the branches of the service send people there. Everybody has a certain number of seats—infantry, medics, transportation, and so on. All the branches are brought together, and for the first time he learns to work with people outside his branch. . . . Simply because it is a selective thing, Leavenworth gets a lot more attention than it deserves. The course isn't really that good, but it does expose you to other people. It lets you know you think differently from another guy. You get the transportation type who's only used to moving trains or planes, and you begin to realize that maybe his job is pretty important, too. If he doesn't move his planes or trains, you don't get fed.

''The number of seats in any one class for infantrymen is limited, and when you're selected, it means you are seen as being one of the best, in quotes. Unless you were selected for Leavenworth, you could almost count on serving your twenty years as a major or lieutenant colonel and being retired.''

By this time, Garland says, Powell ''had the marks; he was a comer, unless he stumbled.'' At Leavenworth, he didn't. Out of a carefully selected group of 1,244 Army officers, Powell graduated second in his class in June, 1968. Of all the reams and reams of magazine and newspaper articles that would ultimately be written about Colin Powell—an avalanche of column inches—a small one that appeared not long thereafter in the *Army Times* may have been the most significant to his military career. The article profiled the top five graduates of the Leavenworth school, and among its readers some months after it first appeared was Charles Gettys, then the commanding general of the American Division, headquartered in Chu Lai, the Republic of South Vietnam, and soon to become Powell's boss. A few weeks after finishing at Leavenworth, Powell was off again to Southeast Asia.

CHAPTER 8

Chu Lai

Some sense of the war that Colin Powell was returning to can be found in the daily staff journals of the Third Battalion, First Infantry, Eleventh Infantry Brigade—the brigade Powell would join as executive officer in June of 1968.

"1200 [hours]: Received word that Co[mpany] C had casualties who were wounded by an enemy booby-trapped 105mm round," the duty officer wrote from Base Camp Bronco on June 11, 1968. "They were: PFC Theodore Paul Raymond who was KHA, SP4 David M. Pruitt KHA also, SGT E5 Larry L. Ploski with possible cracked eardrum, PFC Wines, Thomas L., who is in fair condition and who received shrapnel in right arm and lower extremities, SP4 Harold E. Dickerson listed fair, multiple shrapnel wounds in left and rear portion of the body and fractured left jaw, PFC Ronald Sanchez with shrapnel wounds in abdomen and left leg listed fair, SSG James D. Miller in good condition with shrapnel in left hand and forearm, SP4 Willie A. Pugh listed in good condition with shrapnel wounds in right foot, left hip, left little finger."

("KHA" stands for "killed in hostile action," as distinct from soldiers who die by, say, accidents; all enemy dead are listed simply as "KIA," killed in action.)

More casualties were reported the next day: "1000 [hours]: Monitored radio that Co C had casualties when a booby-trapped artillery round was detonated." Five enlisted men and a second lieutenant were all said to be in "good" condition. "1325 [hours]: Received word that Co D had casualties who were wounded when an enemy booby-trapped 105mm round was tripped.'' Two enlisted men and a second lieutenant were "good"; Sgt. E5 Theodore James Tabbert was "serious."

Still more casualties reports came in the next day: twelve enlisted men of Company D, with injuries ranging from "multiple wounds in both arms, legs, and chest," to "minor frag wounds in back and left arm." All were listed as good. A thirteenth member of Company D, SP4 William A. Johnson, was killed in hostile action. On June 14, at 8:55 A.M. local time, the duty officer "monitored radio that Co B had one casualty, PFC John W. Turner who was in good condition and received a gunshot wound in the hip." Company C also reported "getting 1 KIA VC"—one Viet Cong killed in action. On June 15, Company A reported "some casualties who were injured when a delayed pressure-type (grenade) booby-trap went off." Ten hours later, a little after eight that evening, Company E reported that "SGT E5 Raymond Hernandez . . . had received fragment wounds in his right flank and right thigh, good condition and evacuated to Chu Lai." The next day, on June 16, Company A reported one Viet Cong killed in action and "three VC suspects which we received at South East Pad and turned them over to the MPs." At four that afternoon the duty officer "went to brigade and picked up distribution and the movie to be shown in the rear area." At 6:40, "a movie was shown in the rear area which was enjoyed by all."

Colin Powell had left a South Vietnam with fifteen thousand U.S. soldiers, military advisers and Special Forces for the most part, assisting the Army of the Republic of South Vietnam. When he returned, U.S. troop strength was nearing what he had predicted four and a half years earlier would be needed to prosecute the war: half a million soldiers. (Troop strength would peak at 543,400 soldiers in April of 1969, three months before Powell flew home again.) Three heads of state had come and gone in Saigon in the time he had been away: Duong Van Minh, who took over in November of 1963 with the assassination of Diem; Gen. Nguyen Khanh, who seized power from Minh two months later; and Dr. Phan Huy Quat, who formed a new government when Khanh left the country on February 18, 1965. When Air Vice Marshall Nguyen Cao Ky took over as head of the new military regime on June 11, 1965, South Vietnamese troops—the regulars, the Civil Guard, and the Self-Defense Corps—were deserting at the rate of more than 113,000 a year. (Ky would remain as vice-president when Nguyen Van Thieu was elected president on September 3, 1967.) The first U.S. combat troops, as opposed to advisers and Special Forces, had landed on March 8, 1965, two Marine battalions sent in to defend the air base at Da Nang. Seven months earlier, following an attack on the American destroyer *Maddox* by North Vietnamese patrol boats in the Tonkin Gulf, U.S. planes had bombed the North for the first time.

South Vietnam had been a minor note on the American conscience in November, 1963, when Powell flew back to the United States to see his son for the first time—a note soon to be overwhelmed by the murder of John F. Kennedy. By June of 1968, when Powell returned, the war in Vietnam had nearly overwhelmed American politics and public discussion. The Tet offensive had begun on January 31 of that year—in one prong of the attack, Vietnam commandos dressed in South Vietnamese Army uniforms penetrated onto the grounds of the Presidential Palace and the U.S. Embassy in Saigon. It would be twenty-six days before U.S. and ARVN troops could recapture the imperial capital at Hue, where Powell had stored his foot locker during his first tour. Two months to the day after the Tet offensive began, in a nationally televised address, Lyndon Johnson announced: ''I shall not seek, and I will not accept, the nomination of my party for another term as your president.'' Thus the Vietnam War had claimed an American presidency as well, but perhaps the most shocking incident of the entire war happened some two weeks before Johnson delivered his address. It involved the Eleventh Infantry Brigade that Powell would join three months later, and in one sense, Powell would be the one who first discovered it, a year after it happened, by which time he had moved on to the commanding general's staff at division headquarters in Chu Lai.

''A whole bunch of Army inspectors show up from the Inspector General's office,'' Powell recalls in an interview with the author, ''and the division chief of staff says cooperate with them and give them anything they want. And so they want to see the [daily staff] journals, and they bring the journals to me. And they say, 'We want you, while we're watching you, to go through the journals and stop if you see anything that looks like an unusual incident or a major contact with a large loss of life jumps out at you.' And I say, 'Why are you asking me to do this?' And they say, 'Well, you're the custodian of the journal; you're the keeper [as part of division duties].' So I started going through the journals and came across an entry that . . . had to do with an area called Batangan peninsula, which is one of the worst places in the division's area—a nasty, nasty place. Pirates used to live there one hundred years ago. The French got their butt kicked there and stayed out of it. It was just bad news. You'd come out with fifty traumatic amputations every time you went in there, but every now and then you had to go in. And there was this entry that said there had been heavy contact on Batangan that particular day and had a large body count associated with it, a very large body count. And they asked me, 'Will you please read that into your tape recorder.' So I did. Clearly there was a major investigation under way. But then I left the division and never knew what it was all about until I read it in the newspapers the next year.''

What Powell had discovered in the daily staff journals was the first written evidence that in March, 1968, at the village of Son My on the Batangan peninsula, a platoon led by First Lt. William Calley, Jr., had murdered an estimated two hundred women, children, and old men in what would subsequently become known as the My Lai massacre.

Gen. Samuel Koster, commander at the time of the American (or Twenty-third Infantry) Division, which included the Eleventh Infantry Brigade, had returned to the United States shortly after the incident to become commandant at West Point. He would be relieved of that when the My Lai massacre finally surfaced publically in 1970. The commander of the Eleventh Infantry Brigade, Oran Henderson, who had taken it over just about the time of My Lai, would also see his career cut short by the incident. Calley would be found guilty by a military court of the murder of at least twenty-two civilians. To the war-protest movement in the United States he would become a virtually demonic figure, yet Calley and My Lai have significance that reaches far beyond themselves, military historian Shelby Stanton argues in *The Rise and Fall of an American Army*. My Lai is also a kind of lesson on the theater of action Powell was coming back to, the unit he was joining, and the war the United States was fighting.

"Actually the My Lai massacre itself reflected the stark terror of a war of attrition, in which military success, for lack of terrain objectives, was measured statistically by counting corpses," Stanton writes. "While casualty counts are valid measurements of war, in Vietnam they unfortunately became more than yard-sticks used to gauge the battlefield. Rather than means of deter-mination, they became objectives in themselves. The process became so ghoulish that individual canteens were accepted as authorized substitutes if bodies were too dismembered to esti-mate properly. Guidelines were even issued . . . on factoring additional dead based on standard percentages by type of en-counter and terrain. This appalling practice produced body counts that went largely unquestioned, and were readily re-warded by promotions, medals, and time off from field duty. For example, General [William] Westmoreland [commander of U.S. combat forces in South Vietnam from 1964 to 1968] had issued a special commendation to the Eleventh Infantry Brigade based on its claim of 128 enemy killed at My Lai." Before My Lai, Stanton writes, the Eleventh Infantry was already being called the Butcher Brigade by soldiers.

Just as important, perhaps, the massacre at My Lai is also a comment on the terrain the Eleventh Infantry Brigade was work-ing in and the readiness of the brigade, which had been cobbled together in late 1967, for the task.

"The Eleventh Brigade—a light infantry brigade—was the last brigade to join the Americal," says George MacGarrigle, a historian with the U.S. Army Center of Military History and an Army cavalry officer in Vietnam. "It was not exactly a super brigade when [Oran] Henderson took it over, but he was con-sidered a very decent commander. The area which they worked was Duc Pho, in the southern part of Quang Ngai, the southern part of I Corps. It was a difficult area from the standpoint of the Vietcong. The area had been Vietcong controlled for a number of years even though we were there. That area, at least southern Quang Ngai, was sort of an R-and-R center for the Third Yel-lowstar [Vietcong] division. They would normally work to the south, and they would keep a regiment—one of their three reg-iments—up in southern Quang Ngai for a little rest and recu-peration. . . . It had been worked over by the ARVN, and they had a lot of trouble in the area. The Rock Marines, a very tough-type unit, had worked the area over, too, and they had difficulties there. Sending this kind of unit [the Eleventh Infantry Brigade] in—a green unit into a VC-dominated area—certainly caused some unhappiness because of the mines and booby-traps and things like that. There's no excuse for Calley's performance, but the kind of war you want to fight is when you know where the enemy is. When the enemy is a kid and a little old lady, you get a little uptight and frustrated.''

Powell says simply that ''it was lousy Indian country. I don't mean to be ethnically or politically unconscious, but it was awful. There were nothing but VC in there. I'm not excusing what happened, but when you went in there, you were fighting everybody.''

Powell's battalion commander when he arrived at the Eleventh Infantry Brigade was Ret. Col. Henry Lowder. ''We were primarily engaged with the Vietcong with both the local and the main force and occasional skirmishes with the NVA [North Vietnamese Army],'' Lowder says. ''With the Vietcong, it was trying to locate the places where they concealed their weapons, where they operated from, their command posts and hospitals and communication centers. It was the type of action where we would be constantly searching for them and they would harass us with mines, booby-traps, and sniper fire. Whenever we made a contact, they would flee, and we would pursue. When we did come into contact with the main force, it was a different situation. They were well-trained, well-skilled, very tough opponents.''

A battalion, Lowder says, ''would typically be located with a forward and rear position. The primary duty of the executive officer was to run the rear, insure that all the supplies got forward, make sure all the support activity was provided to the soldiers and units who were forward. . . . [Powell] came in with a good reputation—I don't know how we knew that—but for a short while I didn't have an executive officer. He quickly took over, absolutely did a fine job, and I had absolutely nothing to worry about. I knew we would always be supplied and our administration would be taken care of promptly.''

In recommending Powell for the Legion of Merit in May of 1969, Gen. Charles Gettys, the commander of the Americal

Division, noted—and perhaps one needs to discount slightly the inflated language of such documents—that "Upon his assignment as Executive Officer, Third Battalion, First Infantry, it became apparent that Major Powell was an unusually highly qualified young officer with great potential. His broad knowledge of the military, spirit of cooperation, and unique ability to rapidly sift through voluminous information, extract and analyze pertinent data, and reach a sound decision was immediately recognized. . . . The battalion had been without an executive officer for approximately two months, and there were many problems to be solved. Major Powell immediately assessed the situation, established a schedule for priority of tasks, and in an amazingly short time, revised and strengthened existing procedures, and required high performance standards on the part of all personnel in the Battalion Trains areas. The results were obvious and immediate; the level and quality of administrative and logistical support increased, thereby creating a higher state of morale among the troops in the field. Of particular note was Major Powell's outstanding performance in preparing the battalion for its Annual General Inspection. Starting from the zero point, he logically and systematically prepared the battalion for inspection, receiving minimal guidance from the battalion commander. A measure of the success achieved is best illustrated by the fact that his battalion was selected to represent the Division during the next scheduled Annual General Inspection. . . ."

In what seems an almost unvarying pattern for Colin Powell, he wasn't to hold this job long either. The Eleventh Infantry's daily staff journal for September 21, 1968, concludes: "Maj Powell presided over the awards ceremony this afternoon with Lt Hall, and SP5 Cate receiving BS for Service while Lt Kristan and SFC Shannon received the ACM for Service. Expect a new Bn XO soon as we bid goodby to Maj Powell and wish him good luck with his new assg as Div G3." Three months after he had arrived in Vietnam this second time, Major Powell was on his way to Chu Lai—jumped over senior officers again—to do a colonel's job on the staff of General Gettys. The vehicle of change in this instance was the small article that had appeared in the *Army Times*.

"When Powell's division commander saw the *[Army Times]* story, he hit the roof," Carl Rowan wrote in a 1989 profile of

Powell for *Reader's Digest*. " 'I've got the number-two Leav enworth graduate in my division, and he's stuck in the boonies? he shouted at his aides. 'I want him on my staff!' ''

A division commander's staff consists of four assistant chiefs of staff—and their deputies—designated as G–1, responsible for personnel; G–2, for intelligence (hence the Army slang G–2 for inside dope); G–3, for operations and planning; and G–4, for logistics. Of them all, says *Infantry* magazine editor Al Gar land, G–3, the slot General Gettys plucked Powell from the boonies to fill, is "the most important officer on any staff," largely because planning operations is the work dearest to the boss's heart. "Most senior commanders know absolutely noth ing about personnel and logistics and probably less about intel ligence," Garland says. "What they do know about is operations and planning. Every infantryman is the second coming of Gen eral Patton. They're like Schwarzkopf—Hail Mary and over the top. Planning and operations is what's important to them. G–3 is a sign that [Powell] is going to become an important man."

Powell's battalion commander, Henry Lowder, remembers when Powell was summoned to the division staff: "Typically the general and his G–3 would come around and visit the bat talions daily. On one occasion the G–3 said he was leaving, and he said they were taking Powell up. . . . I protested his depar ture, but it didn't do any good. He was gone for about two months before I went up and became the division G–1. I saw quite a bit of him then."

Powell's position was a temporary one—he would be kicked back to Deputy G–3 once a colonel who had been slated for the job was able to join the division—but the fact that he held it for any period of time is "one of the best indicators that I could cite you from an Army standpoint of his ability early on," says William Abernathy, who had been Powell's commanding officer at Fort Devens. "The G–3 position is one that on the organi zation charts calls for a lieutenant colonel and a senior lieutenant colonel at that, a very experienced person. It is highly unusual that a major will have that position in a division and almost unheard of that he would have one in combat during Vietnam."

Charles Gettys, who discovered Powell languishing on the pages of the *Army Times* and brought him up to his staff, died in November, 1982. Abernathy remembers speaking with him at a party in the early 1980s, marking Powell's promotion to brigadier general: "General Gettys told me that General [Creighton] Abrams [who replaced William Westmoreland as head of U.S. forces in Vietnam in 1968] saw Powell on a visit to the division and asked the general why he had a major as his G-3 when they had hundreds of lieutenant colonels in Vietnam. And General Gettys said it's because he's the best G-3 in all Vietnam. And I bet he was. . . . Mrs. Gettys has been invited to Powell's promotion parties—I've seen her at at least two of them. He doesn't step on people going up, and he never forgets people once he's there."

As executive officer of the Third Battalion, Powell had been responsible for the rear. Now, stationed at Chu Lai, "he was responsible for doing the planning for the entire division," Henry Lowder says. "The Americal had three brigades; each had three or four battalions; and he had to assure that all the planning was done."

Yet with the Americal Division little came easy, and not only because the area it worked was a Vietcong stronghold. The division had first been formed in New Caledonia during World War II—hence its name, a combination of American and Caledonia—and had served on Guadalcanal, Bougainville, and the southern Philippines before being deactivated in December, 1945. It was activated, briefly, in the mid-1950s, with headquarters in the Panama Canal Zone. In 1967 the Americal was once again brought into being, this time by William Westmoreland. In need of an infantry division in Vietnam and aware that none would be arriving soon from the States, Westmoreland took an existing brigade, the 196th Infantry, and added to it the ill-prepared 11th Infantry, which would earn infamy for the My Lai slaughter, and the 198th Infantry, which had expected to be assigned to police duty in the Dominican Republic. The result— shoehorned into Vietnam and made to fit in with the Marines, which still had their large jet base at Chu Lai—was "a very star-crossed outfit," one military historian says. "If anything bad happened in Vietnam, it generally happened to that unit. . . . It had a long and convoluted process of assembly—it was scratched together to fill a void. It got a tough area, a tough, hard-corps enemy area, and a lot went wrong. They fought hard, they were good troops, but this was a sweet hunk of paradise they got, and the unit was jinxed. If you look at the history of this division, it would lead you to superstition. A typhoon comes out of nowhere and just rips through a certain part of Vietnam, and that happens to be where the Americal had its helicopters. It wasn't just Calley—they lost platoons.'' (On April 15, 1970, an Americal soldier tripped a booby-trapped 105-millimeter artillery shell, which in turn triggered mortar rounds and claymore mines that other members of the platoon were carrying. The final tally: fourteen dead, thirty-two wounded.) ''It was one unbroken string of disasters. You know how jokes go around about the Texas Aggies? They had Americal jokes like that in Vietnam. The fact that Powell wears [an Americal] patch [on his uniform] is sort of an act of bravery in the U.S. Army. He's saying he's proud of his service; he had a good unit. When Powell wears that, Vietnam veterans know he's making a statement . . . A lot of times the best people are sent to the worst divisions to try to straighten them out.'' Another major who arrived at the Americal some months after Powell did says, ''I don't doubt there may have been some of that thinking going on. To use the vernacular, it was a bastardized division.''

A feel for Powell's duties and accomplishment as the Americal Division's G–3 and later Deputy G–3—posts he held from September of 1968 until July of 1969—can be gleaned in the perhaps hyperbolic language of General Gettys's recommendation for the Legion of Merit:

''With only a one-day overlap with the departing G–3, he rapidly grasped the scope and complexity of this very important assignment. His performance was unique considering his grade and length of service. . . . Serving as Assistant Chief of Staff, G–3, involved working arduous extra-duty hours seven days a week, intense mental pressure, and frequent exposure to hostile fire while visiting troops, commanders and staffs of subordinate units. He always maintained his calm and cheerful attitude, never reflecting the strain of his great responsibilities. . . . The briefings he conducted for commanders and visiting dignitaries were outstanding and earned him much respect and many compliments from those briefed.

''He was instrumental in developing plans and implementing operations which were highly detailed and complex because of the size of the Americal Division, the largest division in the United States Army. This complexity was further enhanced by the fact that the division was under the Operational Control of a Marine Corps Amphibious Force and that a major reorganization of the division was completed while the division was heavily engaged in operations against hostile forces. During his tenure in the G–3 section, several major combined operations involving the American Division, Marine Corps Special Landing Forces, ARVN units, and supporting naval and air units were conducted and he was highly instrumental in the success of those operations. . . . His ability, knowledge, and helpful, cooperative attitude were so widely known that he was frequently called upon by officers from other staff sections for advice and recommendations far beyond the scope of his assigned duties. He always gave so modestly and so freely of his time and knowledge that friction was never created and, in fact, he earned the respect and admiration of his superiors and subordinates alike."

Among the major combined actions Gettys credits Powell with were Operations Vernon Lake I and II, both against Vietcong and North Vietnamese strongholds in the Song Re valley of western Quang Ngai province. During Vernon Lake II, the quarerly operation report for the division records, U.S. elements "conducted saturation patrols and detailed search operations" in the vicinity, and "air strikes and artillery were utilized to interdict routes of infiltration into the area and to destroy suspected base camps and staging areas." With its emphasis on body count, the operational report lists 303 Vietcong and 152 North Vietnamese regulars killed in action in Vernon Lake II. "Friendly" losses are put at 23 Americans killed and another 158 wounded in action.

Perhaps a better measure of his experience, though, are the entries in his own daily officer's log. In many ways, they sound like a training program for a future Chairman of the Joint Chiefs of Staff:

May 2, 1969, 1100 hours: The deputy G–3 [the position Powell was then filling] accompanied Brigadier General Clement to Landing Zone Buff to observe a combined action of elements of the American Division and the Army of the Republic of Vietnam. Also visited Tra Bong and Tien Phouc in the hills to the west, where a Special Forces camp was located. 1745 hours: Deputy G–3 disapproved a combined action to raid a suspected weapons cache. "Details of C/A had not been worked out in sufficient detail."

3 May, 1300 hours: Deputy G-3 and rest of G-3 section hosted a meeting to coordinate joint plans for Operation Daring Rebel.

4 May, 1000 hours: Operation Daring Rebel began, using elements of U.S. forces and forces from the Republic of Korea and the Republic of Vietnam.

10 May, 1600 hours: "Maj Powell had meeting w/Co F/8 Cav on rearming and refueling points in Tam Ky."

12 May, 1600 hours: Dep G-3 had a conference with G-3 and G-3 Adviser, 2nd ARVN Div, to discuss joint operations.

15 May, 0900 hours: Deputy G-3 departed for liaison visits to Tien Phuoc, Tam Ky, Quang Ngai, and Landing Zone Professional to coordinate receiving and disposition of elements of the 1st Brigade of the 101st Airborne. Returned 1630 hours.

16 May, 1500 hours: Deputy G-3 visited headquarters of the 2nd ROK (Republic of Korea) Marine Brigade at Chung Yung to coordinate recent change in boundaries between the Brigade and the American Division.

21 May, 1000 hours: Powell's counterpart, the Deputy G-3 of the 4th Infantry Division, visited Chu Lai to discuss American patrolling and ambush techniques.

"Major Powell's outstanding devotion to duty, diligent efforts, and high standards have contributed immeasurably to the success of the Americal Division in operations against hostile forces," General Gettys concluded in his recommendation for the Legion of Merit. "His professional competence and outstanding achievement are in keeping with the highest traditions of the military service and reflect great credit upon himself, the Americal Division, and the United States Army."

Beyond doubt or argument, it's an impressive record that Colin Powell assembled during his second tour in Vietnam. If there is any blot on it—and "blot" is a relative term as used here—it is that his record is not that of a fighting man, that in the words of one officer who would serve under him later (and still admire him immensely) "Powell is no warrior."

In part, of course, being a warrior is a matter of opportunity. Powell spent his second tour in Vietnam based at battalion headquarters at Duc Pho and later at division headquarters at Chu

Lai, not stationed at one of the division's fire bases strewn across the southern part of I Corps. He did so because he was clearly so good at the headquarters jobs he was assigned, hardly a sin in any book. Perhaps he did so, too, because he was already a water-walker, one of those earmarked for ascension in an army that even then was beginning to reward organizational talent and personality over unbridled demonstrations of courage and derring-do. In any organization fast-moving careers tend to go in the direction that silent signals from the top are pointing.

"I find it hilarious that the guy who ended up commanding U.S. forces in the Gulf was one of the few fighting officers they have left in the Army—[Lt. Gen.] Calvin Waller [deputy commander of Allied Forces in Saudi Arabia]," says Ret. Lt. Col. William Corson. "If the war hadn't come along, Waller would have been retired because he didn't have the couth to make four stars. You're talking about warriors. When you have to fight, it's like toilet paper—boy, you need these guys. But to get to the position of power, those guys can hardly make it. I doubt seriously that 'Chesty' Puller [the crusty Lt. Gen. Lewis B. Puller, beloved by his troops] would have made major in today's Marine Corps."

On the other hand, Henry Lowder, Powell's battalion commander and later an assistant chief of staff at division headquarters, says the no-warrior contention simply misreads reality.

"[Powell] chafed at being in the rear," Lowder says. "He seized every opportunity to come forward, but there was really no place in Vietnam that was that well protected. The headquarters in Saigon and the outlying areas were subjected to rocket attacks. There were rocket attacks at Chu Lai and at Duc Pho; they were fairly lucrative targets. The units that were located in the rear were responsible for the security of the rear area and the headquarters. They had to be constantly vigilant against sapper attacks and guerrillas that would come in. They probably took as many rocket and mortar attacks as the forward units. They were stationary—the VC could zero in on them. There were no safe havens."

"I'll give you one example," Lowder says later, referring directly to Powell. "We had an action one time. It was a fairly big action. I got a very little scratch, but it was reported as I was wounded. He was on the next helicopter that came up—maybe fifteen or twenty minutes later, he might have ordered it up. He said, 'Look, I'm ready to take over for you.' He was ready to go at any time."

"From my personal association with [Powell]," says an undisputed warrior-general who served with Powell in Vietnam, "he's a soldier's soldier."

There was also at least one act of genuine heroism attributed to Powell during that second Vietnam tour. It happened on November 16, 1968. Powell mentioned it in a 1990 interview with *Washingtonian* magazine: "We were out west of Chu Lai in very mountainous terrain, and a unit had radioed that they had located a capture. We decided to go to the location and get in—get on a helicopter and take a look at it. I was with the division commander [General Gettys]. I was the G-3, the operations officer of the division. The division commander and the chief of staff of the division were aboard the helicopter.

"We found the location, and it was a very narrow landing zone, just barely enough room for the helicopter blades to clear the opening and go down, and as the pilot started down he didn't compensate correctly for the wind blowing back as he started through the trees, and the bird started to shift on him. He simply didn't correct fast enough. I was sitting in the left seat, looking out and starting to realize this was not a good thing to be doing. . . .

"I could see that it was a difficult mission, and I realized that he was starting—I could see the ground, see the trees, and watch the pilot—and I realized he was starting to lose a little control. Then suddenly it shifted left about three feet, and I'll never forget watching the blade hit the tree, and it stopped instantly. And once a blade stops instantly in a helicopter, it is no longer flying. It is a rock. We essentially just went down like an elevator without a cable. I don't know how far—I've never been able to quite reconstruct it, anywhere between eighty and one hundred feet. The engine at that point—the turbine was going—I remember the eerie sound of the turbine engine running but the blade no longer turning. I bent over, put my hands under my knees, and waited for it to hit.

"It hit, and there was a large crash, and I don't think you think about anything but leaving, so I just hit the belt and jumped and ran away for a few feet, turned around and looked, and realized it was starting to smoke now, and I ran back and got the [commanding general] out. He was barely conscious and he had a fractured shoulder. The chief of staff was out of it. He was a foot out of it. I wasn't alone by then, others were coming.

"I pulled [General Gettys] out, and others carried him away, and I went back in and got the chief of staff, who had a concussion and was unconscious, and then I went back to get the [commanding general's] aide, who we thought was dead because the engine had come through the helicopter and he was sitting in the center. . . . Essentially the whole engine and transmission came down on the back of the head and shoved his head into the radio. So he was bleeding, and he looked like he was dead. So I went back to get him, just to drag his body out. As I unbuckled him and started to pull him out from between the radio and the engine—which was starting to smoke; it never caught fire but it was smoking—he moaned. So we got him out and pulled his helmet off. He was wearing a helmet, thank God, and the helmet was all bent out of shape, but it had saved his life. He had a cut around, across his throat, but he was walking a few days later. The pilot we got out—he had a fracture, his back was fractured. Your values and your training and then your instinct just goes to work. Nothing's conscious."

"You made four trips back and forth?" interviewer Kenneth Adelman asked.

"Something like that."

"And you just felt you had to do it? Probably your instincts, your values—"

"I wasn't alone," Powell answered. "There were others doing it. There it was and you just did it. It wasn't anything heroic. It was just instinct and training clicking in, I think." What Powell did not mention in the interview was that the impact of the helicopter crash had broken his ankle.

Powell received the Soldier's Medal for his actions—the award given for bravery in non-combat situations. He would also come home from the Vietnam War with the Bronze Star.

"It was evident" that Colin Powell was a water-walker by the time he departed Vietnam on July 20, 1969, says Henry Lowder. "You didn't know how far he was going to go, but he was clearly an outstanding officer. He had everything that it would take to go on up. Of course, he has risen to the absolute top now, and you know everybody can't do that. But he was certainly one hell of a fine candidate. It was obvious at that point."

To get to the top, says *Infantry* magazine editor Al Garland, there was only one place he could go next: "At this stage of the game, in his career, he needs an assignment in Washington." In one of those wild swings of mood, setting, and tenor that can characterize the military vocation, Colin Powell found himself a graduate student at George Washington University less than two months after leaving Chu Lai and its Vietcong-infested countryside. He would spend all but five years and a few months of the remainder of his military career in the nation's capital.

CHAPTER 9

Ground Zero

A scene: The restaurant is called i Ricchi, on Nineteenth Street, Northwest, in the District of Columbia. The off-white walls in the airy front dining room are decorated with several murals suggestive of Florence, from which the cuisine draws its inspiration. The shrimp appetizer comes laid on a bed of white beans and baby string beans. If it is on the menu, the grilled skewer of quail, veal, and sausage comes highly recommended for an entrée; so do the venison in chianti sauce and La Scottiglia d'Arezzo, assorted meats braised in wine, tomato, and lemon. Dinner for two with an opening round of aperitifs, three courses, a mid-range bottle of wine, tax, and tip runs in the $100-plus range. Moderate lunchers can get out for $20 apiece.

At one P.M. on Monday, January 13, 1992, the curb in front of i Ricchi is taken up with a sight familiar to locals—a black, unmarked van and the conspicuous-inconspicuous sedate black limousine that indicate an important personage is inside. On the sidewalk, men who seldom seem to blink scan the area or talk into their lapel-mounted radio sets. Yet, except for the presence of two gossip columnists—Lois Romano of the Washington *Post* and the *Washingtonian*'s Chuck Conconi, both alerted by the restaurant's manager—there is little evidence in the front room of i Ricchi that something more than the usual lunchtime business is afoot. Platters come and go. The waiters are wise and pleasant and, above all, dignified; they don't introduce themselves by their first names, ever. It is in the sizable back room where the *event* is taking place; one can just get a glimpse of it by veering slightly out of the path to the restrooms. There, seated at a central table and attended to at a distance by two waiters—the room is otherwise empty of humanity—Barbara Bush, dressed in black and white, Jayne Ikard, the widow of a wealthy oil lobbyist and wearing red today, and Alma Powell, in a stylish brown and blue, are enjoying a private luncheon arranged by Ikard. Thus far the three have been served only appetizers: wild mushrooms, a hot salad dressed with feta cheese, and assorted pastas. In the front room chef-owner Francesco Ricchi, who has chosen the dishes, is worrying over whether the women will want an entrée.

A year earlier, when Alma Powell and Brenda Schwarzkopf had joined the First Lady in her private viewing box for George Bush's State of the Union address, the event had been political, meant for public consumption. The husbands of all three were leading the nation through its greatest military confrontation since the Vietnam War—gathering the wives at the outbreak of war is ancient and honorable public relations. The i Ricchi luncheon, by contrast, was private and personal. It was a measure of the distance Alma and Colin Powell had traveled since they arrived in Washington in 1969 and set up house in the sprawling suburbs of Northern Virginia.

Like a good modern politician, Colin Powell is not averse to distinguishing between those Americans inside the Washington Beltway—its circumferential ring of interstate highway—and those outside of it, and doing so to the advantage of those on the outside. "The American people are the smartest people on earth," he told *Washingtonian* magazine. "I don't think they are captives of the evening news. I don't think they are captives of an editorial. When you leave this very intense center of the world—this epicenter here in Washington—and get out, you tend to find that they are able to absorb large amounts of information and dismiss the left and right side of it and pretty much come to a balanced conclusion, a fairly informed and well-balanced and rational conclusion about what they are seeing and what they are reading."

Like a good soldier, Powell also has a military term for the capital: "Ground Zero . . . GZ on the Potomac," he said in the same interview. But while Powell would in time become very much a part of what people both inside and outside the Beltway talked about, while he would become a central player in GZ, he first came into Washington on, so to speak, little cat's feet, with hardly a ripple. For two years, in effect, he disappeared from the Army, dropped off its radar screen, so that he could pursue full-time a master's degree in business administration.

At age thirty-two, Powell would have fit neatly in with the mass of graduate students at George Washington University. The school has long attracted bureaucrats seeking mid-career changes or credential strengthening. Still, Washington in the fall of 1969 must have seemed a strange place for a returning veteran and a man who had lived for more than a decade on one army base after another. The Vietnam Moratorium, the largest demonstration yet held against the war that Powell was just back from fighting, took place on October 15. As Richard Nixon sat resolutely in the White House watching a football game, tear gas filtered across the Mall, past the monuments to Washington, Jefferson, Lincoln—Powell remembers tear gas wafting up from the university cafeteria. However strange the experience must have been, though, graduate school was the fulfillment of a late-rising but deep-burning ambition.

At Fort Leavenworth, during his 1967-68 course at the Army Command and General Staff College, "I became interested in opportunities for an advanced degree in graduate school," Powell wrote for *Guideposts* magazine. "This became a shining goal, and I decided I would apply despite only average college grades." When Powell approached the officer in charge at Fort Leavenworth with a request to go on from that school to a civilian college, he was told, "Your college record isn't good enough." That rejection would have consequences, all, in the long run, to Colin Powell's favor. It made him mad enough to buckle down and finish second in his class at Fort Leavenworth, he once told journalist Carl Rowan—a class ranking that landed him on General Gettys's staff as a major. The rejection also may have helped keep the dream of a graduate degree alive through the long days and nights of his second tour in Vietnam; Powell does not like to fail at anything. Pursuing a second degree might, too, have been part of his own effort to level further the playing field he was competing on with other officers for advancement. As he wrote for the April, 1991, issue of *Black Collegian* magazine, "African Americans . . . start the game with a strike or two against us. We cannot afford to neglect any field of education or any effort at education." Whatever the reasons, though, a masters in business administration turned out to be a very prescient career move.

Powell received his graduate degree from George Washington University in July, 1971, and, now a lieutenant colonel, went to work as an operations research analyst in the Office of the Assistant Vice-Chief-of-Staff of the Army. Both his new academic credentials and his past experience suited him for the work: Research analysts are the ones who determine the RAM criteria—reliability, availability, and maintainability—that Powell had used as a test officer for the Infantry Board at Fort Benning in the mid-1960s. The job was a wholly logical development of his training. But the position also offered proof that the service hadn't forgotten him while he had been away studying. With 3.7 million square feet of office space—three times more than the Empire State Building—the Pentagon is the world's largest office building. Along its 17.5 miles of corridors are many low-profile chambers where new lieutenant colonels toil away unnoticed, but the assistant vice-chief-of-staff is the Army's number-two man and his fiefdom is the place where the real, everyday work of the service gets done. It's a place with profile, and within it, Colin Powell obviously had developed a profile of his own.

One day in 1972, he says, he got a call from "some colonel or major down in the infantry branch" who wanted him to apply for a White House Fellowship. "He said, 'We want you to apply for this program.' I said, 'I just got out of graduate school; I like what I'm doing here.' He said, 'I want you to apply for the program.' So he sent me all these forms."

That Powell might eventually have risen to or near the top of the Army, few who have known him along the way doubt—he had that mark on him almost from the beginning. But that he would have climbed as quickly as he did and in the exact direction he took without the White House Fellowship seems unlikely. (It seems equally unlikely that Powell would have qualified for the program, given its stiff criteria, without a graduate degree. Many elements of his résumé appear to have dovetailed at one time.) The fellowship was to prove Powell's open-sesame to Washington power, and he was to prove a reluctant or, at least, indifferent debutant.

"That happened while we were at the Pentagon," says Joseph Schwar, who had also served with Powell at Fort Bragg and in Vietnam in 1963. "This is recollection of about twenty years ago, but as I remember, we were talking, and he said that he was asked if he was interested in applying. He met the criteria and would he like to do that. If I remember correctly, his initial reaction was that it's kind of a hassle to do the paperwork."

The White House Fellowship Program was begun in 1964 by Lyndon Johnson at the suggestion of John W. Gardner, then head of the Carnegie Corporation. "The underlying thinking," says its associate director, Phyllis Byrne, "was that they needed young people to come in and develop an understanding of how government works at the highest levels. They wanted to expose them to that early in their careers so they could take what they learned back to their respective communities."

Many fellows have done that, with great success. Alumni of the program include former San Antonio Mayor Henry Cisneros; Tom Johnson, the president of Cable News Network; Michael Walsh, the head of Tenneco; Robert Haas, the chief executive officer of Levi Strauss; U.S. Circuit Court of Appeals Judge Deanell Reece Tacha; and Jerry Caruthers, the former governor of New Mexico. Inevitably, too, the program can create a passion for national governance. For some alumni, having tasted from the banquet, Washington becomes a hard town to leave, and for some, Washington is the goal all along. Colorado Sen. Tim Wirth—who would decline to seek reelection—is a former White House Fellow. So are U.S. Congressmen Joe Barton of Texas and Tom Campbell of California; Roger Porter, assistant to President Bush for economic and domestic policy; Peace Corps director Elaine Chau; Peter Krogh, now dean of the School of Foreign Service at Georgetown University; U.S. ambassador to Japan Michael Armacost; and Colin Powell, who has now spent more time in the public limelight than any of them.

In the best tradition of Washington, climbing to this junior Olympus of the national capital means scaling a mountain of paperwork. The current application form—little changed from what it was two decades ago, according to Phyllis Byrne—runs to eight pages. In addition to a lengthy list of short-answer questions, applicants are asked to "describe and explain the purposes of the major extracurricular activities in which you participated,'' and ''describe any outstanding contributions made by you in [your] work.'' ''What do you consider to be your most significant contribution to your community?'' one question goes. ''Explain why or in what ways you consider it to be significant.'' Another asks applicants: ''What do you consider to be your most significant contribution to your professional field? Explain why or in what ways you consider it to be significant.'' Question 25 instructs would-be fellows, using a separate sheet of paper, to ''write a memorandum, *of not more than 500 words*, for the President, making a specific policy proposal. . . . If you exceed the word limit, your application will be disqualified.'' Question 26, again to be answered on a separate sheet, tells applicants to ''describe, *in 300 words or less*, your life's ambition, what you hope to accomplish or achieve in your lifetime, and what position you hope to attain.'' (The answers, it should be noted, are not available for public inspection.) Question 27 allows another 300 words to tell ''why you want to be a White House Fellow.'' And the application goes on from there. Powell says that the infantry branch officer who instructed him to apply, and who wanted a seat for the branch in this prestigious group, gave him exactly one weekend to fill it all out. ''So I hit on some old friends''—among them Gen. Charles Gettys, whom Powell had pulled from the crashed helicopter in Vietnam—''filled out the forms, mailed it in, and thought no more of it.''

But if the paperwork was a bear, what followed only got worse, says James Bostic, Jr., now the president of Butler Paper Company and a fellow contender for the 1972-73 class of White House Fellows. Applications are screened first by the federal Office of Personnel Management, which knocks out more than nine in ten of them to arrive at roughly one hundred thirty contenders. ''Then,'' Bostic says, ''the really tough competition began with the regional competition. You were interviewed by a panel, and out of that they got thirty-three national finalists.'' Like Bostic, Powell cleared both hurdles. Then, says Bostic, ''We all met in Washington for the first time for the finals. We met down at the old Civil Service building and got on a bus to go out to Airlie House [a privately owned conference center near Warrenton, Virginia]. Colin and I chatted on the bus. When we read the short biographies of the other people on the bus, both of our reactions were the same—how in the world did we get here? And frankly, I'm not sure that wasn't good. It kind of put us at ease—we might as well enjoy this because we're not going to get it. I think there were some people there who had planned in the scheme of things that they were going to be White House Fellows.''

At Airlie House the interviewing went on for three and a half days before what are usually three-person panels of the program's commissioners, drawn from business and government and often with some political affiliations to the party in control of the White House. There are also, Phyllis Byrne says, ''a lot of social circumstances—dinners, luncheons; a lot of casual interviewing goes on.'' At the end of the three and a half days, the panelists chose seventeen of the thirty-three finalists to be Fellows. By then, Powell says, what had begun as a bit of a lark, a rote fulfillment of a ''suggestion'' that had all the earmarks of an order, had assumed some *gravitas*.

''It's a great program, and it was a seminal experience in my life. But it wasn't anything I had any personal investment in. I didn't ask for it,'' Powell says. As the selection moved forward, though, he kept surviving cut after cut, ''and by now, with each success in the process, I do have something invested in it. And so finally when we go to the finals, my family [is saying] 'Oh, Colin's going to the White House! Colin's going to the White House!' And by now I'm stuck having to have something invested in it because I'm about to fail. I pass or I fail—it's a line right down the middle. But at the same time I said, God, let's just get it over with and get back to business, and I bounced around the interviews for three and a half days and had a lot of fun.''

''It was obvious Colin was very bright, a friendly person,'' Bostic says. ''And when we finally got selected—and we found out on a Sunday night—we ended up being the two black White House Fellows out of, I think, four black national finalists. I had just graduated from Clemson with a Ph.D. in chemistry; I was the first black person to get a doctorate from Clemson. I was twenty-three years old—the youngest member of my [Fellows] class. He was at the upper end of the class. It was the beginning of a beautiful friendship.''

Bostic says that the two new friends talked frequently during their fellowship year about the larger events of the world around them, but as with many of Powell's later friends, the conversations seem to have been general, without the sort of details that might suggest publically a strong position to either side. "Surely we talked about the war," Bostic says. "We were White House Fellows; we were in Washington. The country was mesmerized trying to get out of Vietnam. We were there when the peace process was trying to happen. I remember that. But people have asked me about it, and I can't remember a damn thing we said specifically. We didn't really talk about the domestic unrest."

Over the course of their year-long program, White House Fellows are brought together regularly for educational programs, luncheons, dinners, and similar affairs. "Colin very quickly became a leader of the group," Bostic says, "and this was seventeen of America's brightest. He was older. He had more experience than most of us. He helped people with the perspective of what was important and what was not. He was a nice guy, a bright one, a consensus builder. All the things people write about him now, they were there then."

Ret. Col. Ben Willis, who served under Powell in Korea, recalls Powell's telling him about one of the educational get-togethers arranged for the White House Fellows to enhance their understanding of feminist issues: "Colin said that some of the people were knocking heads with Gloria Steinem," Willis says. "He said he kept his mouth shut because she was smarter than he was. He could tell if he opened his mouth, he was going to get eaten up. 'I knew when I was overmatched,' he said."

Jobs for White House Fellows are guaranteed, but although fellows express a preference for which slots they would like to fill, particulars are no sure thing. "After we know who the fellows are, we contact all the various cabinet officials and executive branch agencies to see if they have an interest," Phyllis Byrne says. "If they say yes, we fan out these applications. Then, in May, the fellows come in for interviews."

Powell had interviews with George Romney, the former Michigan governor who was then heading the Department of Health, Education, and Welfare, and with L. Patrick Gray, who served for less than a year as head of the Federal Bureau of Investigation, following the death of J. Edgar Hoover. Perhaps because of his recent academic work and his time as an Army research analyst, Powell ended up choosing the executive branch's numbers-crunchers, the Office of Management and Budget.

"I think it was an interesting assignment for him, an interesting job and one that he enjoyed doing," James Bostic says. "And I think he probably surprised people at how well he did and how well he handled the tasks. . . . He always seems to be at ease and comfortable with what he's doing, but at the same time I know he gets intensely involved in what he's doing. He wants to do it the very best it's ever been done. I think he's a competitor, not in aspiring to have this or that job—not in the Washington sense of competition. But once given an assignment, he's competitive in wanting to do it very well, in fact better than it's ever been done before."

If Colin Powell did, in fact, set out to do the job of special assistant to the deputy director of the Office of Management and Budget—his official title from September, 1972, to August, 1973—better than it had ever been done before, he couldn't have picked a better place or time to do so. In one of those fortuitous matchups arranged by what seems to have been sheer serendipity, he had arrived at what was to become the major talent agency of Ground Zero itself.

The Office of Management and Budget is where the executive branch performs some of its most dazzling sleight-of-hand. Projections of revenues are made that often have only the slimmest purchase on reality; dramatic funding reductions are slated for programs that Congress has no intention of allowing cut. Numbers are sometimes pulled out of supposedly protected trust funds; still others seem to materialize out of thin air. Annually all this gets thrown into the federal computers, a federal budget pours out the other end, and for a few weeks OMB is on everyone's lips in Washington. But OMB directors often come and go in Washington with little notice or fanfare. Who today especially remembers Robert Mayo, who took over the agency in January, 1969, or Roy Ash (February, 1973), James MacIntyre (September, 1977) or James Miller (1985) or Joseph Wright, who did two terms as acting director under Ronald Reagan? Some OMB directors do make a name for themselves outside of government—James Lynn, director from February, 1975, to January, 1977, would become chairman of the insurance giant Aetna Life & Casualty. To some a certain notoriety attaches: Bert Lance, who held the job for nine months under President Jimmy Carter, and David Stockman (January, 1981, to August,

1985), who would be taken to the woodshed by Ronald Reagan for speaking out in public about the legerdemain of federal budget-making. Some, like George Bush's OMB head Richard Darman, even have a certain aura of mystery about them. What to make of a man who cuts his own hair, gobbles down fast food, and quotes freely from Joseph Heller's dark novelistic portrayal of capitalism, *Something Happened?* Yet OMB is, in reality, at the very heart of the beast of government. It's where the levers get pulled that begin the battle for money, and the battle for money is always central. OMB is a seeming executive backwater spot with disproportionate clout, and for a little over two years during the first Nixon administration and for a month in the second Nixon term, it was the place to be if you wanted to hitch your wagon to a star. From July of 1970 to June of 1972 the agency's head was George Shultz, who had already been Nixon's Secretary of Labor, would later become his Secretary of the Treasury, and would still later serve seven years as Ronald Reagan's Secretary of State after replacing Alexander Haig. The OMB head when Colin Powell arrived at the agency in September of 1972 was a man who earned the nickname "Cap the Knife" for his budget-cutting ardor and prowess.

Caspar Weinberger was California-born—in San Francisco, in 1917—and Harvard-educated, through both his undergraduate years and law school. He had been an editorial board member of the *Crimson*, Harvard College's daily newspaper and a launching pad for many of Washington's most distinguished journalistic careers. Returning to California after the war, in which he had served from private to captain in the Army infantry, Weinberger practiced law, became a Republican member of the California legislature, chairman of the state's Republican Central Committee and finally state finance director under Gov. Ronald Reagan, in which job he built a reputation as a brilliant strategist of the line-item veto. For that another Californian, Richard Nixon, would bring him to Washington to head the Office of Management and Budget. OMB would prove only the first entry in Weinberger's impressive Washington résumé. He left the agency in 1973 to become Secretary of Health, Education, and Welfare, a position he held through the first months of the Gerald Ford administration before returning to California. There, he went to work as vice-president and general counsel of Bechtel, Inc., where George Shultz also had taken refuge during the Ford and Carter years. In 1981 he followed Reagan back to Washington to become his Secretary of Defense and one of the principal architects of the biggest and most expensive peacetime military buildups in American history. (Weinberger's chief economist at OMB had been another Californian—the buoyant Arthur B. Laffer, whose "Laffer curve" would be a critical underpinning of the supply-side Reaganomics that failed to fund the arms buildup.) In 1983 Weinberger would choose Colin Powell, who had worked in his agency ten years earlier, to be his military assistant.

Caspar Weinberger, though, is only the first part of the OMB story, and perhaps the minor part. Powell's actual boss—his first one—at the Office of Management and Budget was a younger but already more traveled political warrior, Frank Carlucci. Carlucci had been born in Scranton, Pennsylvania, in 1930, and educated at Princeton and Harvard. In 1956 he began a State Department career that would take him to South Africa, the Congo, and Zanzibar before depositing him in Rio de Janeiro as the U.S. consular for political affairs. From there Carlucci moved on to become, in 1965, assistant director and later director of the Office of Economic Opportunity, first under Lyndon Johnson and then under Richard Nixon. Carlucci's next post, beginning in 1971, was associate director and later deputy director of OMB under Weinberger, and it was there that Colin Powell came to his attention for the first time. The impression, Carlucci says, was immediately favorable: "He communicates a lot of energy and personality when he comes into a room, and he always has. He's an enjoyable person to be with—relaxed and humorous but with force. That's unusual."

Carlucci's peripatetic career would see him next become an undersecretary of the Department of Health, Education, and Welfare under Caspar Weinberger, who had by then moved over to HEW; U.S. ambassador to Portugal; and deputy director of the CIA during the Carter administration. In 1981, again under Weinberger, he became a deputy secretary of defense; for his senior military adviser he chose someone already doing that job for his predecessor—Colin Powell. Carlucci left government in 1982 to become president, later chief executive officer, of Sears World Trade, Inc. When he returned in 1986 to become President Reagan's National Security Adviser, Carlucci brought Powell in to be his deputy, and when he left that post to replace

Caspar Weinberger as Secretary of Defense, Powell moved into the National Security Adviser's chair.

In an interview with *Newsday*'s Saul Friedman, Colin Powell refers to Carlucci as his "godfather of godfathers," and understandably so. It's also a characterization Carlucci seems to enjoy. "We've been very close," he says. "He's worked more for me than for any other single person. It was when he was my military assistant—when I was deputy secretary [of defense]—that Cap got to know him well."

Indeed, two careers—perhaps three, including Weinberger's—could hardly be more intertwined, nor does any relationship better illustrate the advantages of a well-placed Washington mentor than that of Carlucci and Powell. (The three, it might be noted, form an odd sight together—Powell is almost a half foot taller and considerably more brawny than either of his wiry former bosses.) Yet Colin Powell's career path in Washington needs perhaps to be seen against a still broader backdrop because there is another salient fact to be weighed: Frank Carlucci wrestled at Princeton University in the early 1950s on the same team as Donald Rumsfeld. And Rumsfeld, too, was to prove an adept network builder.

Born in Chicago in 1932, Rumsfeld apparently caught the Washington bug early in life. By age twenty-six he was an administrative assistant to the U.S. House of Representatives; four years later he was a congressman himself. After four terms representing the Thirteenth District of Illinois, Rumsfeld became director of the Office of Economic Opportunity and hired his old classmate and wrestling crony, Frank Carlucci, to be his assistant director. When Rumsfeld became an assistant to President Nixon late in 1969, Carlucci moved in as OEO director. Four years later, after serving as the U.S. ambassador to NATO, Rumsfeld became Gerald Ford's White House Chief of Staff. As his assistant he brought in one of the protégés he had acquired at the Office of Economic Opportunity, a thirty-three-year-old ex-graduate student named Dick Cheney.

Younger than Powell by nearly four years but without any career interruption for military service, Cheney had come to his own mentor's attention through a route similar to Powell's. He was a doctoral candidate at the University of Wisconsin when a Congressional Fellowship brought him to Washington in 1968. Less than two years later, he was working for Rumsfeld at OEO, and four years after that he followed Rumsfeld to the White House. When Rumsfeld became Secretary of Defense in 1975, Cheney replaced him as Chief of Staff. Another thirteen years later, according to Fred Hoffman, Rumsfeld was on "a very short list" to become Secretary of Defense once again, "but I was told from the White House that Bush vetoed Rumsfeld out of hand, remembering that he had supported Ronald Reagan eight years earlier" when Bush and Reagan were competing for the Republican presidential nomination. Instead, Bush turned to former Texas senator John Tower and—after that bruising and ultimately losing nomination battle—to Dick Cheney, who in the interim had served five terms in Congress from Wyoming. Shortly thereafter, Cheney would pick Colin Powell to be Chairman of the Joint Chiefs of Staff. As has so often been the case in Powell's career, Frank Carlucci seems to have had a hand in that as well.

Carlucci says that he and Cheney got together shortly after Bush had nominated Cheney to the defense post. "I said, 'Dick, you'll get a chance to name your own chairman. In my judgment there's only one person it should be: Colin Powell.' He said, 'You're right,' and I knew it was sealed then. I knew George Bush would accept that recommendation."

And with that, the circle would be, in a sense, completed—the mantle of authority passed on from Carlucci, Rumsfeld, and Weinberger to the new generation of Powell and Cheney.

"It's almost a cabal," one former high-ranking Pentagon official says of the Weinberger-Carlucci-Rumsfeld-Powell connection. "He connected with them in 1972, and he's been hustled along with them ever since."

Carlucci can, in fact, sound almost proprietary when he talks about Colin Powell. Of the fourteen months Powell spent as an assistant division commander at Fort Carson, Colorado—in 1981–82, between stints as Carlucci's and then Weinberger's Pentagon military adviser and during which time Powell was promoted to major general—Carlucci says, "We put him out at Fort Carson to get him another star; then Cap yanked him back to be his aide."

It's true, too, that the interrelationship between Powell, Carlucci, and Weinberger, and Rumsfeld and Cheney is evidence of what the often frenetic pace of change in Washington tends to obscure: that except for the brief interregnum of the Carter years, defense policy and planning has been—for better or worse—in the hands of a very small group of people.

"I often thought as I watched the Gulf War that the same people who brought you the *Mayaguez* tragedy brought you the Gulf War," says author and Ret. Lt. Col. William Corson, an outspoken critic of Operation Desert Storm. (On May 15, 1975, when Donald Rumsfeld was Secretary of Defense and Dick Cheney was White House Chief of Staff, thirty-eight U.S. sailors and Marines were killed rescuing the American merchant ship *Mayaguez*, which had been seized by Cambodian forces.) "They're the same folks recycled. They're worse than baseball managers who lose in the Sally League and end up back in the majors. It isn't a question of shame; you can't get rid of them even when they fuck up."

Yet it is also the case that the Carlucci-Rumsfeld-Powell-Weinberger-Cheney connection is far from unique in the annals of Washington power-making. The capital has long been a place rich in what amounts to interlocking directorates and vertical trusts. Journalist Larry Van Dyne has chronicled dozens of examples, from the Nelson Rockefeller syndicate (Henry Kissinger, who rose to attention on Rockefeller-backed foreign-policy study groups; one-time aide Nancy Hanks, the late chairman of the National Endowment for the Arts; Joseph Canzeri, a Reagan White House aide who was once a right-hand man to Rockefeller; and journalist and television commentator Tom Braden, whom Rockefeller first connected with when Braden was a student at their mutual alma mater, Dartmouth College), to the Felix Frankfurter one (former Secretary of State Dean Acheson, Franklin Roosevelt intimate Tommy "the Cork" Corcoran, Washington *Post* editor Philip Graham, and Elliot Richardson, who held three Cabinet posts under Richard Nixon before resigning in the Watergate-related "Saturday Night Massacre," among others, all worked for Frankfurter at one time or another). All of which is not intended to condemn but to note how Washington tends, for better or worse, to work.

Fred Malek, for whom Powell also worked at the Office of Management and Budget—Malek took over Carlucci's job when he moved on to Health, Education, and Welfare—argues that Powell simply had the qualities to rise, no matter what connections he made.

"Colin functioned as my executive assistant. He screened things before they got to me, and he took on special projects. He was thirty-five then, and I was thirty-six or so," says Malek, who would move on to become president of Marriott Hotels and Northwest Airlines, a business partner of Carlucci's in a Washington investment firm known as the Carlyle Group, and 1992 campaign manager for George Bush and Dan Quayle. (In another one of Washington's well-known circles, Malek also had been on the panel that chose Powell's class of White House Fellows.) "You know," he says, "it was obvious that Colin had just a unique blend of intellectual and people capabilities. A lot of times you find somebody who is very smart and a lot of times someone who is very good with people, and sometimes someone who is very well organized, and he had all three. Another thing that was unusual about him—I've got an Army background, I went to West Point—a lot of times that kind of training breeds a certain amount of stiffness in a person. You're accustomed to a more rigid environment. He never had that. He always maintained such a real good balance."

"I don't think those connections are necessary," Malek says of Powell's mentors and their associates. "In the military, you're promoted on merit. He wouldn't have become a White House Fellow unless he was one of the most outstanding officers in the Army. Once you leave that position, you really move on your own merit."

Arguably, too, Colin Powell succeeded as a fellow and profited from the experience at OMB not because of Frank Carlucci but in spite of him.

"I spent the first three months at OMB frankly just as an action-officer tucked into the new [Executive Office Building]," Powell says. "There wasn't a great deal of interest in a White House Fellow at OMB, so they just shoved me off in a corner. Carlucci likes to claim he [picked] me, but what Carlucci did is, he picked me all right, but then I went off to the new EOB never to be seen by Carlucci again."

To fill what amounted to a great deal of down-time, Powell was handed a study that was to prove in a small way an almost ideal primer for his future White House work. "They asked me to head up a project to keep me out of trouble. . . . Nobody knew what happened to presidential orders when they gave them. Nixon was mad because he kept telling people to do things, and nothing would happen. So I tracked what happened to presidential directives, and I put together a project that resulted in a document that was called 'A Weekly Compilation of Presidential Directives.' And for the first time we started capturing what the hell presidents ultimately do. It's survived in various iterations. That's what I did for two months, and it got me into every department. I was able to go to every department at the assistant-secretary-for-administration level, and that was very useful.''

A high-ranking Reagan official says that Powell was ''hand-picked'' by Carlucci and Weinberger, ''but for obvious reasons. Weinberger had him in his office over at the Pentagon because he trusted the guy and the guy gave good advice. Carlucci got him away from Weinberger because he was looking for a smart military man he could also trust.'' And, notes Powell's friend Harlan Ullman of the Center for Naval Analysis, Powell seems to have risen just fine outside the Carlucci circle.

''There's a guy named Charles Duncan [Deputy Secretary of Defense under Jimmy Carter], who is not part of this cabal,'' Ullman says. ''Duncan picked up Powell to be his military assistant when he was working for [Special Assistant to the Secretary] John Kester. Everybody knew Powell was a great guy. Here's a guy of enormous quality, obvious quality.''

Powell's sister, Marilyn Berns, told the Los Angeles *Times*'s George Frank that the White House Fellowship ''was the real turning point of [Colin's] career. I first realized [then] that this was a young man going someplace.''

Talent had brought him to the attention of Army infantry career-makers who wanted one of their own among the prestigious White House Fellows. Fortune had landed him at OMB in the midst of particularly durable Republican figures in what was to become the Republican epoch of the executive branch, and his personality and dedication to duty seem to have endeared him to them. But Colin Powell was still an Army officer when his fellowship year ended in August of 1973—in need of marking all the right boxes for advancement in a military career—and by then he had been out of the field for more than four years, since leaving Vietnam in July of 1969. One month after vacating his desk at the Office of Management and Budget, Powell was flying across the Pacific again, this time to become a battalion commander in Korea.

"There again was a job he needed," says Al Garland. "He's a lieutenant colonel now, and he needs that to verify his lieutenant colonelcy, to get him up to eagle [full colonel]. Without that, forget it; you're going to retire in twenty years."

CHAPTER 10

Stations of the Cross

"Probably no segment of American society is as little known and little understood as the professional Army," the novelist and Vietnam war correspondent Ward Just writes in his introduction to David Hackworth's *About Face: The Odyssey of an American Warrior*. "It is a nation apart, with its particular customs, laws, language, economy, virtues, and vices. This is a state of affairs that seems to suit everyone; the civilians can retail clichés about the soldiers, and the soldiers retail clichés about themselves, with no one the wiser. The Army is as hierarchical as the church and as class-conscious and snobbish as Great Britain, West Point its Eton and the Army War College its Oxford. The Army today resembles a great ponderous American corporation, but it was not always so. The Army used to be filled with officers who believed their highest calling was to lead troops into battle, not as one more Station of the Cross on their way to the E-Ring of the Pentagon, military Gethsemane; that was why they were in the Army instead of at General Dynamics. There were soldiers who studied infantry tactics with the care and diligence that Picasso devoted to the female face, and so thoroughly that the knowledge became second nature, almost instinct."

Ultimately Colin Powell's career would include a series of stations leading him to the highest post in the United States military—not only the E-, or outer-, Ring of the Pentagon, but its River Entrance, a vast office with an anteroom and a staff of fifty men and women at his beck and call, including a public-affairs office as well-staffed and able as any corporate communications office. When you get to the top of the ladder, everything else below necessarily has been a rung you've climbed on.

Inevitably, too, a military career such as Colin Powell's sends lessons down the ranks. Ret. Adm. Eugene Carroll is among those—a relative handful perhaps—who worry that Powell's rapid rise tends to discourage frontline service.

"Powell never was really in military channels in Washington; he was in political channels. They sent him out from time to time to place an 'X' in a box but you see how long he stayed. . . . When people see that the road to success, the road to the top is through the political agencies, they say, 'Look, I want to be a success; I've got a wife, two kids, a mortgage. This is where the smartest people in the military are. I've got to get aboard.' In the Navy this leads to people declining command opportunities. You've got bombs, weapons. Anyone aboard can make a mistake—the *Iowa* being a good example—and suddenly your career is over." (On April 19, 1989, an explosion in a sixteen-inch gun turret aboard the USS *Iowa* killed forty-two sailors; the ship's skipper, Capt. Fred Moosally, took early retirement.) "So now people are saying, 'Look, I can take the dicey route and become a respected military commander and see where that leads. Or I can become a military aide, get a White House Fellowship and go that route.' If you're smart like Colin Powell and have his personality and intelligence, you succeed, and no one can blow you up. There's an old Navy saying: A collision at sea can spoil your whole day. That's what I'm talking about. It's something you couldn't have prevented, and yet your career is over."

Another critic, retired Marine Lt. Col. William Corson, tells of a conversation he had a number of years back with an active-duty Army general. "This guy is a friend of mine. We got to talking about the problems of the Army. He said we've got this problem with the first brigade of the Eighty-second Airborne—this is the go-go, the first-to-fight outfit. We have had twelve people turn down this command and finally got the thirteenth. The reason was that this is not where you get promoted in one very real sense. You could get in-

volved with a sexual-harassment suit, with racial difficulties,
with drugs in the squad bay. You could be the greatest trainer
and leader in the world but you were guilty—it happened in
your unit. The people who were smart, who were career-
oriented, didn't want command. Get yourself on a joint staff,
fly a desk, and you're home free. In one sense, it's the old
carping criticism of the warriors against the non-warriors, but
what we're getting now are hermaphrodites. We don't have
real staff warriors. . . . In the case of General Powell, who
is obviously very adept at what he is doing, you find yourself—not to have a religious connotation—a rabbi that has
clout, and you sit on his tail, and you wipe his ass, and you
go along if he goes along. Powell has been fortunate to have
an exceptionally astute rabbi [in Frank Carlucci]. Colin Powell is not made of sugar cake, and I'm not raining on his
parade." In one form or another, though rarely so graphi-
cally, Corson's argument does get repeated by some military
officers, active and retired.

Yet Powell's first station of the cross after leaving the White
House Fellow program was *precisely* the sort of posting Carroll and Corson talk about his ultimate career discouraging.
Like much else on his résumé, the assignment to be commander of the First Battalion, Thirty-second Infantry, Second
Infantry Division of the Eighth Army in the Republic of Korea came about mostly by chance, Powell says.

"At the end of the fellowship year, Fred [Malek] asked me
to stay [at OMB], and I said, 'No, I want to go back to the
Army.' I went to Korea because it was the only place I could
get a battalion right away. Everywhere else I would have had
to go wait somewhere for a year or two. I was going through
the little battalion book—in those days before centralized selection they had all the battalions written in a notebook in
pencil—and we went down looking for a battalion that was
open, and the only one they could find was in Korea. So I
went home to Alma and said, 'I've got to go overseas
again.' "

As it turned out, Powell's post was one with exposed flanks,
one where the Army equivalent of a collision at sea was waiting around every corner and where no rabbi or mentor no
matter how highly placed could fly much meaningful interference. The specific issue was racial conflict and, to a lesser

Colin Powell in his Sunday best, at about seven years of age. *(Photo courtesy of the Office of the Chairman of the Joint Chiefs of Staff)*

On Kelly Street in the South Bronx. Left to right, all in their mid-teens, are Victor Ramirez, Tony Grant, Powell, and Manny Garcia. *(Photo courtesy of the Office of the Chairman of the Joint Chiefs of Staff)*

Powell at age 15, following his sister's graduation from Buffalo State College in 1952. With him are his father, Luther; sister, Marilyn; and mother, Maud. *(Photo courtesy of the Office of the Chairman of the Joint Chiefs of Staff)*

Alma and Colin Powell at their wedding reception in Birmingham, Alabama, on August 25, 1962. *(Photo courtesy of the Office of the Chairman of the Joint Chiefs of Staff)*

Captain Powell during his first tour in South Vietnam—December, 1962, to November, 1963. The identity of the other soldiers is unknown. *(Photo courtesy of the Office of the Chairman of the Joint Chiefs of Staff)*

In South Vietnam in 1963, probably in the A Shau Valley, where Powell served as military advisor to the 1st Infantry Division of the Army of the Republic of Vietnam. *(Photo courtesy of the Office of the Chairman of the Joint Chiefs of Staff)*

Lieutenant Colonel Powell as a battalion commander in South Korea—September, 1973, to September, 1974. *(Photo courtesy of the Office of the Chairman of the Joint Chiefs of Staff)*

Speaking to the press at the White House on November 5, 1987, after being introduced as the new National Security Adviser to the President. Looking on are Caspar Weinberger, Ronald Reagan, and, at front right, Powell's "godfather of godfathers," Frank Carlucci. *(UPI/Bettmann)*

The Chairman of the Joint Chiefs of Staff on the firing range at Camp Lejeune, North Carolina—March 15, 1990. *(USMC photo by Sgt. Jim Fitzgibbons)*

The end of the Cold War: General Powell greeting his Soviet counterpart, General Mikhail Moiseyev, at Andrews Air Force Base in Washington, D.C., during Moiseyev's unprecedented visit to the United States in September and October, 1990. *(Photo courtesy of the Office of the Chairman of the Joint Chiefs of Staff)*

The Chairman on a field visit as U.S.-based troops prepare for mobilization to Saudi Arabia. *(USMC photo by Sgt. Jim Fitzgibbons)*

General Powell meeting with members of the 132nd MP Company in Saudi Arabia, December 22, 1990. *(Reuters/Bettmann)*

With Allied commander General Norman Schwarzkopf at the Riyadh, Saudi Arabia, airport on February 8, 1991, more than three weeks into the air war against Iraq. *(UPI/Bettmann)*

Powell listens on in the Oval Office as President Bush talks with Norman Schwarzkopf in Saudi Arabia on February 27, 1991, shortly before the cease fire in the Gulf War was declared. Chief of Staff John Sununu and Deputy National Security Adviser Robert Gates are in the background. Defense Secretary Dick Cheney has his back to the camera. *(Reuters/Bettmann)*

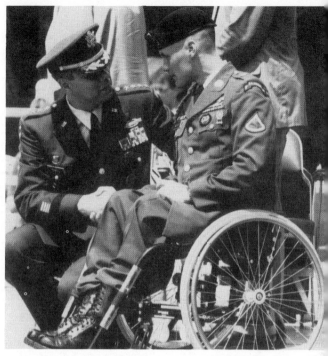

At the Vietnam Veterans Memorial on May 27, 1991. Powell speaks with Corporal Patrick McElrath, who was wounded during the 1989 invasion of Panama. *(Reuters/Bettmann)*

Colin Powell in his Pentagon office. Behind him is the standing desk where he frequently works. *(Photo courtesy of the office of the Chairman of the Joint Chiefs of Staff)*

extent, drugs. Powell's commanding officer with the Second
Infantry in Korea—Ret. Lt. Gen. Hank Emerson, known to
many of those who served under him as "Gunfighter"—says
that Powell passed the test with flying colors.

The military had integrated officially a quarter century before Powell arrived in Korea, but as the larger experience of
American society continues to show, legal integration does
not require racial harmony. In 1973, racial tension, particularly among enlisted men, was very much on the mind of the
United States Army.

"In the late 1960s and early 1970s, you had an awful lot
of racial incidents at [Fort] Benning," Al Garland says.
"Specifically between 1968 and '69 and 1974 and '75 there
were some areas on the post where it was black versus white
all the time. You had a bad situation where you were bringing
men back from Vietnam who still had time to serve. What
were you going to tell them? There was an infantry brigade
here at the time—the 197th, since redesignated—that occupied an area called Kelly Hill. Almost every night it was the
scene of some racial incident. That led to brawls. Tensions
were very tight. The mixture of an unpopular war, drugs,
and race made a volatile situation." In Korea and Germany,
Garland says, the problem was even worse.

"The entire Army and the [Second Infantry] Division [in
Korea] were suffering two things," Gen. Hank Emerson
says—"drug problems and racial problems, both of which
become magnified when you are cooped up. If you tend to
have in the Army a hostile racial problem, it's magnified in
an environment like that. We had to get a handle on it from
two sides. On the command side, there were some guys who
were bigoted and making it worse. And from the minority
side, there were hotheads who were trying to organize."

The Second Infantry Division, Emerson says, "was spread
over five hundred square miles with little encampments here
and there. [Powell] and his brigade were located at Camp
Casey, where my headquarters was. This was at Tongduchon,
a little north and to the east of Uijongbu, almost directly
north of Seoul and south of the [demilitarized zone]. If the
North Koreans made an attack, it was pretty hard to envision
the Second Division wouldn't be engaged. That was part of

the point, I think—to let the North Koreans know that we'd be involved. . . . They were always trying to infiltrate guys south. They'd tunneled under the DMZ. It wasn't like we were going to war tomorrow, but we could have. You get a pretty good handle on whether a commander can handle his guys in the field. Short of getting shot at, it's a good place to test your commanders, and Powell was out-fucking-standing.

"This was a time the Army was in pretty bad shape," Emerson continues. "It was right at the end of Vietnam. We had all the drug and racial problems. They were particularly acute in Korea because there wasn't a lot to do there. That particular battalion [the First Battalion that Powell was assigned to] was a hotbed of dissent. There were twenty-some battalions, but this and another one were the focal points. They had all the hotheads. It was an after-duty problem, at night when the guys got into a recreational mode—two black guys jumping on a white guy [or the reverse], that kind of thing.

"I hadn't known Powell before. He'd had the White House Fellowship. But I'm a field guy—that isn't the best recommendation for me. He didn't come to me with a dazzling combat record, which would have appealed to me more. But you have no choice of whom you get. So I put him in that unit. I assigned him there thinking he's a minority guy, he might be able to get a lid on it, and he goddamn well did. . . . I said, goddamn, this son of a bitch can command soldiers. He was charismatic. He really raised the morale, especially the *esprit* of that unit. It came from very low to very high. . . . He sure as shit showed me what he could do as a commander. I figured, shit, this guy must have it all. I wrote him up as one of the two top battalion commanders I had there, and I had sixty-five, sixty-six battalion commanders. He just showed me. I put on his report this guy should be a brigadier general as quick as the law allows."

(The other of Emerson's two top battalion commanders, Arthur Stang, had also come to Korea from the Pentagon. Stang went on to become chief of staff of the Eighty-second Airborne. He died of a heart attack, Emerson says, while on one of the daily runs required to meet Army fitness standards.)

"Emerson was very fond of me," Powell says, "and he

was forever using me for one purpose or another. I wasn't anywhere near as good as he claims I was. But we were always great friends, and we hit it off, and I was always doing things in Korea that he loved. We destroyed his club one night in a great fight."

The fight—Powell had to find $2,000 the next morning to pay for damages to the club—came at his own farewell party, in a scene that calls to mind the opening moments of *The Great Santini*: "Division staff had brought up some teachers from Seoul to show the teachers from Seoul that animals do not live at Camp Casey, Korea, Tongduchon, or if they do, they're downtown in all those bad places. They're not here at this nice, sedate division officers club," Powell recalls. '*Boom!* The doors open, and in come Powell [and his group]. . . . We didn't plan to have a fight, but one broke out. It started when some of my guys took the foosball machine and, as a test of strength, tried to hit the ceiling with it, which they did, and the foosball machine came down in about a thousand pieces, and then some guy poured a Coke down the jukebox coin slot, and then it was on. The bottom line was when my executive officer punched out the G-1 of the division who objected to this rowdiness. It was a mess."

Out of such moments, Powell says, Hank Emerson developed "this romantic notion" of me.

Powell's executive officer with the First Battalion of the Thirty-second Infantry in Korea was Ret. Col. Ben Willis:

"I was his second-in-command," Willis says. "He was a great guy. I can't say anything but the highest praise for him. He let company commanders command their companies, and he set a great example. He's a fine Christian person. There were no wives over there to speak of, that sort of thing. He cast a very jaundiced eye when any of his officers would stray and go downtown to visit one of the whorehouses. It's certainly something he'd never do.

"We had a big problem when he arrived. There had been some units where blacks had virtually taken over the outfits. Some units had let discipline get away from them. The command authority was being undermined. Virtually you had little pockets of street gangs within the units. His unit was one of them. That was the situation he walked into, and we ended up dealing with it. Of course, there were some ringleaders.

He brought them in, and it wound up in this unit and some of the others with dismissing a number of people from the service. We had to clean house. We had to cut the head of the serpent off. . . .

"General Emerson had this program, and it was one of the best I've ever seen. You take disadvantaged people—black, Hispanic, it doesn't matter—and you try to bring them up by the bootstraps, give them self-confidence. We tried to give these people the best leg-up you can. We created an environment where we didn't think it was possible for this thing to happen again. We had disciplined troops, we cared about their welfare, and we took care of them."

In Korea and out of the public eye, Powell says, Emerson was also able to enforce change in a way that wouldn't have been possible at a Fort Benning: "He did things at Casey you couldn't have gotten away with in the United States with newspapers watching. You know, 'There will be no drugs,' and 'By God, we're going to have race relations and it begins tomorrow morning at eight o'clock. Anybody got any questions?' There used to be a section of town that was where the white soldiers went, and there was another section of town called 'the Crack.' It was a terrible section where all the black soldiers went. And the black soldiers essentially said, 'Don't come in here, don't nobody come in here, or else.' Essentially they declared it off limits. And one night [Emerson] got all the battalion commanders, and he said, 'We're all going to the Crack tonight, every damn one of us, and if anything happens we're going to take the whole division in there and clean it out.' We all went down to the Crack, and he essentially said, 'Enjoy yourself; you don't have to mix with whites or blacks—it's a personal choice—but damn it, we're soldiers. . . . And then we started running them every morning for four miles and working their butts off, and they were too tired to get in trouble. They were too exhausted to think about drugs more than just in passing. When nightfall came, they collapsed. It was one of the best years of my life."

Powell, Ben Willis says, "wasn't the hard-nosed kind of guy that ate nails and spit them out. Some units, it was just terror. You're just so goddamned afraid of your battalion commander that you walk around on pins and needles. You've got to have your own command style—you can't copy anyone else's. The people who get in trouble are the ones who try to copy people and never be themselves. [Powell] was unique. He schooled his junior officers, and we had fun. You can have fun in the Army; you can make it an atmosphere like that. He tried to make it as relaxed an atmosphere as possible yet maintain discipline and get the training done. That's the kind of outfit he tried to run, and did. We did have fun.''

Like virtually everyone else who served with Colin Powell anywhere in his career, Willis says that he could see Powell was "a comer. A lot of us felt that he was obviously going to go a long way. This was the mid-nineteen-seventies. We didn't have a bunch of black generals, and it was obvious we were going to be looking for them. I felt he was going to be a general officer and potentially chief of staff of the Army because we were going to be looking to promote the best blacks we could find and certainly he qualified. But the important thing here is that he would have made it if he was purple. He made the rank not because he was black but because he was the best damn man for the job. His race didn't help him and it didn't stand in his way. He made it on merit. He wasn't handed it on a silver platter.''

The Korean regiment Powell served in is known as the Queen's Own Buccaneers. "It's a famous regiment in the Army," Hank Emerson says. "He was known as Buc 6. When we exchange notes, he still signs them 'Buc 6.' '' General officers are given a retirement ceremony when they leave active duty, a chance for some of the troops who have served under them to pay tribute. At his own retirement ceremony in June, 1977, Hank Emerson—"Gunfighter"—put in charge someone who would eventually make his highest reputation behind a desk: Buc 6.

"I asked for selected units that fought under me in combat," Emerson says, "but I selected him to be commander of troops at my ceremony.''

Powell remembers it as a unique ceremony—in no small part because Powell was by then commanding the 2d Brigade of the 101st Airborne Division at Fort Campbell, Kentucky, while Emerson was the commanding general at Fort Bragg, where the archrival 82d Airborne was stationed. (Although he was at a different fort, Powell was under Emerson's command at the time.)

"Comes time for Gunfighter to retire," Powell recalls "and he designs this retirement ceremony. He says, 'I want Powell to be commander of troops.' *Never* go to Fort Campbell and get a guy from the 101st Airborne Division wearing a Screaming Eagles patch to go to Fort Bragg and stand in front of a formation of Fort Bragg troops with the 82d lined up behind them. You can't be serious. 'I want Powell to be commander of troops!' So I called down there, and I said, 'Guys, get me out of this. I don't need this.' And they came back and said, 'Gunfighter says you're going to be commander of troops. Shut the fuck up and get down here.'

"I went down there three days ahead of time, and the ceremony was all screwed up, so we rehearsed for three days. And it was a little touchy with a guy from the 101st teaching the 82d how to march. The day of the ceremony comes and the whole corps is lined up. We're all standing in ranks I'm the commander in front. And Gunfighter shows up." Powell says that Emerson signaled him several times from the review stand to come to talk to him. "He's waving, Come on up here, so I turned to the staffs behind me and I said, 'I don't know what's going on but I'm breaking ranks to go up and see Gunfighter.' So I go up—'Yes, sir.' He says, 'Colin, I want you to add a little something to the ceremony.' 'Yes, sir, what would you like?' He says, 'When I give you the go, I want you to have all of the officers turn around and face the troops. Just have all the officers turn around.' This is about a minute before the ceremony is to begin. I say, 'Yes, sir, then what?' 'You'll see. You'll see.' So there's no time to tell anybody. . . . I say to the staff, 'Just bear with me.' Sure enough, he's going on, giving speeches and weeping and moaning.

"Finally, at the appointed moment," Powell says, "I make up a command. I turn around and say, 'Listen carefully. Officers—*only* officers, about-face!' So they about-face. They're all in close ranks, so everybody is staring at the guy right in front of him. And what he wanted them to do, he said, 'I want the officers now to salute the troops.' I said, 'Officers, present arms!' And that's what he wanted them to do. That's the kind of guy he was. . . . It was a great ceremony. It was wonderful. [And] I got the hell out of there as fast as I could.''

Despite the unusual nature of the ceremony, Powell says that being asked to command the troops was ''enormously touching.''

''I was trying to make a statement, in part,'' by selecting Powell, Emerson says. ''The Army never admitted it had racial problems, but you had a hell of a lot of racists. It was a measurement of what I thought of him.''

In the Pentagon as on the battlefield—as in real estate, for that matter—location tends to be a determining factor. To gain strategic location at the five-sided military bastion, one progresses outward from the A-Ring to the E-Ring. In general terms, one gains in stature by rising vertically as well. It is not by accident that Secretary of Defense Dick Cheney's third-floor Pentagon office sits on top of the second-floor office of the Chairman of the Joint Chiefs of Staff. The positioning enforces in architecture what the Constitution enshrines in law—that the military is always under civilian control, that the chairman must always come *up* to see the secretary while the secretary *descends* to see the chairman. The distinction is central to American democracy. (The Secretary of Defense also gets a Marine guard posted outside his office while the Chairman has none. The explanation the services offers—that, as a soldier, the chairman needs no one to defend him—can give the perquisite an ironic cast, especially in the case of Cheney, who used a student deferment to avoid service in the Vietnam War.) Other perks accrue to upward—and outward—mobility in the Pentagon. Not the least of them, in the complicated symbolism of the building, is higher office paneling, an outward and visible manifestation of a career itself on the ascent. In September, 1974, Colin Powell returned from his battalion command in Korea to essentially the same job he had held before he left, an operations research-system analyst, but this time he had higher paneling. His previous tour as an analyst had been in the Office of the Assistant Vice-Chief-of-Staff of the Army; this time he was in the Office of the Deputy Assistant Secretary of Defense, up a floor with all that entails in terms of status and a subtly shifting career path. Except for his relatively brief future field commands and one more stint as a student, Powell would not again be outside political channels in Washington.

In any event the analyst's job was to prove a while-you-wait proposition. In August, 1975, Powell moved across the Potomac River to enroll in the National War College at Fort McNair. "I'm sure he swung that to stay in the Washington area," says *Infantry* magazine editor Al Garland. "He was settled by then, and at the level he was at, swinging that wasn't hard to do." The Army runs three war colleges, or officer graduate schools—the Army War College at Carlisle, Pennsylvania; the Industrial College of the Armed Forces, and the National War College, both located within the National Defense University at Fort McNair. Of the three, the National War College is the one that concentrates most on operations and planning, Powell's role as the G-3 and later Deputy G-3 on the staff of General Gettys in Vietnam. Because operations and planning are what the Army and particularly Powell's Infantry Branch most celebrates, the National War College is the first of equals among the colleges, the place "for coming [George] Pattons," in Garland's words.

"Of all the war colleges, that's the magic one," Ret. Col. David Hackworth says. "Making war college is great stuff, but making the National War College is the *crème de la crème.*"

Powell graduated from the War College in April, 1976. By then he was no longer a comer in the Army, no longer a water-walker. By then, says his classmate Harlan Ullman, Powell was a "marked man. Everyone at the War College knew he was going to be chairman or whatever. He had that reputation, that aura, whatever, among his colleagues. Everyone knew he was going to rise to the top, whether National Security Adviser or Army chief of staff or chairman, it didn't matter." Because of Powell's associations with Caspar Weinberger and Frank Carlucci, Ullman says, "he moved possibly more quickly than he might have otherwise, but he had to end up at the top. It was inevitable."

Still, in the rigid hierarchy of the Army, there were other stations of the cross to be performed, other boxes to be marked. The Army promotion ladder descends from a corps command, held by a lieutenant or three-star general; to a division command, held by a major general; to an assistant division command, held by a brigadier general; to a brigade command, held by a full colonel. To get to the next rung and to assume the rank associated with it, you need to have occupied the rung below. Ultimately, Powell—like Alexander Haig—would prove an exception to the hierarchy. He would get his third star without ever having commanded a division. But that was for later. By April, 1976, Powell had led only a battalion. To ascend to the single star of a brigadier general he needed to command a brigade. Fresh out of the National War College and two months a full colonel, Powell took over command of the 2d Brigade of the 101st Airborne Division stationed at Fort Campbell, Kentucky.

If it was not quite the best assignment he could have gotten—the 82d Airborne is generally considered slightly more prestigious than the Screaming Eagles of the 101st—it was a very near second best. For omen watchers it also was still more proof of a career full of momentum and direction. Fort Campbell, David Hackworth says, "was a plum assignment. If you don't have a brigade, your career is finished as a colonel. Then to get this, which is one of the elite units of the Army—he was being well looked after."

For added measure and more proof of how careers begin to overlap as the Army's officers pool is winnowed down to the relatively special few, Powell's overarching boss when he was in charge of the 2d Brigade of the 101st Airborne was the same commanding officer who had not been particularly overjoyed to see him show up in Korea two and a half years earlier—Gen. Hank "Gunfighter" Emerson. "Now," Emerson says, "I know him. I've seen him perform. I'm delighted he's there. And I'm not a damn bit surprised when he does the same thing there that he did in Korea."

As head of the 18th Airborne Corps, Emerson's command included both the 101st Airborne and the 82d Airborne, stationed as Emerson was at Fort Bragg, North Carolina. In between Emerson and Powell in the line of command came Powell's immediate boss, John Wickham, then head of the 101st Airborne and later Army chief of staff. Because of Emerson's enthusiasm for Powell, the chain of command occasionally got a little dodgy, Powell recalls.

"Emerson used to watch me carefully when I was brigade commander of the 101st," Powell says, "because he felt that perhaps John Wickham was a little more straightlaced than he was, which was certainly true. He watched over me like a doting grandfather from a distance. And General Wickham, who is a treasure of my life—he and I had our disagreements from time to time at Fort Campbell, but division commanders and brigade commanders have their disagreements. So he was on my case for a while, and in one or two instances he really got on my case, and word got to Emerson.'' Emerson, Powell says, called him shortly thereafter, offering to run interference in the disputes: " 'You in trouble?' Emerson asked. 'No, General, nothing I can't handle.' 'I'll take care of it!' 'No, General, no! I *don't* want you to take care of it. Please, General, I'll take care of it myself.' And I did, and Wickham and I got along famously.''

As seems to happen with uniform regularity to Powell, John Wickham also would end up helping his one-time subordinate's career along. And, of course, it was while he was at Fort Campbell that Powell would lead the 82d Airborne at Emerson's very singular retirement ceremony.

Powell's next assignment is listed officially as Executive to the Special Assistant to the Secretary and Deputy Secretary of Defense. Unofficially it meant that his first general's star was all but assured. More important, the job was to become the prototype for the positions he would fill on again and off again—but mostly on—for the next eleven years, the positions that would bring him finally into the national limelight. In a very real sense, what Powell was walking into in July, 1977, was a doctoral-level course in the merging points of military and political power. It was very nearly the last bit of education he would need, and as he was to prove in the years to come, he was the perfect student.

In a 1991 interview with Rudy Abramson and John Broder of the Los Angeles *Times*, John Kester, the special assistant Powell became executive to, recalled their first meeting, in the summer of 1977: ''He had a very good, direct personality. He gave me the sense that he was a very straight dealer. Right away, he said something like, 'How did you happen to bring me in here?' And I said, 'I checked you out, and I heard a lot of good things about you.' He said, 'Well, as a matter of fact, I checked you out, too, and it wasn't all good.' '' Powell, Kester told the reporters, delivered the last line with a disarming grin. The scene can seem strangely discordant with the sober-sided Colin Powell that one gleans from his television appearances on, say, "60 Minutes" and "Today." But it has all the trademarks of the more rarely seen private man: candid, street-smart, straightforward, with a perhaps calculated edge of humor and enough sass in it to let the prospective employer know that this soldier was his own man, and geared, as it turned out, for just the right audience. In fact, Kester says in an interview with the author, what Powell seemed to be in that initial encounter was just about what he turned out to be in the long haul.

"I was [Secretary of Defense] Harold Brown's special assistant [under Jimmy Carter]," says Kester, now a Washington lawyer in private practice, "and I was also the political liaison to the White House. I had a little staff of three or four officers. I needed to get a chief of staff for myself, someone to run my staff and do the things that needed doing. The way the Pentagon works, you have a real interface—to use an awful word—between the military and civilians. I knew you needed a smart colonel working for you to get good information out of the staff. Most of the work there is done by the uniformed people. The civilians go home at five; the military guys stay there all night."

Simultaneously, Kester says, Harold Brown was looking for a new military adviser to replace one who was due to shift out, and so Kester piggybacked on Brown's search. "The way the military adviser position tends to get filled is that you go to the services and ask them for nominations. That's a very important job. Each service is slathering to get someone into the SecDef's [Secretary of Defense's] office, so they tend to nominate good people. We got nomination books from each of the services, and each one had half a dozen officers in them."

Neither Powell nor any of the Army nominees was picked to be Brown's adviser—"it wasn't the Army's turn," Kester says—but being included in the nomination book was its own high sign. The names submitted by the Army "wouldn't come up without being seen personally by the chief of staff of the Army. You've got to have good backing," Kester says. "I don't think Colin was ever a protégé of any one senior officer, but he was on good terms with a lot of generals."

With the Army out of the running for the top adviser's spot, Kester went rummaging through its nominations for his own chief of staff. "I had a prejudice in favor of the Army," he says. "I thought they were best at doing what I needed doing. So I grabbed the book and looked at who was there. I saw Colin and he looked interesting. He'd been a White House Fellow, had had infantry commands, was decorated in Vietnam and he was a minority, which was certainly a plus in the Carter administration. I wasn't going to pick anybody on that basis, but having found someone with such a set of qualifications, and his personality as well, I wasn't going to pass him by. I interviewed maybe six people, and I liked him. He seemed to be a very savvy fellow; he was very candid. You could tell he wasn't going to be a yes-man. He didn't seem awed and scared the way [military officers] sometimes do. We quickly got to the nub of what I was interested in without beating around the bush. . . . I needed someone who could walk the halls for me, give me a heads-up on things. If you don't have someone who has decent connections, you can spend a lot of time in needless frictions. Colin could talk to the execs [executive assistants] of the Army or other staff people and say, 'Look, this is what we really want to do.' "

Powell, Kester says, "turned his job into a significant job." In part, Powell appears to have done that by understanding the significance of gate-keeping within the bureaucracy. To control access to someone more important than yourself is, in fact, power; similarly, to know who has access to the top is to know at a gut level the flow of power within any government organization. Powell made sure he knew. "One of the deals" in taking the job, Kester says, "was that he would get a little office constructed outside mine. They're always moving partitions around [at the Pentagon]. I don't see how they have any bearing walls left. He could watch who went in and out of my office, just as I liked to watch who was going in and out of Harold's office. It's all fleas on fleas."

Powell also seems to have had early on in his Pentagon career—and perhaps this, too, flows from his street-smart instincts—an intuitive feel for the complicated politics of the place. "I got a sense he was very acute politically," Kester says. "I was in an intensely political job, and I wanted someone who could understand the role of politics and yet would not get dirty himself. One of the worst phenomena you see are military officers who try to become politicians. They almost always make a mess of it. You want them to understand the political forces at work but not get dirty. A lot of my job was fending off the White House, the crazy ideas that would come in from the politicians there. After I became comfortable with his judgment, I'd sometimes let him talk to the people in the White House . . . and he handled that well."

The result, Kester says, was a kind of fundamental lesson in Washington powermongering, a lesson Colin Powell would have further opportunity to apply as he moved up the ranks of the capital: "There's nothing at all wrong with sexual intercourse, but you don't invite children to watch—that encapsulates how we both felt about some of the political activities we were involved with."

Within the complicated internal politics of the military, Kester says, Powell also managed to keep the proper channels open. "There's a great danger for these guys if they go into jobs like the one he had with me. The Army feels they are becoming estranged. They have to go back out and be regreened. But he always managed to stay on real good terms with the Army . . . When you get up to the lieutenant colonel and colonel rank, you're starting to deal with people who have known each other since they were lieutenants. It isn't just a West Point crowd. Much less than the Navy, the Army isn't a closed society. They know who's real and who's an apple polisher, and they knew Colin was real. There was a certain amount of genuine heroism. He'd been wounded. He'd gotten a real medal, one that actually meant something. He was respected as a real soldier. He wasn't somebody trying to build a career on being a minority. They could tell the difference."

Kester says that he wrote Powell a note late in 1990 or early 1991 "at the time the Gulf War was about to go. I said something like he was someone who understood the human costs involved but would not be immobilized by the necessary decisions. A military commander has to be able to love his troops and at the same time order them into battle, knowing some of them will be killed. . . . [Colin] is not a Hamlet."

* * *

Although he may be associated with the Reagan and Bush administrations, Colin Powell was to work in political channels for virtually all the four years that Jimmy Carter sat in the White House as well. Along the way he would put X's in boxes other than those that stake out a military career. With John Kester, for whom he worked for a year and a half until December, 1978, came Powell's further education in the occasional eccentricities and sometimes outlandish schemes of the White House, where he would eventually become an important player as well as a reluctant participant in one of the more outlandish schemes of them all. By the time Charles Duncan chose Powell to be his chief aide, Powell's résumé was assuming a kind of inevitable force of its own. The experience would only enrich it further and heighten the office paneling once again.

"I was the deputy secretary of defense," Duncan says, "and at one point in time I needed a senior military assistant—like a special assistant, an administrative assistant on [Capitol] Hill—someone who works right with your desk, travels with you, does everything with you. I decided I wanted someone from the Army, and I thought that then Colonel Powell would be a good person to do it. He had impressed me very favorably. I thought he was extremely bright, had all the right sensitivities, understood the functioning of the military and the Pentagon very well, and also had served as a White House Fellow and done some work at OMB. He knew not only the Pentagon but the way the whole system worked. So I invited him to become my senior military assistant, and he performed that task admirably. He was an enormous help to me."

With Duncan, too, Powell would extend his doctoral-level course in government beyond the confines of the military and gain his first close-up look at Congress. In 1979, Duncan says, "I was asked by the president to move to the Department of Energy, and I invited then Brigadier General Powell to go with me after getting appropriate clearances from the Army that this would not be detrimental to his career. He was the administrative assistant—I had someone called a special assistant—but he was the person who just stayed with me during the early months, right through the transition and the confirmation hearings. He was at my side during all that, even though he was an active-duty Army officer.''

In normal times the Department of Energy is not the Cabinet's most exciting spot, but 1979 was far from a normal year. On January 16 Reza Pahlavi, the Shah of Iran and a staunch U.S. ally, fled Tehran. Less than a month later, Ayatollah Ruhollah Khomeini and his Revolutionary Council seized control of the Iranian government and, with that, decades of carefully constructed U.S. oil policy crumbled. Six weeks later, on March 28, the nuclear-power industry was rocked by the accident at Three Mile Island on the Susquehanna River south of the Pennsylvania capital at Harrisburg. A little more than seven months later the U.S. embassy in Tehran was seized by militants and its staff held hostage.

''That was a pretty tenuous period for energy,'' Duncan says with considerable understatement. ''By the early summer of 1979 gasoline lines were at their longest. There was a lot of hostility about that, a lot of public hostility. Things needed to be toned down considerably.'' For Powell, what began as a kind of tutorial in dry government management of resources ended as an object lesson in crisis management and the many tentacles of geopolitics. It couldn't have been better training for what lay ahead.

The keys to Powell, Duncan suggests, are threefold. ''He's a person who has extremely good skills at working with other people, and he's a very fast learner on things.'' And as others have said, he has stamina—he simply outworks the opposition: ''He is totally committed to what he's doing,'' Duncan says. ''There's no limitation to hours or energy. He was there by six-thirty [in the morning] certainly, and by five-thirty if he needed to be. When he was my military assistant at the Pentagon, I'd be there by seven, and he would always be there before me and leave after me, and they were at least twelve-hour days.''

Duncan also gave Powell ''the one rule I always follow,'' he told *Washingtonian* magazine: ''If all else fails and we have no choice, tell the truth.''

While he was working for Duncan, Powell also seems to have gotten his first taste of the recreational side of life at the very top of the military chain. ''David Jones was the Chairman of the Joint Chiefs of Staff then,'' Duncan says, ''and he and I would try to play racquetball several times a week, and often Colin would be my racquetball partner. His game is good. Of course, General Jones would bring in some young Air Force officer, and Colin and I would sometimes have difficulty with them.''

Jones, who flew over three hundred hours of combat missions against North Korea, describes Powell as ''an immovable object'' on the racquetball court. Off the court, Jones says, Powell avoided a problem sometimes visited on fast-rising aides in the acutely status-conscious atmosphere of Washington: ''Every once in a while you run into somebody who—the expression is—'wears the stars of the boss.' He wasn't of that type.'' More than a decade later, when Powell was occupying the chairman's slot, the two men would split over the use of military force in the Gulf.

Except for the time he spent on loan to the Department of Energy, Colin Powell's boss of bosses during the Carter administration was Defense Secretary Harold Brown, now head of the Foreign Policy Institute at the Johns Hopkins School for Advanced International Studies.

''I got to see a lot of him,'' Brown recalls. ''I'd hold a staff meeting at eight every morning to look at what the Congress and media were serving up to us that day. There would be maybe eight people in the room, and more often than not Colin was among them. As is true of just about everyone who meets him, I was very favorably impressed by his energy and ability. He was a very gung-ho type. You gave him something and he'd go do it.'' Like others who have worked well with Powell, Brown remarks on his evident ''street-smarts from growing up in the South Bronx. What it amounts to is an ability to read other people and to get them to do what you want—not sitting back and waiting for things to come to you.''

If there was anything lacking in the Powell package of the late 1970s, Brown says, it was a final touch of what is rarely found among career military types: not so much the political acuity that John Kester talks about—the ability, for example, to see from which way a bad wind is blowing and to avoid it, a nose for what's dirty and what is not—as political polish, the deft feel needed to advance an agenda along through the complex and often competing webs of Washington interests.

"Of course, you get some of that working in the Secretary of Defense's office," Brown says. "Dealing with the White House and Congress and working out of the White House also gives you several additional coats of political polish. He's taken those on very well and very successfully, and he's also learned to deal with the public. All of that, I think, was more than nascent in him, more than inherent, but not fully developed when he worked for me."

"I would say," Harold Brown adds, "that he was ambitious. I don't think unduly so. I think perhaps even then he saw himself—although he never talked about it—as a possible Army chief of staff. It must have been '81 or '82 when his name was put up for membership on the Council for Foreign Relations. I remember writing a note that he had a good chance to be the first black Army chief of staff. I underestimated where he would go, but the fact that others saw this potential in him suggests he saw it in himself."

The extent of Colin Powell's ambition—the degree to which he saw himself as many, many others saw him, as marked for the top, and set his compass in that direction—is difficult to limn. His friend and White House co-Fellow James Bostic says, "I don't think ten or fifteen years ago Colin sat down and said these are the things I want to do: be military assistant to the Secretary of Defense, be this, be that. I don't think he had the slightest idea that those things would happen."

Powell himself says that he has pursued only one position in his military career—the relatively minor spot with the Infantry Training Board at Fort Benning in the mid 1960s—and that that one didn't work out as well as he had hoped, simply because it proved fairly unexciting work. He has always, he has said time and again, had to be persuaded to leave the field, leave the troops, to take new positions in Washington. Some others who have worked with Powell contend that careerism was not wholly alien to his nature. "The whole time he was Weinberger's exec [his military adviser, from 1983 to 1986], he always had one eye on the Joint Chiefs of Staff," says one former high-ranking Pentagon official. "He was going to let nothing stop him from becoming the first black [Chairman] . . . A lot of good people have ambitions. The question is whether he hurt other people because of his ambition or was in some way dishonest in his beliefs because of it.'' If such was the case, the people and the evidence supporting this claim have been difficult to discern, and have rarely come forward.

Frank Carlucci, Powell's ''godfather of godfathers,'' says that he began talking Powell up openly for the position of Chairman of the Joint Chiefs in the mid 1980s and that Powell was uncomfortable with the effort. ''He's never particularly pushed his own career,'' Carlucci says. ''I wasn't certain he even wanted to be chairman—he never expressed a strong desire to me. The only thing he did was to keep telling me to stop talking about his being chairman. He was younger than a lot of people in line; it was causing grumbling. That doesn't win you any kudos in the military.'' Some of that grumbling would continue after Powell was jumped to the top of the pack, but whether Powell resisted Carlucci's backing because he didn't want the post or because he thought it was muddying his opportunity is anyone's guess. Ambition, it should be noted, is almost built in to an up-or-out organization such as the Army; it's the equivalent of a survival mechanism, an instinctive response.

''That's the way the system works,'' says John Kester. ''If you don't go up, you have to retire. The way the promotions go, there are bottlenecks. Once you get to brigadier general, you've entered the club of general officers. Then it becomes more unstable. Half the generals in the Army are brigadiers, and the other half are two, three, and four stars.'' The positions through which one can rise to a second, a third, and a fourth star become ever fewer. Not to aspire to them is, in effect, a form of career suicide, and even if Powell never set his sights on a precise position up the military ladder, he does seem to have been determined to see his Army career through to the end.

On November 4, 1980, Ronald Reagan defeated incumbent president Jimmy Carter by nearly 7.5 million popular votes and won 489 out of a possible 538 electoral votes. Two and a half months later Harold Brown, Charles Duncan, and the entire political structure Colin Powell had been working for in the Department of Defense left office. In their place came an entire political structure he was already familiar with and which was already familiar with him: Caspar Weinberger as Secretary of Defense, and Frank Carlucci as the deputy secretary. For Powell, who stayed on for another five months as Carlucci's senior military assistant, it was old home week.

"In 1981, when we did the transition, Colin was sitting in the chair as the number-one military aide to the deputy secretary, and, of course, Mr. Carlucci came in," says Marybel Batjer, part of the transition team and now special assistant to the Secretary of the Navy. "We were all together from February on, and I was extremely green. I didn't know the difference between an Army and a Marine uniform. Colin figuratively took me by the hand and gave me some very helpful lessons about the Pentagon and the services—fairly elementary stuff that I didn't know. He dealt with us all the way Colin does—with humor and with great insight—and all of us were very, very fond of him."

Eventually Colin Powell would become immune to the normal hierarchical requirements of the Army. Before he could become a permanent part of the Weinberger-Carlucci team, though, there were still boxes to be marked, more stations of the cross to be performed in the field. In June, 1981, Powell left Washington for the first time in four years to become Assistant Division Commander of the Fourth Infantry Division (mechanized) at Fort Carson, Colorado. It was a good position for rising to the rank of major general—in Carlucci's words, "We put him out at Fort Carson to get him another star." In the complicated mythology of the Infantry Division, always driven by the memory of Gen. George S. Patton, it was also the right slot. "Again, he's Patton reincarnated," Al Garland says, "because he's the ADC maneuver guy, as opposed to support. The guy with the brightest future is the maneuver-oriented guy, not the supply guy."

Fourteen months after he had started at Fort Carson, Powell returned to Fort Leavenworth, where he had made his mark as a student fifteen years earlier. This time his title was Deputy Commanding General of the U.S. Army Combined Arms Combat Development Activity, the Army's think-tank for new weapons, new tanks, new vehicles. To an extent, the job was the fulfillment of the other, less glamorous side of his military career: as a test officer with the Infantry Board, he had helped vet new weapons, and as an operations research analyst and an MBA he had acquired the necessary background and academic training to support research-and-development work. The position of deputy commanding general also seems to have been a kind of final rounding out, a capstone of sorts for a résumé that now ran the gamut from combat experience to future planning, from the traditional side of military life to the more chaotic political side of being a thoroughly modern general.

In mid 1983 Gen. Carl Smith, who had been serving as Caspar Weinberger's military assistant, rotated out. To the surprise of no one who had followed his career, Colin Powell rotated in to the position. "I can't imagine we even thought of anyone else," Marybel Batjer says, "much to Colin's chagrin."

CHAPTER 11

Honest Broker

Military assistants to the Secretary of Defense come and go, to varying degrees of success and generally to little notoriety. They are nominated to the position by the various services—all of whom, in the always contentious rivalry between the military services, are anxious to have a man close to the Secretary's ear—and they are most often originally unknown to the Secretaries they serve, with all the attendant need to build up a personal relationship to support the professional one. Colin Powell arrived *de jure* by the same route. He was put forward for the post by the Army at the same time Gen. John Wickham, Powell's superior at Fort Campbell a half dozen years earlier, was named the service's chief of staff. But as Marybel Batjer implies, the position was waiting for him all along. As so often seems to be the case with Powell, he made the job bigger than it was.

"As Weinberger's aide he functioned almost as a deputy secretary [of defense]," says Lawrence Korb, who was an assistant secretary of defense under Caspar Weinberger and would later become director of the Center for Public Policy Education at the Brookings Institution in Washington. "He brought a great deal of experience to the job. He had known Weinberger over at OMB, so it wasn't like the normal military assistant that he had never met before. He helped in the transition [from Harold Brown to Weinberger]; he went out in the field and came back. And in my mind he functioned as Weinberger's deputy."

Powell had been a soldier for almost exactly a quarter of a

century by the time he found himself military assistant to Caspar Weinberger. By then, says a former high-ranking Reagan official, Powell had learned one of the most important lessons that a military career teaches: Pick your fights carefully and anger those above you only as a last resort. "You don't get to be a general without playing some sort of politics and without being a good politician," this official says. "The man had learned to be smooth in his ability to be a politician in the military sense. You have to—to use an old Navy expression—keep your finger on your number. You can't incur somebody's wrath or you get marked and don't make it when you come up for brigadier."

Another high-ranking Pentagon official who worked with Powell under Weinberger says that Powell also kept a kind of proprietorial eye out for the interests of the Joint Chiefs of Staff. "I brought some figures into him once," this official says. "They were out of whack by some exponential number with the figures the Joint Chiefs had expected, and he accused me of putting the Joint Chiefs of Staff on report. He wasn't nasty about it; he's never nasty."

Both views, though, are minority reports on Powell's performance as Weinberger's military assistant. Powell became a major general a month after he moved into the slot; by then, at age forty-six, he had a golden résumé and a line of mentors and supporters behind him unmatched by any of his contemporaries. Perhaps in consequence or by the fact of his maturity, he also seems to have developed a high comfort level with the exercise of power. "His style as I observed it in the three years he was Cap Weinberger's military assistant—a very critical job, by the way—was to be pretty assertive on behalf of the Secretary," says Fred Hoffman, who was the second-ranking Pentagon spokesman from 1984 to 1989. "He wore two stars; he was Weinberger's man in that position, and everybody knew it. He didn't flinch, if necessary, at asserting himself in relation to people senior to him in the military. It wasn't always a safe thing to do."

Federal Washington is a peculiar place. Save for the Government Printing Office—which, appropriately enough, turns out millions upon millions of words a year—the official city runs no factories. Its raw materials are what get charitably referred to in Washington as agendas—shopping lists for this regulation or that exemption, themselves often fronts for larger, unspoken agendas on how the governed shall be governed. Its production lines are the endless staff meetings that fuel government, meetings that in times of crisis can begin well before sunrise, end well after nightfall, and, gridlocked by competing agendas, produce little or nothing at all. Official Washington's competitive drive is shaped not so much in terms of the economic capitalism those in power so often extol as in terms of access. To be the boss is, of course, the first priority, but to be able to get in to see the boss, to have channels through which your memoranda can be carried to the boss, to be able to put "spin," your own interpretation, on the memoranda and other information the boss does receive is nearly as good. Washington's bosses are, after all, running the country—an enormous enterprise—and in some circumstances the world. They can't see everyone, and they necessarily rely on their gatekeepers to sort through the voluminous material that is waiting for their attention.

Two evaluations come up frequently when Powell's contemporaries in government in the mid-1980s are asked about his performance, both of them tied to the federal city's unique nature. One is that he ran a meeting better than almost anyone can ever remember a meeting's being run. "Powell has one ability that may strike a lot of people as trivial but is in fact critical, and it is the ability to chair a meeting," says former Assistant Secretary of State Elliott Abrams, who got to know Powell when he was Weinberger's military assistant and when he was National Security Adviser. "It's the ability to make everyone feel he has had his say. It's the ability to end a meeting with some kind of decision. Now, that can't be done all the time. If you've got [then Secretary of State George] Shultz and Weinberger fighting and Reagan hasn't made up his mind yet, you're not going to end with a decision. However, at a deputy-level meeting he tried very hard and succeeded very often in saying State will do this, Defense or the Agency will do that, and here's the new data we need to collect. That was extremely valuable. It's a rare talent and a real talent."

Part of Powell's talent—and this, too, may trace back to his street smarts—seems to be knowing instinctively what's dross and what is not, what counts and what is window dressing. Ret. Gen. Grant Green, who worked with Powell in the Defense Department in the late 1970s and later at the National Security Council, says, "I've never seen anyone, and I say this with all sincerity, who could run a meeting more effectively with senior people and cut through the crap and get a decision. It's just absolutely incredible." In Ernest Hemingway's famous phrase, Powell seems to have a good "shit detector."

Part of his talent also appears to be understanding the fundamental structure of staff meetings and how to wield power within them. Powell, Caspar Weinberger says, "is very familiar with the general idea that the person who has the agenda normally carries the meeting. He doesn't like to waste his time or [others'] time. He runs a good, tight meeting . . . and he is usually the man who is best informed about the whole subject." With meetings as with many other things, Powell seems simply to have outworked many of the others around the table. The same high Reagan official who suggests that Powell kept a close "finger on his number" acknowledges that in meetings "Powell usually silenced the opposition unless the opposition was very well versed in the subject. People were afraid to challenge him because they felt he knew more than they did." And, Lawrence Korb adds, "Powell has an incredible memory. He never seems to forget anything. You didn't have to repeat something twice either. He knew exactly what you were talking about." Most important, Marybel Batjer argues, is the fact that Powell not only controlled the agenda but had only one agenda.

"He's direct, he's fair, he's quick," Batjer says. "I've never known Colin to go into a meeting not knowing what he wants to get out of it. He knows how to run a meeting better than anyone I've ever known. I've never figured out if it's because he's sat in so many damn meetings in his career or if it's his innate personality. I think I come down in the middle. Part of it is his personality—he's direct and honest, he has humor, and he doesn't waste time. . . . He doesn't understand when someone says, 'Well, they told me to check with that guy and that guy and that guy.' He says, 'Why the hell didn't you check with me?' He doesn't stand on ceremony. He's refreshingly pragmatic."

Batjer tells about a conversation she once had about Powell with Washington *Post* reporter Lou Cannon: " 'Lou,' I said, 'he's just regular. He's normal in a town where people aren't. There's no second agenda. What he tells you is what he means to tell you.' God, that's wonderful, and God, that's refreshing. There is no second agenda, no calculating. And there is in this building [the Pentagon] and in every other building in Washington. Colin doesn't deal with people that way."

Batjer's comments get to the second common evaluation of Powell's tenure under Weinberger—another one steeped in the peculiar workings of Washington, where agendas are a dime a dozen and almost every text comes with a host of subtexts: It is that Colin Powell was an "honest broker," in a position rife with opportunities to be otherwise.

As Weinberger's military assistant Powell did at a higher level some of what he had done for John Kester and, during the Carter administration, Charles Duncan—functioned as the gatekeeper, the channel through which both people and information passed to the Secretary. As is always true in Washington, there are minority opinions on how straightforward Powell was in that role: "A lot of stuff went in to Weinberger that never got to him," one Pentagon official at the time says, but on this front, too, the majority opinion seems convincing. Lawrence Korb says that Powell was closer to being the Defense Secretary's "filter." "If I had a problem and I went to Colin, he'd say, well, you better talk to the boss about that, or this can be handled without bothering him, or we've already discussed that, he's aware of it. He'd also try to orchestrate things. I'd go to him and say, 'Look, we tried to talk to the boss about this but can't get through,' and he'd say, 'Why don't you bring it up at the staff meeting tomorrow?' He didn't abuse it like some people who might have been in that position. He was a very, very honest broker, and he kept the place moving."

Marybel Batjer says much the same thing: "I understood that if I needed to get a message to the Secretary it would be delivered very accurately, and the message back would be very accurate. He was never into spinning things . . . I worked very closely with him under Mr. Weinberger. He was a very trusted confidant and colleague, one [with whom] I could talk about things that were politically and personally sensitive."

In February, 1989, three years after Powell left the military assistant's post, Marybel Batjer's parents were both diagnosed with cancer within two weeks of each other. Either Powell or another friend from the Defense Department, Richard Armitage, called her every day during the months that followed. "Those two got me through a very difficult time," says Batjer, who was working at the time on the stormy transition within the

department to, first, John Tower and, after his rejection by the
Senate, Dick Cheney. "I later learned it was an unspoken rule
between the two of them that one or the other would call me,"
Batjer continues. "It was a difficult time for both of them. Rich
was involved in the transition, too. Colin was down at Atlanta
[as the newly appointed head of the Forces Command]. He had
a very heavy travel schedule and he was decompressing [from
being National Security Adviser]. I literally couldn't have gotten
through that time without the two of them. When a friend is in
need, if you are a very good friend, you know what hurts them,
what makes them happy. Colin, like any friend, hears a voice
over the phone and can say, 'What the hell is wrong with you
today?' " (Journalist and author Bob Woodward, it should be
noted, tells a shortened version of the Batjer story in *The Commanders*, although he places her parents' illness, incorrectly, in
late 1989, just after Powell had become Chairman of the Joint
Chiefs of Staff.)

Perhaps the most compelling testimony to Powell's capacity
as an honest broker comes from someone who might be con-
strued as a hostile witness. Michael Pillsbury was Assistant
Under-Secretary of Defense for Policy Planning from 1984 until
1986, when he was fired for allegedly leaking classified information regarding the U.S. effort to supply Stinger anti-aircraft
missiles to rebel forces in both Afghanistan and Angola. (Pillsbury had failed a polygraph test prior to his firing; he subsequently passed several other polygraph tests and had his Top
Secret security clearance restored.)

"On the outside people joke about leaking," Pillsbury says,
"but on the inside it's like AIDS. It's the worst offense you can
commit. The more secret the material you allegedly leak, the
worse your offense. I learned later that Colin had made a number
of speeches about leakers and how leaking destroys our national
security, and it's gotten back to me that when asked to give an
example he cites me . . . There are those who think I should be
his enemy." In fact, Pillsbury cites the series of events that led
up to the decision to provide the missiles as an example of both
Powell's overarching fairness and his central role within the Defense Department, a role that went far beyond that of the usual
military adviser.

"[Powell] was essentially present for every meeting Secretary

Weinberger held for which any follow-up was required,'' Pillsbury says. ''All documents to and from Mr. Weinberger of any importance went through him. It became understood to those of us [in the Defense Department] that if Colin Powell wasn't present there wouldn't be any follow-up. You had to make sure he was present. He was very well known for his skills as a referee: All points of view, all players with a stake in a decision should be heard from and were heard from. There were no end runs, no hanky-panky.''

Powell, Pillsbury says, ''was particularly worried about people like me because we came from [Capitol] Hill, and he had a certain skepticism about whether people from the Hill were trustworthy. He would tend to suspect political people as capable of tricks, deceptions of one kind or another, which he did not believe was possible for senior military officers to engage in. That was his point of view: manipulation was done by Hill people, and senior officers wouldn't dream of it. Over time I came to believe the opposite was true and that the senior military would do almost anything to defend what they believed was the national interest, especially when it came to their service.''

In the particular instance of supplying Stinger missiles to the Afghan rebels, it was Powell's own Army that was most opposed, Pillsbury goes on. ''The Stingers were being taken from the Army; that was one of the biggest obstacles we faced. The Army was extremely bitter and opposed. It fell to Colin at several points to adjudicate. His fair approach was to convene the Joint Chiefs of Staff with Mr. Weinberger and my boss, [Under-Secretary of Defense] Fred Iklé, and then make the pitch. The Joint Chiefs made their arguments against it, and Mr. Weinberger ruled in their favor, not to send the Stingers. The decision was off; we lost for several months. But the Joint Chiefs had raised two big points. One was that there were only a few thousand Stingers then in existence, and they felt we should have Stingers before we gave them to foreigners. I was able to solve that by telephoning the Stinger manufacturer in California to see if they could increase their production rate so we could buy more, and they could and would. The second big issue was that if the Stingers should fall in the hands of the Soviets in Afghanistan, they could study the technology and make copies and would be able to shoot down American fighters in Europe in a World War Three and we would lose World War Three. It was put starkly to Weinberger that way by the Joint Chiefs. I was able to learn with considerable work that the KGB had already gotten an agent of theirs in Greece to steal the design of the Stinger and some of the parts a year earlier. So the Soviets would not be helped by simply having one in Afghanistan. And Colin, to his credit—this is the fair traffic cop in him—permitted us to revisit the issue, and because the points had been raised before, because these were the objections and there were no others, as soon as we had met them, Mr. Weinberger signed the decision [to supply the missiles to the Afghan rebels].

"If he had been a man of guile, Colin could have simply not let us revisit the issue, or he could have sabotaged it without informing us. This is what assistants often do. Then we would just be told that Mr. Weinberger said no and we can't tell you why. This is the sort of super-secret stuff we're talking about at the time, in 1986. He would have been entitled to spread a veil of secrecy over it and not tell us. The same is true of the Joint Chiefs. Under our system the Joint Chiefs are not permitted to know what the CIA [to whom the missiles were to be provided for shipment to Afghanistan] is doing. Powell to his credit was extra fair to them, too. He let them comment on a covert action, which is usually against the rules. It happened to be their Stinger, but that's not necessary. A third technique for guile is to kill it off at a low level without letting the big elephants in, and he didn't do that either . . . The process was fair. He did chastise me on this because I got four U.S. senators involved in the decision by taking them over to Pakistan on an Air Force plane— Vice-President Bush's plane, Air Force Two; Don Gregg [then Bush's assistant for national security affairs] loaned it to us for a week. We went there and met with the [rebel] chiefs to hear their claims about why they wanted the missiles. Colin's point to me was that it was taboo behavior to involve senators in an internal executive-branch decision. My defense was that the Under-Secretary had officially named me as the liaison to the House and Senate intelligence committees. I had an official duty, and the senators had raised the issue and wanted to know where they could go on a trip around the world during recess in 1985.''

Powell's handling of the Stinger missile case, Pillsbury contends, also offers some insight into his position on the hawk-dove scale, his readiness to use military force to advance causes and settle disputes. "On the Hill we all thought the uniformed military officers were hawks,'' Pillsbury says, ''and nothing could be further from the truth. A lot of left-liberals wear uniforms with four stars on their shoulders. Colin had heard Reagan talk for years about the Afghan rebels and their suffering. If he was a hawk he would have just said, Mr. Secretary, I think you should just sign here [approving the Stingers for the rebels]. A dove with guile would have killed it without telling us why. Here's a case study of Powell's style: he's not a hawk; he's not a dove; he's an owl, in between.''

Michael Pillsbury tells another story about Powell that is revelatory of Powell's profound attention to detail, large and small: ''I'm a horseback rider, and some of the best horses in the Washington area are owned by this elite unit that puts on the parades, the Old First Regiment stabled at Fort Myer. All horses have to be ridden, and so I thought to myself, who is doing this riding and is there some way, as a senior official, that I might be included? So I went over there, I think on a Saturday, and met the sergeant who was in charge of the unit. He said, 'Yes, we ride the horses around here in the ring, and we take them out to the Manassas battlefield park, but it's only sergeants and corporals. What's your rank?' I said, 'Let me see if I can get a memo.' I also asked if it was possible to do it in connection with foreign visitors. I especially mentioned the Pakistanis because they always took us riding when we were over there and I left my name card. I think it was forty-eight hours later when the phone rings and it's Colin Powell: 'There aren't going to be no horse rides for you and the Pakistanis.' I tried to play dumb. I said, 'What are you talking about?' And he said, 'You know what I'm talking about. Leave the horses alone.' ''

As is frequently mentioned about Powell, he is rarely out of the know.

As Caspar Weinberger's military assistant, Colin Powell was generally the first person to see memoranda addressed to the Secretary. His job—consistent with his function as Weinberger's gatekeeper or filter—was to pre-screen the documents and, in many cases, recommend a course of action for dealing with whatever issues had been raised. Powell had been in the military assistant's chair almost exactly two years when a memorandum (see Appendix for full text) addressed to both Weinberger and Secretary of State George Shultz arrived marked ''Secret/With

Top Secret Attachment'' over the signature of Robert C. Mc-
Farlane, then Ronald Reagan's National Security Adviser.
Drafted June 17, 1985, the subject of the memo is stated as
"U.S. Policy Toward Iran." The text—eight single-spaced pages
following McFarlane's cover note—is in the form of a draft Na-
tional Security Decision Directive, ultimately meant for Ronald
Reagan's consideration and signature.

"Dynamic political evolution is taking place inside Iran," the
draft begins. "Instability caused by the pressures of the Iraq-
Iran war, economic deterioration and regime infighting create
the potential for major changes in Iran. The Soviet Union is
better positioned than the U.S. to exploit and benefit from any
power struggle that results in changes in the Iranian regime, as
well as increasing socio-political pressures. In this environment
the emergence of a regime more compatible with American and
Western interests is unlikely. Soviet success in taking advantage
of the emerging power struggle to insinuate itself in Iran would
change the strategic balance in the area . . . [The next two lines
are blacked out by government censors.] While we pursue a
number of broad, long-term goals, our primary short-term challenge must be to block Moscow's efforts to increase Soviet influence (now and after the death of Khomeini). This will require
an active and sustained program to build both our leverage and
our understanding of the internal situation so as to enable us to
exert a greater and more constructive influence over Iranian politics. We must improve our ability to protect our interests during
the struggle for succession."

Four pages later the draft directive suggests a series of "short-
and long-term initiatives that will enhance our leverage in Tehran, and, if possible, minimize that of the Soviets." Among
them: "discreetly communicating our desire for correct relations to potentially receptive Iranian leaders," "providing support to elements opposed to Khomeini and the radicals,"
"avoid[ing] actions which could alienate groups potentially receptive to improved U.S.-Iranian relations," "continu[ing] to
encourage third-party initiatives to seek an end to the war" between Iran and Iraq [then in its fifth bloody year], and "seek[ing]
to curb Iran's collaboration with its radical allies (i.e., Syria and
Libya)." First among the policy initiatives suggested in the
McFarlane memo is this: "Encourage Western allies and friends
to help Iran meet its import requirement so as to reduce the

attractiveness of Soviet assistance and trade offers, while demonstrating the value of correct relations with the West. This includes provision of selected military equipment as determined on a case-by-case basis.''

The following day, June 18, 1985, Powell sent the McFarlane memo on to Caspar Weinberger with a handwritten note that read: ''SecDef, This came in Eyes Only for you. After you have seen recommend I pass to [Assistant Secretary of Defense] Rich Armitage for analysis.'' Weinberger sent the memo back to Powell the same day with his own handwritten addendum to Powell's note: ''This is almost too absurd to comment on. By all means pass it to Rich, but the assumption here is: 1) that Iran is about to fall, and 2) we can deal with that on a rational basis.'' The policy initiatives meant to placate Iranian officials, Weinberger wrote, are ''like asking [Libyan leader Mohammar] Qadhafi to Washington for a cozy chat.'' Powell, in turn, sent copies of the memo and Weinberger's response to Richard Armitage, Under-Secretary of Defense Fred Iklé, and Deputy Secretary of Defense Will Taft IV, the great-grandson of President William Howard Taft.

Two years and a day later, Powell's deposition about the McFarlane memo and the actions that flowed from it would be taken in the White House Situation Room by House of Representatives staff counsel Joseph P. Saba, Senate chief counsel Arthur L. Liman and five other lawyers in the employ of the United States Congress. For his part, Powell, who was by then Deputy National Security Adviser, would be represented at the proceedings by C. Dean McGrath, Jr., Associate Counsel to the President, and Nicholas Rostow, Deputy Legal Adviser to the National Security Counsel.

In fact, of course, Iran did not fall, either to Iraq or internal revolution, as Weinberger had predicted. Nor would the series of policy initiatives that Weinberger characterized as ''almost too absurd to comment on . . . like asking Qadhafi to Washington for a cozy chat'' go gently into that good night. American weapons would be provided to Iran, among the chief sponsors of terrorism against U.S. citizens in the Middle East and the nation that only six years earlier had seized nearly five dozen American citizens and held them for 444 days. As the world now knows, the weapons would be traded for later hostages seized by groups aligned to Iran, although Ronald Reagan had vowed never to do that, and part of the profit from the sale of those weapons to Iran would be diverted to funding the contra rebel movement against the Sandinista government of Nicaragua. What the McFarlane memo did was to lay down the framework for what would come to be called the "Iran Initiative"—Leg One of the Iran-contra affair. Did Colin Powell approve? Did Caspar Weinberger change his mind?

CHAPTER 12

Faithful Indian Companion

Over the years, Colin Powell has collected thirteen precepts to live by. He keeps them typed out on a small white card labeled "Colin Powell's Rules," which he keeps under the glass top of his Pentagon desk:

1. It ain't as bad as you think. It will look better in the morning.
2. Get mad, then get over it.
3. Avoid having your ego so close to your position that, when your position falls, your ego goes with it.
4. It can be done!
5. Be careful what you choose. You may get it.
6. Don't let adverse facts stand in the way of a good decision.
7. You can't make someone else's choices. You shouldn't let someone else make yours.
8. Check small things.
9. Share credit.
10. Remain calm. Be kind.
11. Have a vision. Be demanding.
12. Don't take counsel of your fears or naysayers.
13. Perpetual optimism is a force multiplier.

The Iran-contra affair would test a number of them. It also would lend credence to another rule that Powell frequently men-

tions when he speaks to groups newly arrived in the nation's
capital, according to a Los Angeles *Times* Magazine profile by
Rudy Abramsom and John Broder: "If you think all the sisters
are virtuous and all the brothers are noble, you are going to be
disappointed."

The Iran-contra affair was a stunningly complex web that
ranged from Tehran and Tel Aviv through Swiss banks to the
White House and the CIA, and at the other end to remote jungle
landing strips in Latin America. It was created by and drew into
itself a cast of characters perhaps unmatched by any other government scandal: from the National Security Council's Lt. Col.
Oliver North with his all-American looks, labyrinthian schemes,
and capacity for dissembling; to William Casey, the shadowy
and, as it turned out, fatally ill director of the CIA; to the two
National Security Advisers to the President who served during
the time of the affair—the seemingly implacable, pipe-smoking
Adm. John Poindexter, and his predecessor, Robert "Bud"
McFarlane, who would attempt suicide in the affair's aftermath;
to Ronald Reagan himself, seemingly befuddled by the affair
and finally besmirched by it as well. Iran-contra would come to
include a cast of supporting players that any film director would
love to get his hands on: Ret. Gen. Richard Secord; Secord's
business partner Albert Hakim, a former retainer of the Shah of
Iran; another exiled Iranian, the merchant and go-between Man-
ucher Ghorbanifar; the shadowy Saudi financier Adnan Khash-
oggi; the shadowy Israeli counterterrorism expert Amiram Nir;
soldiers of fortune and sheer opportunists of every stripe; even
North's lawyer, the razor-sharp Brendan Sullivan, who, as he
informed the congressional committees investigating the affair,
was no "potted palm."

Colin Powell's self-acknowledged role in Iran-contra seems,
in the larger scheme of the affair, a relatively minor note: in
mid-January of 1986, at the direction of Caspar Weinberger,
Powell made arrangements for 4,508 TOW missiles to be transferred from U.S. Army stocks to the Central Intelligence
Agency. Four weeks later, on February 13, the CIA took possession of the first 1,000 of those missiles, and the next day the
missiles were flown to Tel Aviv by the CIA-controlled Southern
Air Transport. On two flights over the next two weeks, the 1,000
TOWs were shipped on to Iran, then under an international arms
embargo in which the United States government played the lead

role. Iran, in turn, paid an estimated $10 million for the missiles, through Ghorbanifar and Khashoggi, to a dummy corporation named Lake Resources, which Secord had set up in Switzerland, and Lake Resources transferred $3.7 million of that to a CIA Swiss account for eventual reimbursement to the Department of Defense for the TOWs. The difference—$6.3 million, according to the Tower Commission's calculations—was funneled into covert operations, including secretly funding the contras battling the Sandinista government in Nicaragua despite a 1984 congressional ban against direct military aid to the contras. (The "contra" part of Iran-contra was not a co-equal part of the hyphenate: of the $35.8 million spent on covert operations by "The Enterprise" set up by North, Secord, and Hakim to handle the missile-sale profits, only a little more than one-tenth, $3.8 million, seems to have gone to supporting the contras. $4.4 million alone was paid to Secord, Hakim, and a third associate in commissions.) Ultimately, before the roof fell in on the Iran-contra plotters in November, 1986, 1,500 TOWs would be delivered to Iran as well as spare parts for HAWK missiles, and another 508 TOWs would be sent to Israel to replace missiles it had sent on to Iran in the fall of 1985 in an earlier phase of the North-Casey operation. Ultimately, as well, three American hostages held by the Iranian-backed Hezbollah terrorist group would be released, presumably as a result of the missile sales: David Jacobsen, Rev. Benjamin Weir, and Fr. Lawrence Jenco. During the same time-frame three new American hostages were seized in the Middle East—Joseph Cicippio, Frank Reed, and Edward Tracy—and a fourth already in captivity, librarian Peter Kilburn, was murdered. Three more Americans— Robert Polhill, Alan Steen and Jesse Turner—would be taken hostage early in 1987.

That, in essence, is the Iran-contra affair, and in its vast sweep, Powell's role as a missile-facilitator is indeed a minor note. Powell, Weinberger, and the Defense Department were all set in motion by external forces, by higher authority. The TOW missiles Powell directed the Army to provide to the CIA constituted only one of six separate missile and missile-parts transactions that make up the affair. But it is a minor note associated with considerable reverberations. Without the missiles there was, of course, no Iran-contra: no arms-for-hostages package, no excess profits on the missile sales to be funneled into Swiss accounts, and no funding of Nicaraguan contras with the excess profits.

Powell, however, says that from the time a weapons transfer was first obliquely raised in Robert McFarlane's draft National Security Decision Directive of June 17, 1985, until the Defense Department was in effect ordered to provide the TOW missiles seven months later, neither he nor Caspar Weinberger saw themselves as taking part in a larger enterprise. He insists, too, as Weinberger has adamantly from the time the affair broke open in public, that the Secretary of Defense resisted even what he understood the limited participation of his department to be. And, Powell says, there is "no question" that virtually from the beginning he and Weinberger both saw their assigned part in the affair as a piece of bad garbage to be gotten out of the house quickly, with as few fingerprints as possible on it. Perhaps most notable on the latter front was the decision to provide the missiles to the CIA under the terms of the Economy Act, which allows for such interdepartmental transfers. Treating the transfer as a foreign military sale would have required the Defense Department to inform Congress because it would have exceeded the threshold at which notification is required. And whether they approved the Iran-contra scheme or not, whether they understood it in its totality or not, no one involved in whatever capacity wanted to bring Congress in on the matter.

"The Secretary's record is clear," Powell says, "and it will become clearer if the special prosecutor ever finishes: Weinberger was against it and did everything he could [to oppose it], and I was his faithful Indian companion who tried to help him do that. Every time we thought we had a stake in its heart, it came back. Then, finally, in those days in January when we were told to do it, Weinberger said do it in a way that does not contaminate us any more than we are. And so we did. We used the Economy Act. He insisted that that be the way we do it, and he was able to insist on that. So we essentially provided TOWs for the CIA for however they might want to use them."

"But," Powell adds, "we knew where they were going."

Powell's deposition was taken under oath on June 19, 1987, by lawyers for the joint Congressional Committees Investigating the Iran-Contra Affair. In Powell's telling, the missile transfer becomes a portrait of a Defense Department trying with increasing concern to find a thin line between duty and the preservation of a kind of institutional dignity at the same time that it was constructing a logic to hang its action on.

CHIEF SENATE COUNSEL ARTHUR LIMAN: General, can you remember talking to the Secretary [of Defense] about the structure that was being proposed for the contemplated sale to Iran?

POWELL: I think by this point in time [mid-January, 1986] we knew that the structure would be—the alternatives being proposed were either a direct transfer to Iran or Israel moving it on and then us replenishing Israel.

LIMAN: Do you recall that on one of the alternatives of the direct sale to Iran, the question was being presented of whether the Department of Defense would sell directly to Iran using an agent? Do you remember that?

POWELL: Not specifically, Mr. Liman. I just recall that when we finally got to the seventeenth [of January, 1986], the arrangement that the Secretary had worked out with the others who were these interlocutors in this matter was that regardless of what alternatives had been thought of, the way that we were going to do it was the CIA will do it. And the only involvement of the Department would be to give the missiles to the CIA.

LIMAN: Was that because of price or notice [to Congress] or for some other reason?

POWELL: I don't think it was because of price. I am not sure that price played a part in it. I think it came out that way because it—frankly, I think because it minimized the DOD [Department of Defense] involvement.

LIMAN: Because the Secretary of Defense felt more comfortable saying we will sell it to the CIA, and what the CIA does with it is its business?

POWELL: He did not see it as something that was the Defense Department's role—the transferring of weapons to a country such as Iran. It is not one of the missions, roles of the Defense Department to be involved in that kind of transaction. To the extent that such a transaction was going to take place, it should be handled by elements of the government that are able and agree to handle such transactions.

HOUSE OF REPRESENTATIVES STAFF COUNSEL JOSEPH SABA: So

you would say that the Secretary didn't want the Department of Defense to do it?

POWELL: That was my impression. He didn't want the government to do it, but if it was going to be done, then it ought to be done by those agencies of government that have this as a more appropriate part of their mission.

SABA: And that the reason he didn't want the Department of Defense to do it was one of policy, would you say?

POWELL: I think it is policy in terms of not whether we should be doing this at all, but policy in terms of it is not appropriate for the Department of Defense to be making this kind of exchange. It isn't an FMS sale [Foreign Military Sale]. It was not any one of our security-assistance arrangements. Therefore, it was not something the Department of Defense should be doing. But under the Economy Act, the Department of Defense clearly can respond to a request from another Government agency to provide assets that the Department has that the other agency does not have, but the other agency has a need for.

Several pages later in the deposition, in response to further questioning from House Counsel Joseph Saba, Powell provided more detail on the mechanics of arranging the TOW missile transfer. "Either on Friday night or Saturday morning [that is, either on January 17 or January 18, 1986]," Powell said,

the Secretary communicated to me that a decision had been made and that TOWs were to be transferred to the CIA. The number is 4,000. I can't remember if I had any conversation with John Poindexter [then the National Security Adviser to the President] that same Friday night, Saturday morning, but as a result of that direction, I called General Max Thurman, who was the Acting Chief of Staff of the Army and the Vice-Chief-of-Staff of the Army, and he was a very, very old and dear friend. We were lieutenant colonels together, so I knew him rather well. And because of the sensitivity of the mission, the fact that it was being treated with the greatest sort of compartmentalization—and, frankly, there might have been lives at stake—I told him I needed to see him on a matter of some importance.

He was at work, and I went down to his office [at the Pentagon] from my home at Fort Myers, and one-on-one, I told him that there was a requirement for 4,000 missiles to be made available on demand as they needed them to the CIA. It was a tasking that had come from the National Command Authority, and he knew that to mean the president, and that it had been determined to be legally sufficient to do it, and he could—I was essentially giving him a warning order so he could spend the weekend figuring out how he would do this. And that it was to be held to the closest group of people possible, and I gave him absolutely no indication of the destination of the missiles.

A short time later Saba asked how the number of TOW missiles came to change from the 4,000 Powell first mentioned to Thurman to the 4,508 the Defense Department finally authorized for transfer to the CIA.

POWELL: Some time over the next week—and I can't quite recall how—either from the Secretary or one of my NSC [National Security Council] interlocuters, it might have been Admiral Poindexter or Colonel North, I really don't recall. Or it might have been that the CIA told the Army, once I put them in touch with each other, that the number was up to 4,500, and I became aware of it, it came back to me, and I confirmed it with the—let the Secretary know about it, and there were no objections, and it was at that point that I realized that—well, I have answered your question.

SABA: I am trying to understand where the extra 508 came from.

POWELL: The number that was given to me was 4,000, and sometime in a very—within the next week or two, that number was increased to 4,500. And whether it was 4,508 or not, I don't know. I just recall it being 4,500.

SABA: But you wouldn't have increased it on your own?

POWELL: On my own? Oh, no . . . As a matter of information, once I talked to General Thurman, and he put me in touch with the logistics people in the Army, General Russo, at that point I put General Russo in touch with the CIA, and from then on in I was in nothing but a mongering role.

SENATE CHIEF COUNSEL ARTHUR LIMAN: Is this when you

> learned that the 500 were to be used to replace earlier ship-
> ments to Israel [presumably Liman meant "by Israel to
> Iran"]?
>
> POWELL: Yes. It was at that point that things clicked, and I
> said—I started to find out about the other 500. I just real-
> ized at that point that a transfer must have taken place and
> this is the replenishment of some kind.

Depositions often have a nitpicky quality about them, and in part Powell's is no exception. The same meat gets chewed over and over again. But the close questioning of Powell on the matter of the extra 508 TOW missiles gets to the issue that was always critical to the participants large and small in the Iran-contra affair: What did they know and when did they know it? Powell acknowledges that he knew the missiles he was having trans-ferred from Army arsenals to the CIA were destined for Iran, but if he or Caspar Weinberger knew in advance of mid-January, 1986 that roughly ten percent of the TOWs were to replenish Israeli missiles already sent on to Iran or if he or Weinberger knew that HAWK missile spare parts had also been sent earlier to Iran or that HAWKs themselves had been sent to Iran, then both equally had reason to know that the Defense Department was doing more than fulfilling a one-time need—that it was participating in a continuing effort. Powell says the Defense De-partment used the Economy Act as the means of transfer be-cause "it minimized the DOD involvement." Yet the Economy Act also served the practical end of keeping Congress in the dark about the transfer, and keeping Congress in the dark was clearly high on the North-Casey agenda. In baseball talk, the Economy Act was a trade that benefited both clubs, but it was on just such fine points that the complicated unfolding of the Iran-contra investigation turned, and they were points on which Powell, at least on the surface, tended in some eyes to seem somewhat vulnerable. As certainly, for the same reasons, did his boss Caspar Weinberger.

In mid-November, 1985, two months before the TOW transfer was arranged with Max Thurman, Powell and another Defense Department official, Noel Koch, had asked Dr. Henry Gaffney, then acting director of the Defense Security Assistance Agency, to prepare what are called "talking points" on the possible sale of HAWK missiles, also under the Army's control, to Iran.

Among Gaffney's "points" in response was the possibility of splitting a missile sale to Israel into packages of less than $14 million each, beneath the threshold requiring congressional notification, although, Gaffney wrote, "the spirit and practice of the law is against that, and all Administrations have observed this scrupulously." Simultaneously, on November 21, Oliver North was directing an effort to transport eighty HAWKs out of Israeli stocks to Iran. (It would prove to be one of the more comic-opera efforts of the affair, and in some ways an apt metaphor for the whole operation. The HAWKs were first loaded onto an El Al 747 jet for transport through Portugal to Tehran, but the plane was refused landing rights by Portuguese authorities. Finally, eighteen of them, some still marked with the Star of David, would make it to Iran aboard a plane chartered from a CIA proprietary airline. The missiles, however, did not meet Iranian requirements. After one was test-fired unsuccessfully at an Iraqi plane, the other seventeen were returned to Israel.) House Counsel John Saba pressed the matter of Gaffney's paper and the HAWK transfer in Powell's deposition.

SABA: You mentioned that at approximately this time—and to help with the dates, we'll take November 19th, 1985—that you had received a request to obtain information about HAWKS. Sir, from whom did this information—did this request come?

POWELL: I cannot specifically recall as to whether I got it from the Secretary or from the NSC. If I received it from the NSC, the only two sources possible would have been, I think, Admiral Poindexter or perhaps Colonel North, but more than likely Admiral Poindexter. But I cannot specifically recall which of those three—the Secretary, Admiral Poindexter, or Colonel North—gave me the tasking for that. . . .

SABA: Moving down the page to the paragraph beginning with "The modalities for sale to Iran to present formidable difficulties" . . . There are three points following that paragraph as subparagraphs. Do you recall, sir, your agreeing with those three points or whether there was further discussion of those points at that time?

POWELL: I don't recall any further discussion or agreement or disagreement. We just accepted them as the facts presented by DSAA.

SABA: Moving to the next paragraph, sir, the one commencing, "It is conceivable that the sale could be broken into three or four packages, in order to evade Congressional notice." Do you recall if that paragraph and the two subparagraphs under it were written as a result of a request by you?

POWELL: I don't recall specifically, but I must say that it might have been that. I had a recollection that the question was posed that, is it possible to split a package? . . .

SABA: So if I understand, you had a request coming either from the Secretary of Defense or from the NSC—and in the case of the latter, it would have been Admiral Poindexter or Oliver North—and that request was to determine availability, certain quantities and modalities of transfers for HAWK missiles, whether directly to Iran or possibly by way of replenishment of Israeli stocks. Is that correct?

POWELL: Yes, but replenishment of Israeli stocks, if we were moving forward to provide missiles to Iran, not in the context of missiles already having gone to Iran or about to go to Iran. I took it as a hypothetical question that was presented to me to get some data on before any policy decision had been made with respect to moving forward on the transfer of missiles to Iran.

Some thirty pages later in his deposition, Powell stressed the point again in response to a question from Arthur Liman: Until he was directly told on January 17 or 18, 1986, to provide 4,000, and later 4,508 TOW missiles to the CIA, what would ultimately be shown to be an integral part of an ongoing effort to provide weapons to Iran had been an intellectual exercise. "That was my first knowledge that the United States government, at the right level, had approved the transfer of weapons to Iran," Powell answered Liman. "Up until that day, this, in my judgment and to the best of my recollection, was a conceptual discussion of the initiative to transfer weapons to Iran, and it was heatedly debated within the administration, and no decision was made to transfer any weapons until the direction of January seventeenth, eighteenth. So my recollections of the months before all have to do with discussion about a possible initiative."

Powell had seen reports sent to the Secretary in November of 1985 by the super-secret National Security Agency—reports that they might have indicated that the McFarlane ''initiative'' was either approaching or even had crossed over into reality. On the face of it, however, that would seem to be reading substance into McFarlane's memo. House Counsel Joseph Saba did ask about this.

SABA: Sir, I believe that just after this period on or about November 24th there was information provided to the Secretary of Defense concerning possibility of talks going on between the United States and Iranian officials. Do you recall that incident?

POWELL: I assume everybody here has whatever necessary clearances are required to talk to this subject.

After being assured by Senate Chief Counsel Arthur Liman that such clearances were in place, Powell continued: ''Yes, I was aware of—throughout this period, of intelligence reports . . . [blacked out by censors] that suggested something was going on.''

SABA: In connection with receiving such reports, did you receive reports in the fall of 1985 that weapons had been transferred—United States-origin weapons had been transferred to Iran?

POWELL: Not that I can recall.

SABA: Do you recall what reports you did receive?

POWELL: No, and the reason I have to say that is that in the course of the day I would guesstimate that I dealt with several hundred discrete issues and pieces of paper, and the United States intelligence community is able to provide an abundance of paper in the course of the day, not all of which I read, and even that which I read, I doubt I could recollect much longer than several days later because of its abundance. So I read a great deal of material, and to specifically say that I saw . . . [blacked out] without me having seen it again and refreshing my memory, I simply can't do that.

Perhaps it is simply that as Weinberger's military assistant, Powell was of necessity at the center of a blizzard of paper, not all of which any human being, no matter how prodigious his memory, can be expected to recall. Or perhaps it's that just as he compartmentalized knowledge of the missile transfer within the Defense-Army system—assuring, for example, that Max Thurman did not know where the TOWs were headed for—so in effect he perhaps compartmentalized that knowledge, keeping *himself* intentionally in the dark as to the larger workings of the Iran "initiative." Whatever, under the circumstances it surely wasn't a bad policy to follow.

The other central thrust of Iran-contra on which Powell seemed to have, again, some surface vulnerability was the pricing of the missiles—the effort to derive a profit from the sale that could then be turned to funding covert operations. Perhaps the primary indication of this was a January 15, 1986, note from Oliver North to John Poindexter. At the very best, though, it is circumstantial evidence, and not convincing even as that. But assuming North's note is accurate—and there is always room to wonder with North—it does suggest the extent of Caspar Weinberger's resistance to the missile transfer and, at the same time, the breadth of Powell's knowledge of the players involved. (Weinberger is referred to by his nickname "Cap" in the excerpt that follows. "Casey" is CIA Director William Casey. "Copp" is the code name used for Ret. Gen. Richard Secord, who had been recruited by North to help with the mechanics of the affair.)

"Casey believes that Cap will continue to create roadblocks until he is told by you that the President wants this to move NOW and that Cap will have to make it work," North wrote to Poindexter. "Casey points out that we have now gone through three different methodologies in an effort to satisfy Cap's concerns and that no matter what we do there is always a new objection. As far as Casey is concerned our earlier method of having Copp deal directly with the DoD as a purchasing agent was fine. He did not see any particular problem w/ making Copp an agent for the CIA in this endeavor but he is concerned that Cap will find some new objection unless he is told to proceed." (Two days later Ronald Reagan signed the order that broke the logjam. That evening Reagan wrote in his diary: "I agreed to sell TOWs to Iran.") North goes on in his note to say that on January 14 he had sat next to Colin Powell during a speech

Caspar Weinberger delivered at the National War College at Fort McNair in Washington and that Powell asked him two questions: "Does Copp deal w/ Iranians or Israelis?" and "What cost are the Israelis willing to pay for the basic TOWS?"

"Do you recall why you would have asked about the price?" Joseph Saba asked Powell during the deposition.

"No, I do not," Powell answered. "I don't know—I can't remember what motivated me to enter into discussion with Colonel North that evening . . . I can't remember why I entered into a conversation with Colonel North and the subject that night, but we did."

"The Secretary never really concerned himself much about price," Powell said elsewhere in his deposition. "He had no reason to, and neither did I, frankly. It is just that there was always a lot of discussion about price because depending on the model of TOW missile that you bought, the price varied considerably, and as we will learn later, you could really get into a swamp talking about the price of the TOW. But in the context of the times, the price issue was not of great import. It is not anything that would have locked into my memory because we didn't—all we knew is that at some point a price had to be determined."

In his sworn testimony before attorneys from the Army's Inspector General office, Richard Armitage—Assistant Secretary of Defense while Iran-contra was unfolding and a good friend of Powell—could recall Powell's saying only that the Army wasn't to "lose any money on the deal." Given Powell's abiding interest in the welfare of the service he had then been a part of for nearly thirty years, that seems a plausible explanation for his interest in the missile pricing. Understanding his attachment to that service also can help frame Powell's memo to John Poindexter sent some two months after the missile transfer to the CIA had been arranged:

"The attached memorandum from the Director of the Army Staff is self-explanatory," Powell wrote Poindexter. "It reflects the unease of the Army General Counsel's Office over the transfer of items with which you are familiar. As you know, we have been handling this program on a very close-hold basis, and the Army has been told nothing with respect to destination. Per guidance received from NSC, the Army has been told that they have no responsibility for Congressional notification. The Army also has been told that whatever notifications are to be made will be taken care of at the appropriate time by the appropriate agency and that the Attorney General has provided an opinion that supports this position.''

The attachment—sent to Powell from Lieutenant General Arthur B. Brown, Jr.—concludes: "This memo is to assure understanding of statutory requirements should this issue be raised by one of the Congressional intelligence committees in the future." As events transpired, writing the memo was a prescient act.

In his testimony to the Army Inspector General's Office, Richard Armitage said of the Defense Department and the Iran-contra affair: "You know, we lost our virginity. I was appalled at it all." For Armitage—a veteran of closely held government operations—it seems a somewhat overwrought assessment. He had no reason to think that all the sisters were virtuous or all the brothers noble. No more so than elsewhere in society.

In his autobiography, *Under Fire: An American Story*, Oliver North argues that neither Weinberger nor Secretary of State George Shultz, who also opposed the arms shipments, were quite the warriors for right that they subsequently have painted themselves to be: "Had Shultz and Weinberger been as strongly opposed to the Iran initiative as they later claimed, it would never have continued," North writes. That may be closer to the truth, even though it assumes that the aftermath of the affair can be read back into how one should have behaved at the time. Hindsight, as the saying goes, tends to be one hundred percent accurate. Still, it seems highly unlikely, had either man quit over the initiative and gone public with their reasons for doing so, that the Iran-contra affair would have gone forward. But quitting in Washington—especially at the highest levels of power—tends to be a one-day wonder, and Weinberger at least appears to have been constitutionally incapable of finally doing anything but standing by his President right or wrong.

"Weinberger was intensely loyal to Ronald Reagan," Powell says. "He believed in the man, had been with him for years. And so I don't believe on this issue Weinberger would have walked out on his President . . . It looks like a very big deal from this distance, but at the time it was a judgment call. It was legal according to the Attorney General. The Secretary just felt that this was not the correct thing to be doing, and he did not share the President's judgment about it. But Ronald Reagan was the President, and when the President makes his judgment loyal supporters follow.''

And, Powell contends once again, neither he nor Weinberger was aware of anything other than the small piece of the mosaic that had been directly presented to them: "What we saw was simply a bad judgment call having to do with fiddling around trying to buy out the hostages, even though there was a feeling it would also open up a new relationship with Iran. I don't know what [Weinberger] might have done if he had known about all these other things. I have not a clue, not a clue.''

As for Colin Powell, Weinberger's "faithful Indian companion" in the matter, he seems to have followed the orders he was presented with, done what he was told to do, learned perhaps no more than he had to learn. Although he had arranged for the transfer of missiles to the CIA, Powell was never dragged before the television cameras of the joint congressional committee investigating the affair. The reason, one committee source told Washington *Post* reporter Walter Pincus, was that to have Powell testify alone would "overlap" the testimony of other witnesses and "was not practical in terms of the best use of time." Another source told Pincus that committee members "didn't want to be seen beating up on a general.''

"Obviously Powell had exposure," says Malcolm Byrne of the National Security Archives, a private research center that has followed the Iran-contra affair closely. "Was he left off the hook on the merits of the case or for other reasons? I think it's probably for other reasons if you define 'other reasons' as, 'Look, we have other fish to fry, and we're not really interested in frying them.' ''

Iran-contra would not go away easily. In the spring of 1992 Powell was still being questioned informally by Walsh's team on the Pentagon's role in the missile transfer. As for Caspar Weinberger, a federal grand jury handed down a five-count indictment on June 16, 1992, charging that he had repeatedly misled investigators about his knowledge of the affair. But barring some tectonic shift in the evidence, Powell has emerged from the affair with his reputation intact and his career trajectory still decidedly upward. Less than five months after he instructed General Max Thurman to ready 4,000 TOW missiles for transfer to the CIA, Powell was flying to Germany to one of the Army's prime assignments, command of the V Corps, the front line against the Soviets.

Elliott Abrams, who would spend many hours before the TV cameras of the joint congressional committee defending his role in the Iran-contra affair as Assistant Secretary of State for Latin American Affairs, recalls a plane ride on Air Force One shortly before Powell left for his new post: "I have a very distinct memory of Cap Weinberger saying to the President, 'My military adviser is going to Germany to take over the V Corps there, and I want you to just shake his hand and say what a great job he did and bon voyage.' And the President came in and said, 'You've done a great job' and so on. There was no sense that Reagan knew who he was, but it was obvious that Weinberger thought a lot of him."

Six months later a call from Ronald Reagan would bring Powell back to Washington, and less than a year after that he would finally have his own government shop to run—the National Security Council.

CHAPTER 13

The Adviser

The National Security Council was created by the National Security Act of 1947, the same legislation that also abolished the 158-year-old position of Secretary of War and brought the Secretary of the Navy and a number of other sub-cabinet positions under the single aegis of a new Secretary of Defense, James Forrestal. (Henry Knox, of Fort Knox fame, had been the first Secretary of War under George Washington; Kenneth Royall of North Carolina was the last.) Two years later, in August of 1949, the act was amended to limit membership on the National Security Council to four principals: the president as chairman; the vice-president; and the secretaries of state and defense; with the director of the CIA and the chairman of the Joint Chiefs of Staff serving in secondary capacities. Although the staff that supports the council has grown enormously in the years since, those remain the principals today.

The work of the Council was established by its very first policy paper: NSC-1/3, which approved U.S. covert involvement to prevent victory by the Communist Party in the Italian elections of late 1947. To manage this coordinating agency for intelligence operations, to give it infrastructure and serve as referee among its principals, Harry Truman chose an old friend, Navy Rear Adm. Sidney William Souers, the owner of the Piggly Wiggly supermarket chain, to be its first executive secretary. Souers would vacate that position in early 1950 to become Truman's "special consultant" on national security—in effect, the

first National Security Adviser, although the position would not
bear that official title until Henry Kissinger filled it in the Nixon
administration. Souers also would leave behind a description of
the traits that should be looked for in his successors. In his
history of the National Security Council, *Keepers of the Keys*,
John Prados writes that Souers's outline "still stands as a fine
description of the qualities necessary in a national security adviser."

"*He should be a non-political confidant of the president,* a
trusted member of the president's immediate official family . . ."
Souers wrote. (The emphasis throughout is his.) "*He must be
objective and willing to subordinate his personal views on policy
to his task of coordinating the views* of all responsible officials."
The adviser, Souers went on, should see himself as "only a
servant of the president *and the other members of the Council* . . . His job is not to sell the president an idea with which he
is in sympathy, but rather to insure that the views of *all* interested
departments and agencies are reflected." And, Souers added,
the adviser "*must be willing to forego publicity and personal
aggrandizement.*" The National Security Adviser to the president must be, in short, an honest broker, someone without an
agenda, someone who doesn't put a spin on issues, someone with
a high sense of duty and loyalty and without an overweaning ego.
By November of 1986, when the Iran-contra affair finally bubbled
into public view, people inside the military-defense establishment had been saying those things about Colin Powell for a number of years. By then, too, the National Security Council was in
flat-out shambles.

Paralyzed by the seemingly never-ending battle between Secretary of State Shultz's advocacy of military solutions and Secretary of Defense Weinberger's preference for diplomatic ones,
and chaired by a president who often appeared disengaged from
the issues and unwilling to offend either Weinberger or Shultz,
the work of the council fell more and more into the hands of
staff members such as Oliver North and his political-military
office, where the detail work of Iran-contra was hatched and the
scheme executed. Meanwhile, as Fred Barnes wrote in *The New
Republic*, the position of National Security Adviser became
Ronald Reagan's "Bermuda Triangle, swallowing up more ap-
pointees than any other job in his administration." In the twelve
years from the beginning of the first Nixon administration to the

end of the Carter years, there had been four different National Security Advisers to the president, including the one who would put the position on the national map, Henry Kissinger. In the first six years of the Reagan administrations alone, five different people held the post: Richard Allen, William Clark, Robert McFarlane, John Poindexter, and Alton Keel, who served as acting adviser after Poindexter's resignation was tendered.

To solve the paralysis, to restore order and structure to the council, Reagan turned for his seventh National Security Adviser to someone with government experience dating back three decades, including service under presidents of both political parties and, just as important, someone who had been out of government while the Iran-contra scheme was unfolding: Colin Powell's "godfather," Frank Carlucci. Almost inevitably, Carlucci turned to Powell to be his deputy—his gatekeeper and second-in-command.

"I was desperate," Carlucci says. "It was no easy chore to walk in there. You've got a traumatized staff, a demoralized president. The press has a stakeout at your house. I needed all the talent I could get. Colin said, 'Frank, you're going to ruin my career.' I said, 'Colin, I'm not.' " According to Carlucci, getting Powell to take the job was no easy chore, either.

Command of the Army's V Corps had brought Colin Powell his third star less than a month after he arrived in Germany; he was now forty-nine years old and a lieutenant general. The command also had brought him to where, he has said time and again, he always wanted to be—in the field, with the troops and away from Ground Zero on the Potomac.

"I have been in a number of Washington assignments," Powell told *Washingtonian* magazine, "and I have never gone away saying, 'God, I hate the Pentagon. God, I hate the White House.' I have enjoyed all those assignments, but nothing is quite as much fun, as exciting as being a commander out somewhere where . . . you are not trying to satisfy nine constituencies at once, and you are not being bludgeoned daily by our free and open democratic system of government in Washington, and you're a little more insulated from the daily push and pull of the Washington environment."

As for the Pentagon and White House positions that have consistently brought Powell back to Washington, he says, "You will not find me having volunteered for any of these positions. In fact, you can check with the people who hired me; you'll find almost in every case I said I don't want to do it.''

"I think it took two phone calls," Carlucci remembers of the effort to convince Powell to return from Germany and become his deputy as National Security Adviser. "And then he said it's really the decision of the commander-in-chief, so I got the president to call. But once the president called, I think he knew it was the right thing to do for the country."

Ret. Gen. Grant Green, who joined the Carlucci team to become executive secretary of the National Security Council, has a similar memory: "We were trying to decide on a deputy, and when Frank said, 'Well, that's who I really want,' I talked to Colin. He said, 'Please, try to talk him out of it. I've been in Germany six months. I'm just getting up and running this corps. I don't want to come back to Washington.' Well, what did that one move result in? If he hadn't come back he would have continued as corps commander, stayed in Army circles, come back eventually, and maybe even been chief of staff of the Army. But he came back and was reinstated in the diplomatic-military circle and gained the confidence of Reagan and then Bush, and the rest is history. If he hadn't been good, he would never have had the offer, but Frank was very comfortable with him, and Colin is a good fit."

Another high-ranking Pentagon official at the time says Powell "was reluctant to come back. He had a three-star plum Cold War job, back when there still was a Cold War. I talked to him when he came back from Germany, and he wasn't all that happy. But now, of course, he's emerged much higher than he would have been otherwise."

The Powell legend, and by now there is one, holds that this is the way it always is with him. He is forever finding himself happily ensconced in the field when some new crisis beckons in Washington and he is called back to help solve it, and with each successful resolution of each succeeding crisis, his stock rises still higher and the pressures pulling him reluctantly back to the White House and the Pentagon become that much greater. As one of his former commanding officers puts it, in what amounts to a tidy and perhaps completely accurate summation of the legend, "He's just too damn good for his own good."

Someone close to the transition from John Poindexter to Frank

Carlucci recalls the events that brought Powell back a little differently: "Bill Casey called me one day and said they were looking for a new National Security Adviser," says Kenneth Adelman, who was head of the Arms Control and Disarmament Agency from January, 1983, until December, 1987. "Casey said he was pushing for Jeane [Kirkpatrick, who had been U.S. Ambassador to the United Nations from 1981 to 1986] and for me. This was Thanksgiving of 1986. He said he thought Frank Carlucci was going to get it, though. Then Carlucci called Sunday night and said, 'I hear rumors it's going to be me.' Monday he calls and says, 'The president wants to see me.' A few days later, or maybe a day later, he called again and said, 'Meet me at a restaurant on Capitol Hill and we'll talk about the transition. I can't do anything until January 1 because my contract runs out then. I'll lose my benefits if I leave before then.' [Carlucci was then chief executive officer of Sears World Trade, Inc., based in Washington.] That's the day Frank was announced [to be the new National Security Adviser]. At the restaurant Frank says, 'I'm thinking about a deputy.' He gave me two names of Foreign Service officers and Colin Powell. I said, 'Frank, it's not even close.' So he says, 'All right, I'll call Colin.' And he does it. He goes to the phone right then and there in the restaurant and calls Colin in Germany, and he comes back and says, 'I talked to him. What we need is a call from the president.' It was all set up.

"Three days later, Colin calls me and says, 'What's the buzz?' Three days later, it's the same thing—'What's the buzz? Where's the president's call?' He's calling me all the time saying what's the story. So I go to these little round-faced guys who work for [White House Chief of Staff] Don Regan, and I say, 'What's the buzz on this call to Colin Powell from the President?' They say, 'Well, we never got a form requesting a presidential call.' So I use the typewriter right there. I give the secretary two bucks to go get coffee, and I use her typewriter and fill it out right there. Regan apparently had his own candidate for the deputy's job . . . Reagan didn't give a crap. When he got the slip, he made the call to Colin. Colin has been seen [by some] as the reluctant warrior, but he wasn't so reluctant. He wanted it. He was delighted to do this job."

One impediment still existed to Powell's taking the position of deputy to the National Security Adviser—his at least apparently tangential relation to the Iran-contra affair that was only then being laid out for public inspection and that Carlucci was supposed to be cleaning up after. Donald Regan, Adelman remembers, was trying to use Powell's ties to the weapons transfer to lever his own person into the deputy's slot. However much he did or did not want the job as deputy, Powell, too, realized that Iran-contra was a potential stumbling block, according to Carlucci: "He did mention to me right at the outset: 'You should be aware when I was Cap's aide, one of the things went across my desk, something about moving some of the missiles along. Therefore, I'll probably be called.' I, of course, mentioned that to the President and to A. B. Culvahouse, who was the White House lawyer on it, and they said it wasn't a problem."

Arguably, too, Powell's familiarity with the broad outlines of the Iran-contra affair gave him a running start in the deputy's position. For him it wasn't virgin territory. "The most impressive time I ever saw Colin was during the transition [from Alton Keel to Carlucci]," says Adelman, who helped the new National Security Adviser settle in. "I was saying, there's going to be all kinds of stuff about Iran-contra. You don't want to spend six months doing nothing but that; you want to get this place squeaky clean. But there were all these documents scattered all over the place, some with the Tower Commission, some with [David] Abshire [who Ronald Reagan brought in as his special counselor on the affair]. Colin gets the documents right away, and he goes right through them. He dove into it in a way that was very nonmilitary, very non-hierarchical, very non-rigid."

Just as the White House fellowship had been the vehicle of Powell's debut into the civilian side of government, so the Deputy National Security Adviser's post was his coming-out party into public attention. As Weinberger's military aide, Powell had developed a following inside the White House; now, as the number-two person to Carlucci in an agency that had been rocked to its core by Iran-contra, he began to develop a following beyond 1600 Pennsylvania Avenue and its dependencies. One person who has worked closely with him says, without malice, that Powell was not averse to the attention: "He has a relish that's very human for being in the limelight, for getting the job. He's not a Cyrus Vance faceless public servant." The limelight, though, did not fall on Powell haphazardly; his presence simply commands attention. Journalist Peter Ross Range says that Powell had "star quality from the very first day, even when he was the Deputy National Security Adviser. The guy had a presence, a clarity of mind that was astounding."

"Carlucci had already cleaned the place up," Range says of the National Security Council. "The impression with Powell was a real breath of fresh air. Frank was a legend, a lion, a dinosaur of the Washington bureaucracy. Powell was this unknown thing."

In fact, Carlucci replaced about half the professional staff of the council during his first one hundred days on the job, according to John Prados, as well as abolishing the entire political-military staff and Ollie North's special office within it—in effect, taking the NSC out of directing covert operations itself. As Lou Cannon recounts in *President Reagan: The Role of a Lifetime*, Carlucci also "restored a mood of professional normalcy to a workaholic staff that often seemed driven by an almost frantic sense of mission. Soon after arriving at the NSC, Carlucci asked Colin Powell why the NSC had so many secretaries. Powell checked and told him it was because the staff was accustomed to working eighteen hours a day, seven days a week. 'Colin, get rid of half of them,' said Carlucci, who sent out the word that 'henceforth we go home at six at night and we don't work weekends.' Carlucci set the example by walking out of his office at 6:00 P.M. his first day on the job with a tennis racket under his arm." Cannon also notes that Carlucci kept his own office door open and shut down the computer on his desk that staff members had used to communicate with John Poindexter. "We weren't working through machines," Carlucci told Cannon, "we were working with each other as human beings."

If Carlucci's out-by-six decree jolted Powell's own workaholic sensibilities, the deputy's job played to his proven strengths as a facilitator, a meeting chairer, a face-to-face cajoler, and—as he had shown with Weinberger—a loyalist to his boss. "I never saw any daylight between [Powell and Carlucci]," says Elliott Abrams, who dealt frequently with the National Security Council. "I wasn't over there, obviously, but it seemed to be an ideal relationship." The position also gave Powell a critical chance to broaden his range of acquaintances in government, at a time when many of his patrons were doing their last hurrah in official Washington. "When Colin was my deputy," Carlucci says, "we were stabled right next to George Bush. They had a terrific relationship. It was clear George Bush was very fond of Colin Powell.'' As almost everyone who first meets Powell notes, he is immediately likable. And as deputy, Powell could do what is always too rare in government—get things done, move the cumbersome apparatus of government. That, probably more than anything else, is his *modus operandi*.

''I spent my time with the care and feeding of the president and with one-on-one meetings with Cap [Weinberger] and George [Shultz],'' Carlucci says. ''Colin ran the day-to-day. He chaired a lot of interagency meetings. I also delegated a task I despise—clearing all the speeches. Colin put in an awful lot of time on the Iran-contra Oval Office speech. Landon Parvin was brought in to do it, and Colin worked with him on that.''

The Oval Office speech Carlucci refers to was perhaps the most eagerly awaited speech of Ronald Reagan's administration—the March 4, 1987, speech in which the president said, ''A few months ago I told the American people I did not trade arms for hostages. My heart and my best intentions still tell me that's true, but the facts and evidence tell me it is not. As the Tower Board reported, what began as a strategic opening to Iran deteriorated, in its implementation, into trading arms for hostages. This runs counter to my own beliefs, to administration policy, and to the original strategy we had in mind. There are reasons why it happened, but no excuses. It was a mistake.''

The words were largely the work of veteran Republican speechwriter Landon Parvin, with the counseling, among others, of Nancy Reagan, Republican political operatives Stuart Spencer and Richard Wirthlin, and new White House Chief of Staff Howard Baker, who had replaced Donald Regan only a week earlier. Powell, as Carlucci says, sat in on many of the meetings in the days leading up to Reagan's address, but perhaps his major proposed contribution to the address never made it into the president's final text. That contribution, an insert delivered by Powell at a March 3rd meeting in the Oval Office—the day before the speech was aired—would have had the president tell the nation: ''As a matter of simple fairness, however, I must say that I believe the [Tower] commission's comments about George Shultz and Cap Weinberger are incorrect. Both of them vigorously opposed the arms sales to Iran and they so advised me several times. The commission's statements that the two secretaries did not support the president are also wrong. They did support me despite their known opposition to the program. I now find that both secretaries were excluded from meetings on the subject by the same people and process used to deny me vital information about this whole matter.'' Instead, ten days later and as a sop to both men, the president said on his weekly radio speech of March 14 that ''both Secretary Shultz and Secretary Weinberger advised me strongly not to pursue the initiative.''

For Powell, it was a rare setback. The proposed insert was also something Weinberger badly wanted. ''If Weinberger had fought as hard against the arms deal as he did to get this in, I'd think better of him,'' Parvin would later tell Lou Cannon. But, Parvin said in an interview with the author, Powell's advocacy of the insert was kept well within bounds. ''Colin is sort of like a son to Weinberger,'' Parvin says, ''and so Colin did pass along what Weinberger wanted . . . But I just found him direct and easy to work with, and I never worried about his having ulterior motives.'' Powell would also work with Parvin on a second Iran-contra speech for Reagan. ''After Ollie North testified at the congressional hearings in August, we did another speech,'' Parvin recalls, ''and we basically said nothing because the president had sort of reverted in terms of how far he would go. I had done a first draft that I remember Colin really liked a lot, and then the president didn't want to go that far.''

In any case, the proposed insert brought Powell's participation in the Iran-contra affair full-circle. From McFarlane's June 17, 1985, draft National Security Decision Directive to the January 17, 1986, transfer of TOW missiles to the CIA to the March 4, 1987, address to the nation that may well have saved the Reagan presidency, Powell had continued to be Caspar Weinberger's faithful Indian companion. Now it was time, in John Kennedy's memorable phrase, for the torch to be passed to a new generation.

Caspar Weinberger resigned as Secretary of Defense in November, 1987. He had been in the job nearly seven years and had presided over the largest peacetime military buildup in American history. The reason he cited for leaving was his wife's poor health. After Weinberger had delivered the news to White House Chief of Staff Howard Baker, the two met with Ronald Reagan in the Oval Office to discuss a successor. ''My original recommendation for a Secretary of Defense to follow me was [then Deputy Secretary of Defense] Will Taft,'' Weinberger says, ''but I also supported Frank Carlucci,'' whom Baker was touting for the post. Once Carlucci was decided on, the meeting turned to who would succeed him in the job he was vacating. ''I urged President Reagan to appoint [Colin Powell] National Security Adviser,'' Howard Baker says. ''He was deputy from the time I first went to the White House, and we soon got acquainted there, initially at the 8:30 [A.M.] senior staff meetings. He often gave the NSC report as Frank was often otherwise occupied. I was impressed with the succinct clarity, which is not always typical of national security experts. He had a pleasant disposition and personality. It didn't take long for me to realize that he was not only very talented, but he also was delightful to be around.''

Reagan announced Powell's selection on November 5 at the White House. That same day on Capitol Hill, the joint congressional committee investigating the Iran-contra affair approved a recommendation that, to keep the lines cleanly drawn between civilian and military authority, the National Security Adviser not be what John Poindexter had been and what Colin Powell, though he wore a coat and tie to work, still was: an active-duty officer. The recommendation, Carlucci says, ''was one that Colin favored, but we were so consumed with other issues that we didn't worry about it. Whether it was a military person or not was the least of my worries. There were some grumblings in Congress, but as soon as they got to meet him, it was all right.''

In December of 1987 Colin Powell formally took office and so became the first African-American to hold the position of National Security Adviser. Measured not by title but by the capacity to effect events worldwide, he had become the most powerful black person ever to serve in the executive branch of the United States government.

''On the day of the transition—the day Carlucci went to Defense to replace Weinberger and Powell took over at the National Security Council—the passing of the torch was held in the Rose Garden [of the White House],'' Peter Ross Range recalls. ''Carlucci spoke, then Powell. Powell's presence towered over Carlucci's. I don't just mean height. He seemed so much more statesmanlike, and Carlucci is his godfather.''

* * *

To a degree, Caspar Weinberger had to vacate the Defense Secretary's seat not only so Carlucci could rise to his position and Powell to Carlucci's. He had to do so, too, so the impasse between himself and George Shultz could be broken and the National Security Council—on which they constituted half the principals—could begin to function again. Fellow Californians, veterans of the Nixon administration, even once co-executives of the Bechtel Corporation in San Francisco, Weinberger and Shultz had been paired together at Defense and State in the expectation that they had enough commonality of interests and experience to cooperate. Nothing, as it turned out, could have been further from the case. By the time Powell became Deputy National Security Adviser, the relationship had broken down to almost schoolyard taunting. Kenneth Adelman remembers one NSC meeting he and Powell attended in the summer of 1987: "Weinberger and Shultz were going on at each other. Shultz said, 'Mr. President, I wanted to talk to the military about this, but Weinberger wouldn't let me do it.' Weinberger said, 'You could have called up on the telephone. My number is listed.' It kept going on and on like this. Colin handed me a note that said, 'It's going to be a long eighteen months.' A little later I poked my head in his office, and he said, 'Adelman, have you ever? My God!' "

As the Deputy National Security Adviser, Adelman says, "Colin didn't do much better than anyone else had done" at reconciling Weinberger and Shultz, but "once Weinberger left, he could work with Carlucci, obviously, and with Shultz. He was an honest broker. Shultz liked him." Nor could it have hurt that Powell had served Shultz's cause as well as Weinberger's when he tried to persuade Ronald Reagan, in effect, to absolve the two men publicly of any guilt in the Iran-contra affair. In Washington what goes around has a way of coming around: it's a city of long memories. Nor, for that matter, could it have hurt that Powell had long shown a knack for pleasing competing constituencies and helping them find common ground. Fairness seems to be endemic to him, even when one of the competing constituencies was represented by his longtime mentor.

"Powell was really quite scrupulous," Elliott Abrams says. "There was an enormous fight between State and Defense, between Shultz and Carlucci. I think Powell was too smart to want to be in the middle of that fight, and I think he was a really faithful observer of the rules.''

One official who sat in on many NSC meetings while Powell was adviser to the president says, ''Powell is smarter than Carlucci, and he was better at the job than Carlucci, and so the switch was one that most people in the administration were comfortable with. He was better at the personal level, at managing relations among the principals.''

Powell also appears to have been successful at rooting out the few remaining rough spots from the Carlucci transition. ''I had put my organization in place,'' Howard Baker recalls. ''Frank had done the same with his, and the Tower Commission had reported, so the institutional work was done. But Colin brought a special dimension to the job. In addition to being thoroughly familiar with the changes that had been put in place, he also brought a smoothness of operation that's awfully rare.''

Another high-ranking Reagan official who also sat in on many of the same NSC meetings says that ''Powell was very good at coordinating. He moved things along. He was far less operational and less laborious than McFarlane had been. His style is pretty much the same as Carlucci's, but in a sense Carlucci had a stronger ego. If he was meeting with Reagan on, say, Latin America, he'd take along a Latin American expert from the NSC staff. If Reagan asked a question, Carlucci would have the Latin American expert answer it. Powell didn't do that very often even though it's very motivating to the staff, who work very hard with very few benefits and accolades. It's a week-making thing to spend fifteen minutes with the president. In that sense, Frank's way was the better way to operate.''

A journalist who covered the Reagan-Mikhail Gorbachev summit in Washington in early December, 1987, very shortly after Powell had officially assumed the National Security Adviser's position, also seems to take Powell to task for his report to the press on the status of negotiations between the two superpowers on the Strategic Defense Initiative—the so-called Star Wars anti-missile plan that Reagan favored and Gorbachev opposed.

''There was a briefing the night before the summit ended at the J. W. Marriott Hotel, which was the press center,'' this journalist says. ''One of the big issues of the summit was whether Reagan and Gorbachev could somehow deal with, neutralize, put aside, or somehow get around the issue of SDI, which had brought the Iceland summit of the previous year to a halt. The briefing was given by someone who was reported to be a 'senior administration official': in fact, it was Powell. This was like two thousand people he was doing it for. He came in, did his briefing, then took questions. He was asked questions about SDI. They were ultimately not pinning questions, not ones that got to the heart of the matter, but he essentially gave the impression that Reagan and Gorbachev had put SDI behind them, that it was no longer a problem. The next day Powell appeared on one of the morning news shows, maybe the 'Today' show, and said, 'Well, yes, this still does stand to be a problem.' I remember saying to myself, 'File that away. Put that in the Colin Powell file.'

"Maybe I held Powell to a higher standard because I figured he was coming out of the Army, but he lied that night [even though he corrected it on the record the next day] at the press briefing . . . it was a very impressive performance. He did what the administration needed him to do, and he did it deftly . . . At the same time, and this is the most exculpatory element, I don't think he had ever been thrown into that sort of situation before. You've got two thousand reporters. He wasn't familiar yet with the White House press corps or the diplomatic corps, but you also have guys from all over the world who want to know all sorts of wild stuff . . . For all I know," this journalist adds, "it's the only blemish on his career." By Washington standards, that's virtually dirt-free.

Arguably, too—at least from a strictly pragmatic point of view—the larger ends of the Washington summit and the one that followed it half a year later in Moscow were worth serving, even at the risk of some dissembling before the international press. The INF treaty that was agreed to in Washington and finalized in Moscow resulted in the dismantling of nearly 2,700 intermediate- and short-range nuclear missiles, more than two-thirds of them Soviet, and provided for on-site monitoring—certainly important for what it symbolized regardless of the limited access it allowed in practical terms. In fact, Howard Baker says, the success of the Washington half of the superpower summit was assured by a meeting held in Florida nearly three months before Gorbachev arrived in the nation's capital.

"Frank [Carlucci] and his people had put together the critical talking points that had to be resolved by the president," Baker recalls. "We went down to Miami to greet the Pope, and there were about four hours in there when the Pope had a separate schedule [from President Reagan]. Frank and I took the president to a hotel, just the three of us, and we went over those points one by one. I'm sure Colin had a lot to do with the presentation of those points . . ."

By the Moscow summit, Baker says, "I was more familiar with how these summit procedures went, and Colin was familiar from his time as deputy. The Moscow summit and the preparation for it were a much more procedural matter than the Washington summit. It went smoothly; there were no untoward events. Most of the hard work was out of the way." The Moscow summit was perhaps the smoothest run from the American side of any summit in modern memory. At least a lion's share of the credit for that goes to Powell and his passion for tough detail work. He is not a man to let even small things slide.

Powell put one piece of old Reagan administration business to bed while he was National Security Adviser—a piece that, in part, had led it into scandal and poisoned the well with Congress: military aid to the Nicaraguan contras. In February, 1988, over the objections of George Shultz, among others, Powell succeeded in reducing the administration's request to Congress to $3.5 million in military aid to the contras. "He was the driver," a senior White House official said at the time. "He was the one everyone looked to." When even that reduced package failed to win support, Powell, though a contra supporter, essentially abandoned the fight. "This was in the dying days of the Reagan administration," Kenneth Adelman says. "Everyone was exhausted. Not funding the contras was Colin more than anyone else. He knew that politically there was no way to do it." With that ended the oldest and perhaps the ugliest of the many *leitmotifs* that floated through the National Security Council during the Reagan years; it was the final proof that pragmatists, not ideologues, were finally driving foreign policy. "I've known him very well for quite a few years, including when he was at the National Security Council," Arizona Sen. John McCain says of Powell. "It was a very tough time. They were going through the aid-to-the-contras issue, and a lot of those guys were very badly tarred. Yet he was able to conduct himself as he should have. He supported the president and his policies, yet he escaped not only untarred but enhanced. He said it like it is, and he was always scrupulously honest. He never deceived anyone.''

What is perhaps most telling about abandoning the fight for military aid to the contras was that it was accomplished by the most junior member of the new inner circle. "Powell moved the Reagan administration towards where it should have been all along, and he did it effortlessly,'' says his friend Harlan Ullman of the Center for Naval Analysis. ''Yet he wasn't a big player—he wasn't Shultz or Carlucci. He was the least among equals.''

Powell was less successful at achieving resolution on two other fronts: Manuel Noriega and Panama, and the Persian Gulf, both of which would spill over into the Bush administration and ultimately come to occupy much of Powell's first term as Chairman of the Joint Chiefs of Staff. "Ironically, because it wasn't like him, Powell fiddle-faddled on Panama,'' says one Reagan official very close to the workings of the National Security Council. "It was all, 'Let's have another meeting.' He didn't bring any resolution to it. He was immobilized between State wanting to use the military and Defense wanting to use diplomacy.''

Powell had been National Security Adviser less than three months when Noriega and his PDF, the Panamanian Defense Force, toppled the Panamanian civil government of President Eric Arturo Delvalle in February, 1988, and forced the National Assembly to install Manuel Solis Palma as the new president. Simultaneously Noriega had been indicted by a U.S. federal grand jury in Miami on charges of drug trafficking—it was Delvalle's attempt to oust Noriega after the indictment was handed down that had brought on the coup. On the first front Powell sided with his mentor Frank Carlucci and Adm. William Crowe, then the Joint Chiefs chairman, against the State Department's advocacy of the use of force to restore Delvalle and overthrow Noriega. Although he could have invoked national-security considerations to cripple the grand jury investigation, Powell stood on the sidelines as the proceedings ground on toward an indictment that neither he nor the administration generally appears to have considered enforceable. In effect, Howard Baker says, the indictment temporarily put Justice Department officials in charge of U.S. policy towards Panama: "The initiative sort of passed to the U.S. Attorney in Miami. I do remember one day in the Oval Office the president saying, 'Since when did the U.S. Attorney in Miami start setting national security policy?' Colin had mentioned it more than once to the president.'' The shaky result of that arrangement became evident on a May 22, 1988, airing of CBS's ''Face the Nation'' when correspondent Lesley Stahl asked about the controversial administration-backed plan to have Noriega voluntarily step down from power in return for dropping the grand-jury indictments. It's an interview segment wholly unlike Powell—filled with the language of indecision, with hints of a policy that was in effect a floating craps game.

STAHL: What about the charge, though, that because [Noriega] leaves his man, Solis Palma, in as acting president, that he will be able to run the government from someplace in exile and come back in ten months and run for president, or whatever? I mean, the criticism is that under this deal he keeps making more and more demands and we keep giving in to him, and we look weak and our image is being hurt.

POWELL: The elements of the negotiation have not changed significantly in recent weeks. There are not new and more important demands being put on the table. The elements are pretty much in place. He would leave, and he would not be in a position to run in the next election, which is scheduled for May of 1989.

STAHL: He would not be able to run?

POWELL: The elements that are on the table would remove him from the political process and he would not be a candidate for election in 1989. What I'd like to get to, though, is the most controversial part of the deal that's causing all the debate—it has to do with the indictments. The indictments that were handed down are indictments that would be very difficult to follow up on because of the Panamanian constitution and Panamanian law. There is no provision for anybody who is a Panamanian citizen to be extradited to the United States. So it is unclear that we would ever see anybody, General Noriega included, who is indicted in Panama to be brought before a U.S. court. For that reason the indictment has some value, and its value is in negotiating removal of General Noriega from power. The president has not yet decided whether to go forward with this deal because dropping an indictment of this nature is a very serious matter. But if the result of dropping the indictment is to remove General Noriega from power—it's not clear that we can remove him from actions behind the scenes, but the important thing is he loses the levers of power that he currently has a complete hand on as commander of the PDF.

STAHL: The ball is in whose court? Has [Noriega] accepted these terms, and now it's up to the president to decide? Or is it up to him to decide where—you say it's on the table.

POWELL: It's on the table; all the elements have not yet come together. The president has yet to make a decision.

STAHL: But the president has agreed for the deal to be put on the table, didn't he?

POWELL: The president has agreed for the deal to be put on the table, but it has not gone to closure. There are some outstanding elements.

STAHL: What about the report that the president has ruled out the use of military force? And I ask you that because if this deal falls through, what are our options, just to leave him in power, or what?

POWELL: We continue to have options. We haven't ruled out any options but—

STAHL: Military options haven't been—

POWELL: We haven't ruled out any options. But at the same time one has to be careful when you talk about let's go in with military force and invade. We are trying to get a non-violent solution to this problem. And I think it's very irresponsible to talk about military options which might involve the loss of Panamanian lives as well as U.S. lives.

One can almost hear the discomfort in Powell's answers. He is a man who prides himself, and rightfully so, on achieving consensus, on finding a bottom line; yet consensus is the one thing the principals of the National Security Council could not reach on Panama. "What [Powell] could not do was substitute for presidential decisions when they weren't being made, as in Panama," Elliott Abrams says. After years of hard-line advocacy on Central America, the final chapter of the Reagan administration became the Epoch of Indecision. It would take a new president, 26,000 U.S. troops, nearly four more years, and a federal jury in Miami to finally write an end to the Manuel Noriega story, and even then, only the ease with which the Panamanian invasion was pulled off and a somewhat surprising conviction would keep the entire policy from being a tragedy of errors.

As for the Middle East, neither Powell nor anyone else in the administration had a finely tuned antenna. Powell had been Frank Carlucci's deputy for less than two months when the Security Council made the decision to allow foreign oil tankers operating in the Persian Gulf to ''reflag'' themselves as American ships, subject to the protection of the U.S. military. Thereby the United States finally did directly what years of administration policy—including the missile sales to Tehran—had done indirectly: inserted itself into the Iran-Iraq war. On May 17, 1987—ten weeks after the decision was made but before the reflagging operation began—an Iraqi warplane either intentionally or otherwise attacked the USS *Stark* with missiles, leaving thirty-five crewmen dead. By July the Navy was escorting merchant ships in the Gulf—the *Bridgeton*, the very first supertanker to be escorted, struck a mine—and had moved some of its sophisticated cruisers into the region. There followed a series of mining incidents and other attacks that finally resulted in April of 1988 in a limited U.S. military strike against Iranian targets. By then Powell was in charge of the National Security Council. Another three months later, on July 3, 1988, the Navy cruiser USS *Vincennes*, equipped with the new AEGIS radar system, was on a so-called neutrality patrol in the Gulf when it misread Iran Air Flight 655 for an attacking plane and fired. The 290 passengers on board were killed. Lost in the uproar that followed was the proximate cause of the National Security Council decision to reflag tankers in the first place: a request by Kuwait to the Soviet Union to allow Kuwaiti tankers to carry the Soviet flag. In the years ahead, the Soviet Union would simply disappear. Kuwait, decidedly, would not. Nor, of course, would Colin Powell. As 1988 drew to a close, though, and the Reagan administration with it, Powell had to decide what he was going to do next.

Lt. Col. Oliver North, who along with William Casey had been the driving force behind the Iran-contra scheme, retired from the Marines in May 1988 to write what would become a best-selling book and to give speeches at a reported $25,000 apiece. Alexander Haig, the former Secretary of State and retired four-star general, whose résumé closely parallels Powell's, earns in excess of $1 million a year as a consultant and has received handsome book publisher advances for two memoirs. The second is still in progress; like the first, it is being written with the author of spy thrillers, Charles McCarry. Donald Regan, White House Chief of Staff during part of Powell's tenure as National Security Adviser, also used McCarry's services in compiling his own memoirs for a reported $1 million advance. Henry Kissinger, who held the National Security Adviser's chair under Richard Nixon, reportedly makes at least that much annually as head of his own consulting firm, Kissinger Associates. Jeane Kirkpatrick, the fiery ideologue who had vied with Frank Carlucci for the National Security Adviser's post in 1986, has earned millions of dollars on the speaking circuit. Caspar Weinberger, Powell's boss from 1983 to 1986, also went on the speaking circuit after he left the Reagan administration, as well as receiving a reported $500,000 advance to write his memoirs and becoming publisher of *Forbes* magazine, the self-described "capitalist tool." Powell's "godfather of godfathers," Frank Carlucci, became vice-chairman of the Carlyle Group, a major Washington investment firm, after stepping down as Ronald Reagan's Secretary of Defense. It's a familiar Washington scenario perhaps best summarized by an offhand comment Carlucci made to reporter Harry Jaffe in January, 1992: "I lunch with the Russian ambassador. Dick Cheney is one of my best friends. Jim Baker was in my college class. And God knows, I know George Bush well." In Washington access is power, and power is ultimately money.

In *The Commanders* Bob Woodward writes that Powell "had been quietly circulating résumés in the business world" in the final months of the Reagan administration—résumés that "had drawn only a mild response in any case." Powell's friends, though, say that that assertion is exaggerated. "Colin was at the NSC, waiting for his next Army assignment; there was no doubt about it. He was a soldier waiting for his next assignment, and that's no bullshit," says Marybel Batjer. "He wasn't stupid. Knowing this was a political town in a political world, he knew there might be opportunities. People were bringing opportunities to him, but he was anxious to get back in the Army. There was probably a month after the election when we were waiting to get booted out of our offices, when people obviously were coming to Colin from the outside, from business, asking him what he wanted to do—people with speaking opportunities, book opportunities. But he was waiting for his next assignment. If Woodward read that as Colin's circulating résumés, that was a wrong read.'' As for memoir opportunities for Powell, Simon and Schuster editor Alice Mayhew, who has shepherded many such projects, told a reporter for *The Economist* that ''Those books are only worth something if you're willing to spill the beans. The trouble with him is that he's a gentleman.''

After he was elected but before he took office, George Bush would offer Powell the directorship of the Central Intelligence Agency, a number-two position at the State Department, or a chance to stay on at the National Security Council until his successor was determined. Powell turned them all down, and in April, 1989, he went off to Fort McPherson, Georgia, to become commander-in-chief of the Forces Command—the head of all U.S.-based Army personnel and a post that would earn him his fourth star. It goes almost without saying that he would stay in the job only five months and be out of pocket much of that time. ''We couldn't control him,'' says one of his staff officers. ''Our major problem was getting access to him because he was gone all the time.'' In any practical sense, Forces Command was a job too small for Powell by the spring of 1989, but it was necessary work all the same. Subarticle b of Article 3 of Section 152 of the Goldwater-Nichols Department of Defense Reorganization Act of 1986 requires that the president, except in extraordinary circumstances, appoint as the Chairman of the Joint Chiefs of Staff an officer who has served as ''(A) the Vice-Chairman of the Joint Chiefs of Staff; (B) the Chief of Staff of the Army, the Chief of Naval Operations, the Chief of Staff of the Air Force, or the Commandant of the Marine Corps; or (C) the commander of a unified or specified combatant command.'' But nowhere does it say how long an officer has to hold any of those positions. Until he took over the Forces Command, Colin Powell had done none of those things. Forces Command was the last box he would have to mark on his résumé, his last station of the cross.

Fittingly, too, Powell, who had arrived in the Reagan administration as a minor player in July, 1983, would be perhaps the last person to visit Ronald Reagan in an official capacity during his tenure, according to Kitty Kelley's *Nancy Reagan*. "The world is quiet today, Mr. President," Powell told Reagan during his daily national security briefing on the morning of January 20, 1989. A few hours later, in a sunny but bitingly cold ceremony on the Mall, George Bush was sworn in as the nation's forty-first president.

CHAPTER 14

The Chairman

It could almost be a trivia quiz: Name four chairmen of the Joint Chiefs of Staff, none of them Colin Powell. Current-events buffs might recall Adm. William Crowe, Jr., Powell's immediate predecessor. Those with a sense of history can perhaps bring to mind the first official chairman, Gen. Omar Bradley, appointed in 1949, but they are more likely to remember him for his performance in World War II, where he commanded the First and, later, Twelfth Armies in Europe. (Adm. William Leahy had been, in effect, chairman of the Joint Chiefs of Staff during World War II, although the position didn't exist statutorily.) The urbane Maxwell Taylor, recalled to active duty in 1961 to be John Kennedy's military representative and later Chairman during the early U.S. buildup in Vietnam, might also come to mind. Unlike Bradley, Taylor cut a dashing figure. The others, though, stretch memory: Arthur Radford and Nathan Twining, who both served under Dwight Eisenhower; Lyman Lemnitzer, who preceded Maxwell Taylor; Earle Wheeler, who was Chairman for the maximum six years during the height of the Vietnam War and is now almost forgotten; Thomas Moorer and George Brown, Navy and Air Force respectively; David Jones, who served under both Jimmy Carter and Ronald Reagan; and John Vessey, Jr., who preceded Crowe.

The job, however, invites anonymity. Although the Chairman is, by law, the nation's highest-ranking military officer, he has no divisions, no fleets, no tactical fighter wings under his command. His principal job is to be military adviser to the president, who is under no obligation to take his suggestions. (Eisenhower, for example, was his own military adviser.) While the Chairman of the Joint Chiefs of Staff has one of the longer titles in Washington officialdom, he heads his own Pentagon staff, nothing more. That Colin Powell has risen in the position to recognition as perhaps the most widely known general since World War II is, in part, a result of sheer good fortune and the forces of history: Powell is the first black to hold the position, and he was in the chair when a popular war was waged and won with a minimal loss of American lives. To the victor belong the spoils, including public esteem. Powell also has benefited by good fortune in another sense. Prior to the passage of the Goldwater-Nichols Act of 1986, the chairman was, in effect, a kind of glorified executive secretary and legman for the combined joint chiefs. He set the agendas for their meetings and presided over them; he carried the chiefs' advice to the commander-in-chief, which made him first among equals; but he otherwise held no special sway. His job was to represent the *collective* wisdom of the service chiefs. Consensus under the old system was frequently hard to achieve and slow in arriving and was often bought at the cost of assuring that military ventures were four-service shows. By the mid-1980s the system by which military authority was exercised seemed to many in Congress and elsewhere simply to have broken down, and the services appeared to lack the resolve to fix it. Vietnam and the demoralized armed force it left behind were still fresh in memory. So were the disastrous October 23, 1983, bombing of the U.S. Marines barracks in Beirut that left 241 American servicemen dead and, two days later, the hastily assembled U.S.-led invasion of the small Caribbean island-nation of Grenada, an invasion that had awkwardly included elements of all four services. The 1986 Goldwater-Nichols Act—named for its chief sponsors, former Sen. Barry Goldwater and the late Rep. William Nichols—was Congress's revenge, says author and retired Col. Gordon Kaiser, now director of operations for the Naval Institute and the author of *The U.S. Marine Corps and Defense Unification: 1944–1947*. ''It was punishment for not listening to what Goldwater and those guys kept telling [the services] to do,'' Kaiser says. ''Finally, they said screw you guys, here's the rule. We, the military profession, didn't pay attention, so Congress said, all right, we're going to fix your wagon; we're going to arbitrarily provide a solution and you are going to follow it. It's bureaucratic discipline. That's the way Congress does it.'' It was, Kaiser adds, necessary discipline: ''I said in my book, either give this guy [the chairman] something to do or get rid of the position.''

Goldwater-Nichols gave the chairman something to do by changing the power equation within the joint chiefs. Henceforth, the chairman and only the chairman was to be the principal military adviser to the President, the National Security Council and the Secretary of Defense. Secondarily and as a consequence, the law also downgraded the importance of the individual service chiefs, who now served in part as the chairman's advisory panel, not as his co-equal. Under the old system when the chairman was away from Washington, as he frequently was, his spot rotated among the other chiefs; under Goldwater-Nichols, a new vice-chairman took over in the absence of the chairman. ''Our intent,'' says Rep. David McCurdy, who helped write the law, ''was to streamline the chain of command . . . When we were going through the process, the [service chiefs] railed against us like we were the worst people on Earth.''

The first chairman to serve under the new Goldwater-Nichols rules—William Crowe, an admiral with an academic bent, a Princeton graduate degree, and a think-tank manner—had been in place when the legislation was passed. The second, first appointed in the late summer of 1989, was Colin Powell, who already had been National Security Adviser and for all practical purposes an assistant secretary of defense. From his tenure in the White House, Powell also knew George Bush well, and that, says one retired general, is perhaps the most critical factor in the effectiveness of any chairman. ''The president will do whatever he wants, no matter what the law says. If he wants the chairman to be important, he'll be important. The job is in the eye of the president.'' One measure of George Bush's preexisting relationship with Powell is the fact that the president jumped him over more than thirty senior officers to make him chairman and the military's highest-ranking officer. In effect, though, Goldwater-Nichols had created its own imperative: the position as newly configured was almost custom-fit for Powell.

"The services often did a pretty good job in their own ambits," former Under-Secretary of the Navy James Woolsey says of the genesis of the Goldwater-Nichols Act. "The problem was the things that crossed service responsibility—airlifts and sea lifts, running operations in such a way that you always picked the best force and didn't have to have contributions from each of the services in equal amounts. I think it was probably more than anything else the operational side growing out of dissatisfaction with Vietnam, the bombing in Lebanon, and Grenada that led people to become interested in a clear operational scheme. Military operations require an integrating intelligence, and the chairman was the obvious person to do that. To a lesser extent, it helps to have an integrated military view of budgetary and planning matters . . . The powers of the chairman are considerably broader now that Goldwater-Nichols is in, and I think Colin has filled it in its broadened sense. He has not been hesitant about making recommendations on his own on policy and budget, which is what Goldwater-Nichols envisioned the chairman doing." But as Powell has done at so many stops along the way, he also seems to have made the job more than it was envisioned to be.

"The guy is different from any chairman that has previously been," says Charles Corrdry, the veteran defense correspondent for the Baltimore *Sun.* "I don't know for sure if he thinks he took a demotion, but no one has ever gone to the chairmanship from being the National Security Adviser to the president. There's not much about how government and the executive branch works in his field that he doesn't know. And he's a terribly bright fellow anyway. He also has the benefit of Goldwater-Nichols, which makes him not just first among equals but the boss. Yet I've talked with all the service chiefs at one time or another, and I haven't heard anyone bellyaching."

Powell's reputation as an honest broker and as someone who doesn't put his own twist on information is equally important, says former Chairman David Jones: "The main thing you have to do is make sure the leaders have all the information on which to make a good decision as opposed to 'This is what I think.' Not that 'This is what I think' isn't an important ingredient, but the main thing is to make sure the leaders have all the information, all the options, and I think he does well in that regard.

"Also, in that job chemistry is very important," Jones adds. "To a great extent you have very little authority; your effectiveness depends on persuasion. You're not in the literal chain of command—that runs through the president and the secretary of defense—so you are in the job of persuading others."

With Congress, one of the constituencies Powell must persuade, he "plays very, very well," says Pat Towell, who has covered defense issues and Congress since the mid 1970s for *Congressional Quarterly*. "Powell has a capacity to project a sense of authority and frankness, which are the key. The thing that sinks senior uniformed officials is when members get the sense that their institutional right to information is not being respected. I've seen senior uniformed people do this not just with liberal critics of the Pentagon but even with some of the old boys who think of themselves as the military's tribunes on the Hill. There really is a sense of the members' right to information, and when they feel that is being toyed with, their wrath can be terrible. Powell gets a lot of credit for apparently—and as far as anyone knows actually—leveling with them, treating them as a people in a collateral branch of government who have a right to know."

Powell appears to play well, too, with the service chiefs, his most immediate constituency, in some ways his most touchy one, and one that historically has resisted any strong-arming from the top. "What you can't do is steamroller the joint chiefs of staff," says Alexander Haig. "These service chiefs all preside over powerful fiefdoms, and they're very sensitive to being bulldozed by a chairman whose authority has been enhanced immensely in recent years. But Powell has exercised it with great sensitivity. I never hear carping from the services." On Capitol Hill, Haig says, Powell "has a large measure of credibility because he's articulate, able to deal with domestic politics, and able to logroll, which is a compliment, not a criticism. I think he's also exercised great influence with George Bush, who has a vested interest in his success because he reached down to pick him up."

With his immediate boss, Secretary of Defense Dick Cheney, the match is also very good, says NBC-TV Pentagon correspondent Fred Francis: "Frankly, [Powell] is running the Pentagon. When Admiral Crowe was there he just stayed with the military end; he let Weinberger and Carlucci handle everything else. Powell has such a relationship with Cheney that Cheney lets him run the place, militarily and operationally, until it spills over too much into the political side. Very often you'll ask [Pentagon spokesman] Pete Williams a question, and he'll pick up the phone and call Powell, not Cheney." Powell plays the Goldwater-Nichols Act "like a maestro," Francis says. "He doesn't overplay it; he plays it perfectly. He's inventing the chairman's job, defining what that position will be for all time." (During the Persian Gulf War, Powell and Cheney were sometimes referred to by the collective nickname "Lethal Weapon" around the Pentagon, after Danny Glover and Mel Gibson, the black and white stars of the three movies by that name.)

The chemistry with the president, ultimately Powell's most important constituency, has been equally good, says someone who has been close to George Bush for many years . . . "It's a funny thing, it has to do with class in a sense. Powell has a manner that is very reserved in public, very white-bread. He's not rough-hewn, and Bush is more comfortable with that. Powell doesn't get on his nerves. There's a part of Bush that's volatile inside; people like [former White House Chief of Staff John] Sununu can get along with him, but modulation means a great deal to Bush. He's comfortable with that. Cheney stands well with Bush for the same reason; he's got that modulated quality, too. Nixon had to have it the same way—keep it calm. Ford also was comfortable with that; that's why he didn't like [his first Secretary of Defense James] Schlesinger; he was always getting excited, lighting up that pipe, and blowing off at the mouth. If I had to train someone for success in Washington—*Pygmalion* fashion—I'd say, Don't be George Patton. If you sit there and modulate yourself, you can get away with murder . . . Bush is comfortable with Powell, and that gives him a certain leeway."

The Patton reference gets obliquely at the one sustained rap on Colin Powell—the one that seems to come up in any negative critique: that he is, in fact, no George Patton; that he is a political general. In part, the criticism is a double-bind: Without having served in political posts Powell couldn't have accumulated the experience he brought to the chairman's job or developed the rapport he had with the president before he came to his position, but by having accumulated that experience and rapport he is, for some, tainted by the amount of time he has served in political posts. In military terms, it's a catch-22. The criticism also misreads Powell's history somewhat: He may not have resisted his Washington postings as Norman Schwarzkopf, for example, appears to have done, but Powell did fight, twice, in the only war available in his military career. The criticism also misreads the nature of the chairman's job, one retired general and historian says: "The chairman is, to begin with, a political position. The thing you have to disabuse yourself of is the notion that the person is picked for field experience or any other reason." And to a large extent, says Ret. Gen. Mike Lynch, that is simply a function of the complex modern world that chairmen operate in—a world in which military issues are inseparable from geopolitical and domestic ones.

"If you look back on the history of that particular job, the key thing is the old expression: a man for the times," Lynch says. "The first chairman, Omar Bradley, would have been so lost today in this world that it's unbelievable because of the tremendous number of factors that impact on the military. We used to assume that all you required was a military force and you could get anything done. As we found out in Vietnam, using military force only gets you into a situation that perhaps you can't get out of. The greater the penalty you pay for making a mistake, the greater the need for someone who has a tremendous perspective on the job. That's where Powell is particularly effective."

Although the peak of U.S. military involvement in Vietnam came more than two decades ago, Powell is also the first chairman of the Joint Chiefs of Staff to have served on the ground in that war below the rank of lieutenant colonel. (Indeed, and it is fascinating to consider, Powell is the only one of the twelve chairmen to have served on the ground in *any* war below the rank of colonel. Omar Bradley, who was an Army first lieutenant when the United States entered the First World War, spent the war with the Fourteenth Infantry Regiment in the American West. Earle Wheeler, who was a captain at the outbreak of World War II, spent the first part of the war at stateside camps before being promoted to colonel and joining the European theater as chief of staff of the Sixty-third Infantry Division in 1944. John Vessey was a lieutenant colonel when he arrived in Vietnam as the executive officer of the Twenty-fifth Infantry Division in 1966.) As much as that says about the vagaries of timing and about the route by which one arrives at the chairmanship of the Joint Chiefs, it also is critical to understanding Colin Powell's readiness for the position, General Lynch argues.

"One of your greatest challenges in the Pentagon is trying to explain to other people the problems down at the fighting level. So many of those guys started out as vice-presidents and worked their way up. They never had an appreciation of what goes on down there at the lowest level. Powell had the advantage of going up through those levels. For the younger leaders in Vietnam, there was a tremendous moral and ethical challenge that was never faced by the commanders in World War Two. When a guy is steeped in the moral and ethical issues down at the fighting level he's more inclined to back off from gross solutions and try to equate what they are saying to how difficult it would be to implement it down where he remembers it. Powell was the first chairman who had that experience and was able to carry it up through the ranks.

"The fact that Powell is black on top of this meant that he was exposed to the same things domestically that had occurred on the battlefield. There was a tremendous discrepancy in Vietnam in the role the fighter played versus the role the guy in charge played—[Gen. William] Westmoreland swept his hand across the map and put kids in terrible situations and exposed them to terrible discrimination. The average guy could have come out of there and forgotten all that, but in Powell's case he'd already experienced that, being in a minority in a world dominated by a majority. That wasn't any different really than what the poor infantryman was facing in Vietnam. All of that gave Powell a tremendous advantage in perspective that no other chairman of the Joint Chiefs of Staff had ever had.''

Colin Powell became Chairman of the Joint Chiefs of Staff at midnight on Sunday, October 1, 1989. He was asleep the next night at his new home—Quarters 6, the spacious red-brick official residence of the chairman at Fort Myer—when Gen. Thomas Kelly called to relay a message he had received only minutes earlier from Gen. Max Thurman, head of the U.S. Southern Command based in Panama City. "Got a report for you. There's a coup going down," Thurman had told Kelly, according to Bob Woodward in *The Commanders*. An hour later, still well in the pre-dawn, Powell and Kelly met at the Pentagon. The chairman's job was to be a baptism by fire.

As events turned out, the would-be Panamanian coup was one the United States would decline to participate in in any meaningful fashion. Maj. Moises Giroldi, the thirty-eight-year-old Panamanian major who led it, was at least suspect: he had played a role in helping Noriega crush another coup attempt in March 1988, according to the CIA station in Panama City. Like Powell, Max Thurman also was new to his job—he'd taken over the Southern Command only the day before Powell became chairman—and Thurman suspected the coup was an attempt to sucker him into precipitous military action. And although the rebels did have Noriega in their custody for several hours, Powell's message authorizing Thurman to assist in the coup if it could be done without overt U.S. military intervention arrived hours after Noriega's PDF forces had come to his rescue and crushed the revolt.

For Powell, Dick Cheney, and George Bush, the failed coup was a public-relations debacle. Noriega—who had become in the public mind what Bush would later make Saddam Hussein into, a kind of drug-trafficking Adolf Hitler—had slipped through the U.S.'s fingers at a time when removing him would have risked few American lives and minimal force involvement. Conservative Sen. Jesse Helms called the administration's war planners "Keystone Kops." Rep. Les Aspin, the powerful head of the House Armed Services Committee, told a reporter that "We ought to be ready at any opportunity to use the confusion and uncertainty of a coup attempt . . . to do something about Mr. Noriega." Noriega himself appeared in public soon after the coup was crushed, shaking his fist and telling reporters, "The gringo piranhas want to do away with me." Ten weeks later the Bush war council found the right pretext, had the right plan in place and did just that. The coup attempt—botched or not, from the American side—had given Powell and his commanders a wake-up call. To have responded to it would have required a Grenada-like response, what Powell has called "a come-as-you-are in about two or three days' time." By the time events in Panama provided adequate cause again for intervention, the U.S. military was ready.

"We had weeks to put on the shelf a plan in case a plan was ever needed," Powell told *Washingtonian* magazine. "That's what General Thurman and I spent a good part of our first two months in office doing. Not looking for a war but making sure should we ever be called on we knew what we would do. That's what we did, down to the level of rehearsing, down to the level of finite review of details. So all things were in our favor in Panama. We also happened to have a headquarters right there and 12,000, 13,000 soldiers to begin with. We had everything in our favor in Panama. The command structure [was] in place. Also, General Thurman and I have known each other for twenty-five years. General [Carl] Stiner [commander of the Army's 41,000-troop Eighteenth Airborne Corps] and I have known each other for twenty years . . . All of the units involved belonged to me when I was the FORSCOM Commander. So I knew the capabilities of those units; I knew the commanders involved."

On December 16, 1989, the bottom began to fall out on Manuel Noriega. That evening four off-duty U.S. officers were returning to base from a dinner in Panama City when their car was forced to stop by a roadblock set up by Noriega's PDF forces. When the Panamanians started to pull the Americans from the car, the driver tried to speed away. The car was raked by gunfire and one of the officers, Marine Lt. Robert Paz, was killed. Two other Americans who had been stopped earlier—Navy Lt. Adam Curtis and his wife Bonnie—had looked on while the shooting took place. From the roadblock, the Curtises were taken to a nearby PDF office. Over the next four hours, before they were suddenly released, Adam Curtis was beaten and kicked in the groin repeatedly and his wife threatened with sexual acts. Noriega tried to paint both incidents as American-provoked, but U.S. eavesdroppers had listened to him plotting his responses. It was all the pretext the Bush war council needed. Three days later, a little after midnight on December 20, Colin Powell, in his words, dropped "eighteen thousand teenagers with guns" into Panama, and Operation Just Cause began.

At 7:20 that morning George Bush appeared on national television to deliver an eleven-paragraph overview of the American action in Panama. He was followed by Cheney, who delivered his own prepared statement, and by Powell, who spoke without notes and then answered questions. "We have not yet located the general," Powell said of Noriega, "but as a practical matter, we have decapitated him from the dictatorship of this country, and he is now a fugitive and will be treated as such." "We will chase him," Powell said, "and we will find him," even in the unlikely event he tried to go to roost in the jungle. Noriega was "used to a different kind of lifestyle, and I'm not quite sure he would be up to being chased around the countryside" by U.S. Special Forces, infantry units, and Rangers. "This reign of terror is over." When the questions finally ended, Powell added one more thought: "Could I just say that I hope you recognize how complicated an operation this was and how competently it was carried out by the Armed Forces of the United States. We all, the Secretary and I, all of our associates, deeply regret the loss of American life [then preliminarily set at nine dead and thirty-nine wounded]. But that's sometimes necessary in pursuit of our national interests and in the fight for democracy." From the crisp sentences to the near arrogance of the vow to run Noriega to the ground to the sentimentality of his closing comments, the public national performance—his first as chairman and first ever in a time of major crisis—was vintage Powell. Alma Powell, who describes herself as the toughest critic of her husband's TV appearances, says it was his most impressive one ever.

None of it, of course, would be as easy as Powell's press-conference performance had made it sound. Manuel Noriega remained at large for four days, despite a $1 million reward for information leading to his capture. On Sunday, December 24, he finally came to ground at the Papal Nuncio's residence in Panama City, where he would stay for ten days, bombarded part of that time by heavy-metal music (to prevent eavesdropping on U.S. negotiations with the Nuncio), before surrendering to members of the Army's Delta Force. Casualties, too, would climb to 23 Americans killed—including three American civilians living in Panama—and 324 Americans wounded. Panamanian fatalities would top 500, split roughly between soldiers and non-combatants. Civil order also would break down in Panama City. "The U.S. Defense Department may have been in charge," Kevin Buckley writes in *Panama: The Whole Story*, "but as December 20 wore on, U.S. troops made no effort to prevent looters from ransacking the city. These looters did more damage to the economy than all the economic sanctions [imposed against the nation under Noriega]. They emptied department stores, supermarkets, pharmacies, boutiques, fast-food shops, and whatever could be entered easily. The looting cost $1 billion, according to the Panama City Chamber of Commerce." And although U.S. forces never attacked the Papal Nuncio, they did storm the residence of the Nicaraguan ambassador, in violation of international law. Powell learned about it while watching CNN. "The camera," Bob Woodward writes in *The Commanders*, "revealed a sign the size of a manhole cover showing unmistakably that it was the ambassador's residence." Later, when Powell talked to Max Thurman on the phone, the head of the Southern Command explained that the house had been full of weapons and that there had been confusion over whether it was a diplomatic residence. " 'It's undeniable,' Powell snapped," according to Woodward's account. " 'I just saw it on CNN. Stop bullshitting me. We did it.' " Whatever glitches there were, though, it seems undeniable that Manuel Noriega had drastically underestimated the U.S. resolve to involve itself militarily. Saddam Hussein would make the same mistake.

"I am cautioning my staff and cautioning all the people that are studying this to see Panama for what it was," Powell told *Washingtonian* interviewer Kenneth Adelman in February, 1990, a little over a month after the conclusion of Operation Just Cause. "It was a unique set of circumstances and a unique operation. Make sure we've learned the right lessons out of that: readiness of troops, thorough planning, attention to detail, making sure you bring the right capability to the problem. Those are the lessons learned, [but] don't take Panama and don't take Operation Just Cause and all the maps, all the overlays, and go look for another piece of ground to put the overlays on."

In fact, Powell went on, he had learned only one real lesson from Panama, and that was a matter of "relearn[ing] things that I have known all along. The main one is that in the final analysis it's the quality, training, professionalism, morale, and esprit of the individual soldier, sailor, airman, marine, and his leaders that will either make the operation a success or a failure. The goofiest plans of the goofiest generals can turn out well if you have the right kinds of guys executing it. The best plans of the best generals can turn to zip if you don't have the right kinds of people to execute."

But if Panama was unique in its details, in broad view it was exactly what Operation Desert Storm would later become: a distillation of nearly every lesson learned from the Vietnam War. The first and perhaps most important of the lessons was put forward by then Secretary of Defense Caspar Weinberger in a November, 1984, National Press Club speech that became known informally as the "Weinberger Doctrine." U.S. military forces, Weinberger said, should be committed only "with the clear intention of winning." In other words, bring everything you can and then some. "Everybody thought I used too much stuff in Grenada," Weinberger says. "I'm perfectly frank to say that whenever the Joint Chiefs made a recommendation I would automatically double it. If anybody had told me that the [1980] Iranian hostage rescue attempt [in which eight American commandos died] could have been done with eight helicopters, I would have sent forty-five. As far as I know, Colin agrees with that completely . . . We tried to get Vietnam over with with small, incremental increases that we thought the public wouldn't notice." (Weinberger says that the speech that became known as the Weinberger Doctrine "happened to be one I wrote myself. That was completely my idea, but I sent it around and Colin never expressed any disagreement with it.")

The Panama invasion force whose assembly Powell would oversee was precisely and in all likelihood intentionally the opposite of the force that fought in Vietnam. It involved not a gradual buildup but twenty-five thousand troops employed simultaneously against a nation the size of South Carolina—and with a million fewer people—and against a Panamanian Defense Force with few resources at its command. The Powell plan even included two F-117A Stealth fighters, although Noriega's forces had no air defenses to evade.

"Panama was like a light rehearsal for the Gulf," Ret. Col. David Hackworth says, "and certainly what Powell is about is his experience in Vietnam. You've got to understand that whole generation was scarred by Vietnam. The David Hackworths, the Colin Powells, we'll be forever painted by that experience. It was the hot stove, and we learned never to touch it again." The moral that has been learned, Hackworth says, is "overwhelming superiority. [Powell] went into Panama with twenty-five thousand troops when twelve Special Forces guys could have done the job."

It is, Hackworth goes on to suggest, a dangerous moral applied universally: "The thing I find frightening is this application of the military solution, and now it's being done with a sledgehammer instead of a ball-peen hammer. It's very similar to Cuba in 1962. If you look at the actors then—the President, Maxwell Taylor, all the dudes, the chiefs—the only voice that came out loud and clear for restraint was [Secretary of Defense Robert] McNamara, who said, 'Yes, let's use the blockade.' In retrospect, we find out they had not only strategic nukes [on Cuba] but even tactical nukes. My paratrooper unit was set to go in there if we invaded. We would have formed our airhead, and some Soviet soldier would have pushed the button and melted us, and there would have been one mushroom cloud after another. That can be what happens when you insist on the military solution."

"The one lesson from Vietnam is clear and absolute, and that's the issue of decisive force," Rep. David McCurdy says. "It may be a sledgehammer, but if we are going to be in conflict and going in on the heavy side saves American lives, then we ought to lean that way. I think that's the most significant lesson from Vietnam. [In the Gulf and in Panama] we played to win."

The second lesson, not unrelated to the first, is to have a clear political objective going into battle and, once you have one, "to make sure you have the right statement of strategic military objectives to achieve the political objectives and that you put the resources to bear on it," Powell said in the *Washingtonian* interview. "Then you give enough flexibility to the commanders to make sure you can achieve it." In Vietnam, Powell adds, "I don't think it all worked out that way." Indeed, it's a lesson that's applicable only if the president and to a lesser extent the Secretary of Defense allow it to be, and on that score, George Bush and Dick Cheney get generally high marks. They've let the generals be generals. Just as important, in Powell they've had a general in place who was, to both of them, a known quantity. It is not just Colin Powell himself that has to be factored in; it is the cumulative weight of his résumé.

Powell "had the advantage of a very close rapport with the president, having been in the White House before when George Bush was vice-president. That's a very valuable asset," says Adm. Thomas Moorer, who was chairman of the Joint Chiefs of Staff during the closing years of the war in Vietnam. "I guess General Powell is the first chairman since World War Two who has been permitted to conduct military operations based on professional military rather than political guidelines. In the Vietnam War I was even getting told how many bombs to put on each wing of the airplanes."

The third lesson—inseparable from the others, as all the lessons are—is that military operations must have finite time spans. "You simply also have to have buried deep in your psyche the fact that the American people are not that patient," Powell told the *Washingtonian*. "They like to see rather quick results whenever possible. Panama gave quick results. If it had lingered for a while longer, it might not have been the success it was." In practical terms, Powell says, that means that "if you are going to conduct a military operation, try to do it in a way that gets it over quickly. That doesn't necessarily mean big. . . . Put the right amount of force in to make sure that you get a success and you get a success quickly. You control the situation quickly, and then you can go back to business as usual and leave if possible."

The fourth lesson, a necessary corollary to the third, is that as a modern commander you have to deal not only with the situation on the battlefield but with the perception of the situation back where the home fires are burning. "The other thing that's changed over the years is the public attention or public awareness of what you're doing wherever you're doing it," Powell continued. "With minicams and with jet travel and with satellites and with twenty-four-hour-a-day instant communication around the world—imagine what would have happened if [during the Civil War] you had filmed Marie's Heights and the

American people all over the country had been able to see some of the carnage that took place in Antietam and the Wilderness. . . . What would it be like had it been shown every night live? But that's the environment you're in now. It's live. So you have to keep that in the back of your mind. It's being seen, analyzed, commented upon, critiqued, and public conclusions are being made in real time, changing hour by hour as an operation unfolds. I saw that rather vividly in Panama.'' The American people, Powell said, ''like to kibitz about everything. But that's not wrong, and it should not be a pain. It just means it is an additional element that we have to work with. We have to work with it well; we have to work with it smartly—not to deceive or stiff, we're not going to show you to put a spin on it. My own view is the more you tell the American people and the more you can give to the American people, then nobody can put us down.''

In fact, press coverage of the Panama invasion—the assurance and protection of the American people's right to know—was a failure. Several weeks after Operation Just Cause was launched, Fred Hoffman, who by then had stepped down as the Defense Department's number-two spokesman, was asked to put together a study on what went wrong. Hoffman's conclusion, essentially, was that just about everything did. Despite the presence of a sizable U.S. press contingent already in place in Panama, the war-planners opted to use a press pool comprised of Washington-based reporters to cover the war. The planners, though, didn't begin notifying the pool reporters until 7:30 P.M. on December 19, five and a half hours before Operation Just Cause was set to begin and only three and a half hours before their flight was set to leave from Andrews Air Force Base outside Washington. Dick Thompson of *Time*, who was at the magazine's Christmas party when he got word, flew off to Panama, wearing a wool suit. Like the other pool reporters, he also arrived after much of the decisive fighting had taken place. On the ground in Panama things deteriorated even more. Pool reporters were shuttled off to non-events; transmission machinery kept breaking down, both in Panama City and at the receiving end in the Pentagon. Film disappeared in ''in'' boxes, and favoritism, apparently drifting south from either the White House or the Pentagon, began to rear its head. ''Members of the pool resented what they regarded as special treatment accorded to ABC personality Sam Donaldson, who arrived with an entourage the day after the main attacks,'' Hoffman writes in his report. '' 'When Sam Donaldson arrived, it was like the President had walked into the media center,' said one military escort who shared the pool's feeling of resentment. This officer said [Col. Ron] Sconyers [Public Affairs Officer for the Southern Command] was 'given over basically to supporting Sam Donaldson.' Sconyers and his deputy, Lt. Col. Bob Donnelly, made it clear they were unhappy at what they hinted was pressure from Washington to give Donaldson favored treatment.'' To an extent, it is the usual moaning that journalists so often fall into about their treatment, but, Hoffman writes, ''the result of all this was that the sixteen-member pool produced stories and pictures of essentially secondary value.''

In Hoffman's report, Powell is quoted as saying that ''the final judgment'' on using the Washington-based press pool ''was made in the Oval Office.'' He himself had been ''left out of the pattern'' on the decision and unaware of the consequences. '' 'I thought everything went smoothly,' Powell said. He said he 'didn't have a single clue' the pool was bogged down until newsmen informed him.'' In an interview with the author, Hoffman says that Powell's self-assessment is entirely accurate. ''What it comes down to at the bottom is that Powell was not the one who made or significantly influenced the critical public-affairs decisions. Those were made by Cheney . . . Powell was forthright. His hands were clean.''

There's a final lesson, a summary lesson of sorts from Vietnam, distilled in the Panama invasion and Operation Desert Storm—and in Colin Powell—says Sen. John McCain, who spent five and a half years in a Hanoi prisoner-of-war camp. In essence, it is: learn the lessons of that war but don't overlearn them. That Powell had not overlearned them became evident in December, 1990, during the Senate Armed Services Committee's hearing on the potential use of force against Iraq. McCain says: ''We had witness after witness who had been in the Vietnam War—guys you and I respect very much—saying, 'We can't do it. There will be all these body-bags.' That's understandable among people whose life's experiences were defined by the Vietnam War. [Powell] also watched soldiers die in combat, in a war for which there was no blueprint for victory, but rather than react by believing that we should never embark again in military operations outside the continental limits of the United States, his thinking matured to the degree where he was convinced we should never embark into conflict again without a clear blueprint for victory and without devoting whatever resources are necessary to winning.''

Although the Panama invasion was, as Powell says, a unique operation, it was also a tutorial on warfare as the United States under George Bush, Dick Cheney, and Colin Powell intended to wage it. Had he been a better student, Saddam Hussein might have gone to school on it.

CHAPTER 15

Desert Storm

The Persian Gulf War that expelled the Iraqi army from Kuwait lasted 45 days, from the onset of the aerial bombardment of Baghdad shortly after midnight on January 17, 1991, through the cease-fire declared in Washington by George Bush on February 27 one hundred hours after the ground war had begun, to the March 3d meeting in the desert of southern Iraq, where Norman Schwarzkopf laid out for Iraqi Lt. Gen. Sultan Hashim Ahmad the terms for peace. As wars go, it was a short span, yet Operation Desert Storm managed to squeeze into its brief history some extraordinary numbers. Coalition air forces flew 112,000 sorties and dropped 88,000 tons of bombs, yet their losses were almost unimaginably light. Forty-two went down in combat and another 33 were lost due to equipment failure or accidents. Adjusting for combat missions only, Allied forces lost 52 aircraft for every 100,000 sorties. The loss rate for U.S. aircraft in the Korean War was 440 per 100,000 sorties; in World War II, it was 620. The disparity in human losses between the two warring sides is virtually unparalleled. Two hundred forty-four Allied troops, including 146 Americans, were killed in action, perhaps thirty percent of those by friendly fire. Another 159 Americans died outside of combat. Iraqi deaths in the war are far more difficult to calculate. Using a variety of sources, *Newsweek* has estimated that 70,000 to 115,000 Iraqis were killed before the cease-fire went into effect. Even at the low end, that would be 287 Iraqis dead for every Allied combat death.

Another 65,000 Iraqi troops were captured or surrendered, and there were far more of the latter than the former. And, of course, for many Iraqis the war with Allied forces was only the beginning of the suffering. Beth Osborne Daponte of the U.S. Census Bureau's Center for International Research has estimated that more than 150,000 Iraqis—86,194 men, 39,612 women, and 32,195 children—were killed by Allied forces in the domestic unrest that followed the war in Iran, or from postwar deprivation.

Inevitably, too, millions upon millions of words have been written about the war, and millions are yet to come. Millions more were spoken as it was being waged. It was a war that legitimatized a TV network, CNN; a war waged in part and on both sides in desert briefing rooms, Washington press conferences, and live feeds from Baghdad and its al-Rashid Hotel. (If Saddam Hussein proved one thing in the Gulf War, it is that he recognizes the value of a satellite dish.) TV analysts became a war mini-industry of their own, turning out everything from psychohistories of Saddam to nearly nonstop analyses of bombing missions and troop maneuvers.

But of all the words the war produced, none would be anywhere so instantly famous or as enduring as the twenty-seven words Colin Powell uttered at a Pentagon news conference on the morning of Wednesday, January 23, 1991—a week into the air war and after the bloom of Allied success was fading in the faces of captured American airmen being paraded in front of Iraqi television. Powell first laid out the broad Allied plan for the continued prosecution of the war. Then, in a voice strangely reassuring in its sternness and lack of overt passion, Powell told the reporters and the nation watching on television: "Our strategy for going after this army is very, very simple. First we are going to cut it off, and then we are going to kill it."

As usual, Powell worked without notes, but the twenty-seven words he used to calm the American people were not off the cuff. For Colin Powell, God is in the details and in planning. "We came in on Tuesday," Powell says, "and things were getting very wobbly. The whole building was shaking. The whole country was wondering, 'My God, [CNN correspondent] Wolf Blitzer said it would be over in twenty-four hours. It's not!' So it was a very awkward time, and by Tuesday we knew we had to do something. And we started to pull together charts. The

Secretary and I talked about how we would handle this. As I reflected on it, I just thought that we needed to lay out the entire campaign so that people would recognize it was a total campaign and don't panic because we're just beginning. I was looking for a way to sort of give it—not just looking for a sound bite but to give some clear statement of what we were trying to do that's understandable to human beings and not just to a foreign-policy community or an infantry-school audience . . . People like to focus on that line, but the more important part of that was what I said before that line. It was the windup to that. So I knew what the line was, and I already had it in my mind. I had sort of shared it with my folks around here to get a sanity check, but it was not that extemporaneous. It was *given* extemporaneously, but the thought was not an extemporaneous thought. I'd thought of it beforehand, about twelve hours beforehand.''

(When the author asked Powell whether his famous twenty-seven words were off the cuff, he at first replied, with a laugh, ''You little bastard.'' That, too, was vintage Powell.)

To the extent that Panama had been a light rehearsal for the Gulf War, as David Hackworth suggests—a practice session in the application of overwhelming force—so the December 20, 1990, press conference in which Powell vowed to chase Manuel Noriega and find him was a light rehearsal for the more famous one a little more than thirteen months later when he vowed to cut off Saddam Hussein's army and kill it. The tone and the sound are the same; even the syntax has a symmetry. George Orwell wrote in his 1946 essay ''Politics and the English Language,'' ''In our time, political speech and writing are largely the defense of the indefensible. . . . A mass of Latin words falls upon the facts like soft snow, blurring the outlines and covering up all the details.'' With Colin Powell, political speech seems to be almost the opposite of that. The words are monosyllabic; instead of tripping over themselves, the sentences run clear and brief from beginning to end. The language is meant not to blur but to drive a point home. ''The great enemy of clear language is insincerity,'' Orwell went on. ''When there is a gap between one's real and one's declared aims, one turns as it were instinctively to long words and exhausted idioms, like a cuttlefish squirting out ink.'' At moments such as Powell's press briefings on Panama and on Operation Desert Storm, there seems to be no insincerity, no room for questions of intent. On the other hand, the road that the Bush administration generally traveled from the massing of Iraqi troops on the Kuwait border in late July of 1990 to the onset of hostilities against Iraq more than five months later appears to have been not altogether straight. To many, there did appear to be a gap between real and declared aims on the part of the Bush administration.

A year after the Gulf War had been concluded, Colin Powell appeared on the "MacNeil/Lehrer Newshour" to defend the need for a continued global American military presence and to do battle against the so-called "Fortress America" proponents. "The last time we adopted a policy like that, or one time we adopted a policy like that was when somebody said, 'Well, gee, I don't see a particular threat in Korea. We don't have to maintain any forces against a particular threat that might come from Korea,' " Powell told interviewer Jim Lehrer. "And that was in 1948, and two years later American troops were dying in Korea because we had signaled to the aggressor in that part of the world that we had no vital interest there and we were not prepared to defend the interest of our neighbors, our friends, as well. We should not take that chance now in this very curious world in transition that we live in."

The U.S. Department of State, though, seems to have been at pains in the week before the Iraq invasion of Kuwait to signal its similar if carefully couched indifference to the longstanding border dispute between the two nations. Iraqi Republican Guard units were already positioned on the Kuwaiti border when State Department spokeswoman Margaret Tutwiler told reporters on July 24, 1990, that "We do not have any defense treaties with Kuwait . . . And there are no special defense or security commitments to Kuwait." The next day U.S. ambassador to Iraq April Glaspie met with Saddam Hussein for the first time in the more than two years she had been in residence in Baghdad. Accounts differ on the substance of the meeting—Iraq sent out its own version some months after it had taken place; the State Department has provided only limited insight into Glaspie's version. But at one point, the State Department acknowledges, Glaspie did tell Saddam that the United States has "no opinion on the Arab-Arab conflicts, like your border disagreement with Kuwait." Glaspie did apparently warn the Iraqi leader that the United States "can never excuse settlement of disputes by any but peaceful means," but an April 12, 1990, meeting with a delegation of U.S. senators may well have inclined Saddam to interpret the American response to his own best advantage. The senators had come to Iraq officially to deliver a stern condemnation of Saddam's development of nuclear and biochemical weapons. Unofficially some of them sought to mitigate whatever insult the condemnation might bring about. Minority leader Robert Dole, a member of the delegation, assured the Iraqi leader that he had friends in Washington. Another Republican, Wyoming's Alan Simpson, blamed Saddam's bad image in America on a "haughty and pampered" press, according to a tape of the meeting secretly made by the Iraqis.

If the message being sent by the State Department and the Senate delegation to Saddam Hussein was mixed, so, too, was George Bush's initial response to the invasion, at least on the surface. Iraqi tanks had been in Kuwait about eight hours when Bush told reporters—just before an emergency meeting of the National Security Council—"We're not discussing intervention." Bush said that his desire was for "this invasion [to] be reversed and have [the Iraqis] get out of Kuwait," but asked again if he was thinking about intervening in the occupation or sending troops to the Gulf, Bush answered, "I'm not contemplating such action." Three days later, on Sunday, August 5, Bush had just returned to the White House by helicopter from the presidential retreat at Camp David in Maryland's Catoctin Mountains when a reporter asked, "Are you going to move militarily?" "I will not discuss with you what my options are or might be," Bush said, "but they're wide open. I can assure you of that . . . I view very seriously our determination to reverse out this aggression." Then Bush, his anger appearing to rise, provided his own sound-bite epigram for the war that was to follow: "This will not stand. This will not stand, this aggression against Kuwait." In three days he seemed to have traveled a long way toward war and to have made the invasion of Kuwait a personal insult. "There's a proclivity on the part of this president," one general says, "to make—*rash* is the wrong word, because he has the power to back it up; when you're a Major Leaguer and you spend the afternoon in Triple A, you can be pretty good—but there's almost a preppy decision-making process in which we're going to get the bad guys." Quite possibly to his great surprise, Saddam Hussein had just become one of them, and markedly so.

Powell, who had spent part of that weekend at Camp David with the president, Dick Cheney, Norman Schwarzkopf, and Under-Secretary of Defense Paul Wolfowitz, says that Bush's suddenly heightened war rhetoric was more a matter of evolution.

"People read more into that than is deserving to be read into it," Powell says. ". . . Over a seventy-two hour period the president quickly came to grips with the importance of the situation. It took him a few hours, a few days to understand what we could do, to consult with some people and do some soundings and some checks and to watch what actually was happening. The people who expect him on the morning of [August] second, based on early reports of an invasion, to say what he subsequently said on the fourth are asking a bit much. So I don't see a sort of a light on the road to Damascus. I see a very prudent man seeing the invasion, saying 'check it out,' talking to [then British Prime Minister] Margaret Thatcher, which he did that day, and getting some advice. We spent the whole morning with him Saturday at Camp David, and then on Sunday, having it fairly clear in mind—I don't know how much he had thought about what he would say when he got off the helicopter, but that is what he said. It goes in the history books that way."

In the long and exhausting postmortem to Operation Desert Storm, Powell's own ambivalence about the need for military action against Iraq has been a central theme, thanks to Bob Woodward's book, *The Commanders*. Woodward's book is a work that doesn't document its sources yet puts the reader in the midst of events, knee-deep in details and conversations as the United States sweeps into Panama and builds up to the Persian Gulf War. It is also a book that started out to be something else— a more general account of civilian and military leadership in the Pentagon until history intervened and gave Woodward an invasion and a war to rally his work around. It was on the former basis that Powell, Dick Cheney and others initially gave Woodward extensive access to their thoughts and actions, but it is the latter—the war and the invasion—that gives the book its rich perch on momentous contemporary events. In his foreword, Woodward writes that *The Commanders* "falls somewhere between newspaper journalism and history." Marybel Batjer, who was interviewed for *The Commanders* and knows many of its leading characters, says that "Bob Woodward was about eighty-percent accurate at any point in that book.'' In Powell's case the accuracy rate is important, nowhere more so than in Woodward's account of the Friday, October 5, 1990, meeting in the Oval Office between Powell, Cheney, Bush, and National Security Adviser Brent Scowcroft.

As Woodward depicts the event, Powell used the meeting as something of a last chance to present what Powell called the ''strangulation'' policy against Saddam Hussein, including the United Nations-backed economic blockade of Iraq that stopped short of waging actual war against him. Powell ''tried to speak as an advocate, adopt the tone of an advocate, support it with his body language,'' Woodward writes. ''He sat on the edge of his seat, his hands were in the air emphasizing his points, he spoke with conviction. But he did not go so far as to say to the President that containment was his personal recommendation . . . No one, including the President, embraced containment. If only one of them had, Powell was prepared to say that he favored it. But no one tried to pin him down. No one asked him for his overall opinion. Not faced with the question, Powell was not sure what his answer would have been if he had to give it without support from one of the others . . . Afterward,'' Woodward concludes the scene, ''Powell said his conscience was clear. He had presented the military implications of each choice. There was only so much he could do.''

Powell's response to Woodward's version of the meeting: ''I don't know who Bob's source is,'' he says. ''I've never discussed what my recommendations were to the President, didn't do it to Bob, won't do it now. The President knows what I said to him, and that is a fairly fanciful piece on Bob's part. If you read it very carefully, he has to get me where he wants me, but he never attributes it to me. He essentially mindreads without a basis to mindread. So I've got to leave it there because I've never tried to defend myself against what Bob said. The President knows what I said, and that's all I care about.''

Woodward, too, according to Frank Carlucci, feels too much has been made of his account of Powell's advocacy of containment in the Gulf. ''I've had one conversation with Bob about it,'' Carlucci says. ''He feels his book has been abused, misrepresented, and he's a little pissed off about it. I suspect neither Colin nor Woodward expected it to be used as it was . . . You're damned if you do talk to the press and you're damned if you don't.''

Bob Woodward himself says that in the reaction to his book, too often "everything gets reduced to one sentence. In that period of October, he made those recommendations as I report. Again, a lot of it is done with body language, as I carefully lay out there. That's in October; then in November, when the President says, 'No, we're going to double the forces, put us in this position,' nobody works harder for it [than Powell]. It's been read as he opposed the war, which he did not. It's carefully constructed, carefully sourced . . . There were multiple sources; there were other people at the meeting besides him.'' Read Powell's comments on his characterization of the meeting, Woodward responds: "That's not disputing; that's what we used to call a non-denial denial . . . Bush almost confirmed what I wrote when the book came out, saying Powell made his recommendations, then he saluted. Now, come on.''

Still, whether or not Woodward was accurate, whether or not he indulged in mindreading, whether or not Powell was damned if he did or didn't talk to a famous journalist-author—whether, for that matter, Powell with no particular hedging in mind did exactly as Woodward describes—*The Commanders'* rendering of the October 5th meeting would cause Powell perhaps his rockiest moments in high-government service. From Woodward's account would flow the accusation, particularly from those who opposed U.S. military action in the Gulf, that Powell was once again being a political general, that he was holding back on delivering his best advice because the administration winds were blowing in the wrong direction, that he was too reluctant to bear news contrary to what the boss wanted to hear.

"If *The Commanders* is to be believed, when it came time to go to war in Iraq, Colin Powell had reservations about the need for and the timing of the military operations but did not express them, sensing no political support for his position,'' retired Adm. Eugene Carroll says. "In my estimation, the worst possible thing that could be said about the chairman [of the Joint Chiefs of Staff]—any chairman—is that sensing no political support he failed to give the military advice that it is his statutory responsibility to give. It doesn't appear to me that the door was closed on raising concerns about the military operations. There were plenty of expressions of concern about a precipitous, in-

evitable war in Iraq being expressed by former chairmen of the
Joint Chiefs of Staff [including Powell's predecessor, Adm. William Crowe, and his one-time racquetball opponent, Gen. David
Jones], former Secretaries of Defense [including Powell's former boss during the Carter years, Harold Brown], influential
members of Congress. It doesn't appear to me he would have
had to climb out on a limb or walk the plank in order to offer
the military counsel the law says he's required to supply. If he
had given it and been told it wasn't the policy of the president
and the Secretary of Defense—that they had made the political
determination we would go to war—then he can say aye-aye, sir,
and his job is to supply the best advice on how to do it.

"I don't know him personally. I don't know to what extent he
consciously balances the competing pressures he faces, but it
sounds terribly expedient to say 'I felt one way, but recognizing
the political winds, I didn't offer that advice.' I always felt I
owed my commanding officer the best advice I could give. I
hope he had the fortitude to say, 'Do this' . . . but it's awfully
hard to outgrow the habits of twenty years of being in the top
echelons of official Washington.''

Of course, this is all based on the material and implications
in *The Commanders*, and Powell disputes it. Still, Woodward's
account of Powell's alleged hesitancy to advocate containment
also would cause him a problem with Sam Nunn, the powerful
head of the Senate Armed Services Committee. An outspoken
proponent of sanctions, Nunn was "mystified by the certitude
with which the president went the other way," according to a
person close to the committee. One reason, this person suggests, is that "Nunn was getting through back channels at the
highest level of the Pentagon a sense that sanctions were the way
to go." Powell may not have been those back channels—indeed,
Nunn may not have been so informed or as mystified as this
source implies—but if one can read backward from the September, 1991, hearings before the Senate Armed Services Committee on Powell's reconfirmation for a second two-year term as
chairman, Nunn was at least visibly exercised by the time Powell
appeared to have spent with Bob Woodward.

Powell's relationship with Nunn, Eugene Carroll says, "is
apparently terminal . . . Sam knew [Powell] had a major tour
of the Pacific on his calendar. He held off the confirmation hearing until Powell had to cancel this whole trip, then summoned

him up and expressed some annoyance that Powell was as forthright with Woodward as he apparently was and yet denied information to Congress.''

Indeed, the reconfirmation hearing held September 27, 1991,
and continued on September 30 is a study in congressional dis-
ciplining. Powell was required to answer in writing four broad
questions about *The Commanders*, each with five to seven
subquestions. Some examples: ''Did you or anyone on your
behalf have any conversations or written communication with
Mr. Woodward?'' ''Was the Secretary of Defense aware of these
conversations or written communications?'' ''Did you provide
any classified or sensitive information or material to Mr. Woodward?'' Given that Secretary Cheney himself talked extensively
to Woodward for the book, the second question seems especially
odd. Given, too, that Powell was at the time the hearing was
held probably the most popular chairman in the history of the
job, that there was virtually no chance his second term would
be denied, and that the final day of the hearing came less than
twenty-four hours before Powell's first tour as chairman was to
expire, the whole process seems particularly penny-ante and
indicative of a deep rift with Nunn.

Powell, though, seems to harbor no grudge over the experience. ''I like a good fight,'' he told interviewer Brian Lamb on
C-Span's ''American Profile'' series, ''and there's no better fight
in town than testifying before Congress. It keeps you on your
toes. It forces you to think through your positions. It's in the
best tradition of the democratic process. Not all military officers
like to testify before Congress, and, in fact, if I had a choice, if
there was something else I could do that day, I would do it. But
I don't shrink from it . . . What's happening up there is not
personal; it's business. And you can be friends with each and
every one of them, and I am friends with most of my interlocutors on the Hill, but we can also have a helluva debate in open
hearings . . . It's kind of like the old story out of *The Godfather*—'nothing personal, just business' as they throw the wire
around your neck.''

When Lamb asked specifically about Nunn and the reconfirmation hearing, Powell said, ''I don't know whether he did or
did not like the book *The Commanders*. He had some questions
with respect to some information that was in the book, and he
had some questions with respect to my role with respect to the

book and what I might or might not have said to Bob Woodward. And so we worked through those questions, we resolved them, and I was reconfirmed in time to not have a break in tour. So all's well that ends well.''

Indeed, it is possible to read a certain fighter's glee into Powell's answers to Nunn at the reconfirmation hearing. ''I always protect contingency operations,'' he told Nunn on September 27. ''I always protect the advice I give to the president, to the Secretary of Defense, and to the other members of the National Security Council. So I have no second thoughts. I have no conscience problems. I said nothing to Mr. Woodward that would have betrayed any classified information, and I conducted myself in no way that might be considered inappropriate.'' At another point in the hearing, this time on September 30, Powell was grilled by Sen. Malcolm Wallop about another contention in *The Commanders*, this one having to do with the more general readiness of the U.S. military for Iraqi adventurism against Kuwait. The transcript of their exchange follows:

WALLOP: It is clear that both you and the Secretary [Cheney] made a judgment that there was no likelihood of an Iraqi attack on Kuwait.
POWELL: That is absolutely wrong, Senator.
WALLOP: Well, that is what the book said.
POWELL: I do not care what the book said, Senator. The Defense Planning Guidance that the [Defense] Department wrote anticipated just such a scenario. And that is why General Schwarzkopf had plans in place for just such a scenario eight or nine months before the attack occurred.

Neither the response to Nunn nor to Wallop is the reaction of someone who runs from a brawl, even with a senior committee member and especially a chairman who has all manner of ways to make life difficult. And as John McCain, who also sits on the Senate Armed Services Committee, notes, ''Powell is one of the few guys who could get away with doing that [to Nunn].''

The Commanders also may have done Powell some long-term harm with George Bush. Although Woodward's style prohibits any special insight into who is providing the information, Bush and National Security Adviser Brent Scowcroft are generally portrayed in the book as the most bellicose of the administration's senior circle as the nation marches toward Operation Desert Storm. Therein, suggests one source who has been close to Bush for many years, lies the problem:

"There's a reservation that would never be expressed to Powell, but Bush would feel it now," this source says. "Powell would not have his full confidence any longer. [Secretary of State] Jim Baker does a lot of talking, and stuff comes out in the papers that is not the way George or Barbara Bush would like to see it, and you know it came from Jim, and that's been going on for years. But with Powell it's different. I think it's reflected this way. I would have no inhibition now in saying to George Bush, 'Look, this guy Powell has done so and so.' I don't think I would have done that before because I would have gotten, 'Well, he's doing a good job. I hear what you're saying, and I appreciate your telling me that, but he's doing a good job.' You wouldn't get that now. It's not vindictive, it's not anger, it's just a kind of disappointment, a feeling this guy has his own agenda here.

"I think everyone feels Powell was in a CYA [cover-your-ass] situation in talking to Woodward. Cheney talked to him, too, but it wasn't the same. There wasn't this war-crazy president with this Gulf plan and this war-crazy National Security Adviser . . . There's no confrontation there. I think the president still has confidence in Powell's military judgment, his professional judgment. Scowcroft could win any head-to-head confrontation there because Bush knows that Scowcroft has his best interests at heart. But if Powell said we need fourteen brigades here and Scowcroft said seven is enough, George might go with Powell. That's his professional judgment. It's just a disappointment that he talked that much with Woodward at all.

"There's also a lot of feeling in the administration that Powell is a Democrat. There was talk in 1988 about Powell for vice-president, but now you hear it more and more, 'Well, you know he's really a Democrat.' "

Powell's suspected political leanings may well have something to do with how his participation in Woodward's research has been read by those in the Bush inner circle, especially those with a predisposition to favor Dick Cheney in the 1996 presidential campaign. A Cheney-Powell ticket is probably inconceivable—it leans too heavily toward defense and military expertise—but a Cheney-Powell face-off on the national ticket, in either slot, does not overly strain the imagination. One senses at least a backing off of unalloyed praise for Powell by those with Cheney ties, even those who have also been close to Powell over the years. As one such person says, "Colin did talk too much with Woodward. It's not a proper role for a sitting military officer. It was not a tribute to him. It was a bad moment in his career." At least in part, the implication is that it has the sound of building a case for the future.

The frequent press speculation in the immediate afterglow of the war that George Bush might make Powell his 1992 running mate caused Powell problems elsewhere in the administration as well, according to veteran NBC Pentagon correspondent Fred Francis. "For a long time after the war, Powell wouldn't go on the air," Francis says. "He'd say, 'I have too much to do.' But the fact is that Dan Quayle's people would go bonkers whenever he was mentioned for the vice-presidency. Powell went off the air for eight months because he didn't want to upset the Quayle folks. Can you think of anybody who was such a hero as Powell was and took less credit for it? And there was one reason for it, and that was Dan Quayle."

Perhaps Colin Powell did trim his sails to the political winds when he held back on forthrightly recommending containment at the October 4 White House meeting. Perhaps he was, to an extent, covering his rear by letting Woodward record for posterity his concern about an offensive against Iraq. (Elliott Abrams, a Powell admirer, suggested as much in his review of *The Commanders* for the Washington *Times*.) Hindsight does make the Persian Gulf War seem a cakewalk, but in October, 1990, it seemed far from that. "Nobody really thought we were going to do as well in the Gulf as we did, not even Powell," says Harlan Ullman of the Center for Naval Analysis. But even assuming Woodward's rendering of Colin Powell's actions during the buildup to the Gulf War is accurate, it is just as possible to read them in a wholly different way—not as someone who was throwing his advice to the political winds but as someone who was trying to apply a reality check to a grave and awesome undertaking. In fact, such a reading seems far more consistent with the totality of Powell's career.

Former Under-Secretary of the Navy James Woolsey argues that Powell's conduct as described by Woodward is, in fact, precisely in line with a chairman's role. "What you got [in *The*

Commanders] generally was the notion that he was slow to anger and wanted to make sure that if we went into this, we went in with all four feet in such a way as to win and win quickly, and once the president decided to go, [Powell] went along," Woolsey says. "That's what you want a chairman doing. You don't want him jumping up and saying at every meeting, 'Hey, we can do this.' You want a professional who can use the drastic remedy to have a sense of balance about using that remedy. You want your soldier to say, 'You know, war is a terrible thing. If you want to do it, I'll do it for you, but make sure you go in with your eyes open.' Once you find a surgeon licking his chops because he wants to cut or a lawyer who can't wait to get your case into court, you need a new doctor or lawyer."

Nor is strident advocacy in either direction—for or against military intervention—the proper role of a chairman, says a high-ranking Pentagon official: "The chairman of the Joint Chiefs of Staff is not supposed to be decisive. He's supposed to be a consensus guy. You want him to move the system, not be argumentative and confrontational." Moving the system is almost a *leitmotif* with Powell.

Arguably, too, on October 4, 1990, the United States was in at best a poor position to be considering a military offensive to expel Iraq from Kuwait. The buildup in the Gulf then was still struggling toward the 230,000-troop level that planners deemed sufficient to deter Saddam from extending his aggression into Saudi Arabia. Ratcheting the U.S. force in the Gulf up to the half-million-plus level that the Pentagon felt was necessary to assure a swift victory over Iraq would require reserve units to be called up and transported overseas; ultimately it would mean shifting the "Big Red"—the Army's VII Corps—from the NATO front lines in Europe to the Gulf region; it would require the construction of a massive infrastructure in Saudi Arabia to supply the forces there with everything from food to fuel to mail and another massive infrastructure to get the troops there; it would stretch even more a federal budget perilously out of whack; and it would require a whole new level of cooperation with Saudi officials. And if Vietnam and the Panama invasion had taught Colin Powell one thing, it was to play to win. "I don't believe in doing war on the basis of macroeconomic, marginal-analysis models," Powell told *U.S. News & World Report*. "I'm more of the mindset of a New York street bully:

'Here's my bat, here's my gun, here's my knife. I'm wearing armor. I'm going to kick your ass.' ''

At an October 30 meeting in the White House, this time in the Situation Room, with the same principals he had met with on October 4, Powell made his recommendation after consultations in Riyadh with Schwarzkopf: an offensive against Iraq would mean bringing the VII Corps from Europe for their high-speed tanks; it would mean three more aircraft carriers; it would mean more than doubling the troops already in Saudi Arabia; and it would mean perhaps three more months to put the whole package in place. The additional man- and machine-power were themselves a form of acknowledgement of the potential difficulty of the war that more and more seemed to lie dead ahead, says Harlan Ullman. ''Powell's uncertainty was clearly addressed in his recommendation that if we go in, we go in with half a million troops and clean their clocks. That's Powell.''

In practical terms, Ullman says, Powell's recommendation provided a final test of the Bush administration's war resolve at the same time that it sealed the fate of Saddam Hussein's army. ''I think the reason we won the war was that sometime in October—don't forget, the election and the budget summit were preoccupying the White House—sometime in October there was a briefing, and the president wanted to know what it was going to take, and Powell said half a million troops. That was brilliant, and it was shrewd. It was going to shock George Bush into reality. If he wasn't dead certain, he wasn't going to go. That received very little credit at the time, but that was the strategic decision point of the war, and that was Powell. I'm sure there were a bunch of tight jaws when they heard that.''

And although Powell's presumed advocacy of containment in the early going in the Gulf would become one of Washington's bigger post war stories and lead him into difficulties both in the White House and with Congress, it was at the time one of the capital's most poorly kept secrets, according to CNN Pentagon correspondent Wolf Blitzer. ''We knew all along that the last people in Washington pushing for the war early on were the Pentagon,'' Blitzer says. ''They were the ones who were going to have to fight it. Only when they felt they had overwhelming military readiness in place, only then would they do it. At 250,000 troops, the Joint Chiefs didn't think it was enough. They wanted to go beyond anything that was reasonably necessary. I was surprised when it became such a big story.''

Powell knew, too, what the Bush war council generally seemed to have come near to forgetting in the months before the air raids commenced on Iraq and Iraqi positions in and around Kuwait—that overwhelming firepower is only part of the equation in waging war in the modern age. Further, as the only member of the inner circle to have spent ground time in Vietnam, Powell had more reason than any of the rest of them to know the necessity of bringing Congress and the people along for the ride, not only to assure that the president would be granted the power to make war but also to make certain that once the power was granted the prosecution of the war would be as free as possible of entangling politics. (Although he is a West Point graduate, National Security Adviser Brent Scowcroft saw no combat in Vietnam; in his early twenties when the Vietnam buildup began in earnest, Scowcroft had a draft deferment.) Among the Hill members Powell nurtured along was Rep. David McCurdy. A member of the important House Armed Services Committee and a captain in the Army Reserve, McCurdy was given a briefing in Saudi Arabia weeks before the air war began.

"When I was in Saudi Arabia in December, I saw the first forty-eight hours of targets, the targets themselves, which aircraft was going to which target," McCurdy says. "When I saw it was Baghdad, that it was intended to deal a blow to Saddam directly, I came away convinced it could be done. And I give Powell some credit for that. He understands the political process, the fact that you have to bring the public and Congress along with you. By even allowing me as a reservist to spend time there—which was a risk, a gamble—he came away with an advocate. I worked my colleagues on the Armed Services Committee and others. I said it was important we support this effort." On January 12, 1991, George Bush would win from Congress the authorization to wage war in the Gulf, by five votes in the Senate and sixty-seven in the House. At least while the war was underway, it would be largely free of serious second-guessing from Capitol Hill.

Powell's time as National Security Adviser, his experience

in dealing with foreign governments at top levels, even his brief tour as commander of the V Corps in Europe also appear to have played a role in the Allied success in the Gulf. To a significant degree, what was fought there was a U.S.-led NATO war, transported from the battlefields of central Europe to the desert sands and with the addition for diplomatic purposes more than military ones of a variety of Arab-speaking forces. It was a combination that required a deft touch to assemble and an even more deft touch to manage, says Harlan Ullman. "What you had was a brilliant yet simple assignment of forces. A lot of it was done to keep things simple—commonality with the British and Americans, no language problems. If you step back and review the assignment of forces, there's a political design that has to come from Powell. He's one of the very few people who have that simplicity as well as that feel for politics."

Powell's other political challenge in the Gulf War—human politics, not domestic ones or geopolitics—was the care and feeding of the Allied commander in Saudi Arabia. In his April 15, 1991, speech to students at his alma mater, Morris High School in the South Bronx, Powell said he was "flattered" when people talked about him as a role model. But, he went on, "there are lots of role models in this nation. One other role model who has become very famous in recent weeks is my good buddy Gen. Norman Schwarzkopf. Norm and I are the best of friends, and he is now looked up to around the country as a role model as well. The point I want to make to you is, role models can be black. Role models can be white. Role models can be generals. Role models can be principals, teachers, doctors, or just your parent who brought you into this world and who is trying to give you the best of everything . . . So as you dream about what you might want to be, don't think you have to be like a Colin Powell because he happens to be from the South Bronx like me, or he's black like me. Dream of being a Norm Schwarzkopf and commanding 500,000 men. Dream of being the president. Dream of being the governor."

It's an idealistic sentiment, and more proof of Powell's willingness to risk being what some may call corny in his public addresses. To some extent, it is also an accurate portrayal of the relation between Powell and Schwarzkopf, but only to some extent. The Gulf War also appears to have strained the "best of friends" to near-breaking point.

For all the glowing attention that would be paid to him as the Gulf War progressed and for all the authoritative bonhomie that he could project during desert press conferences, Schwarzkopf was not universally loved within the military community when the Iraqi forces began massing on the Kuwait border. One of ten U.S. commanders-in-chief under the Joint Command system, Schwarzkopf was in charge of the CENCOMM—or Central Command, responsible for the Middle East—but because no U.S. bases were welcome in Arab countries, Schwarzkopf operated out of MacDill Air Force Base near Tampa, Florida, and his command was generally considered a second-tier one. Still, Powell apparently had fought to save the post for him several years earlier when a movement began to give it to a Navy admiral, on the theory that the Navy had been doing the most work in the region. Whether Powell acted out of friendship or because he believed a ground war was the greater challenge in the Middle East or simply to preserve a command for his Army is anyone's guess. As a role model, though, the mercurial Schwarzkopf begins to be problematic. "I would suspect that one of the great chagrins of the war was that Schwarzkopf was the man sitting in that seat at the time the bell rang," Eugene Carroll says. "I don't think there were many people in the military who wanted to see him become the Lion of Saudi Arabia."

Schwarzkopf's tirades against Gen. Frederick Franks, head of the VII Corps, during the ground war have been documented by the staff of the *Army Times* in their "After-Action Review" series. His other tirades in the months leading up to the war—against his own staff and against the armchair generals in the Pentagon—are broadly hinted at. One retired officer tells of a conversation he had with someone who worked very close to Schwarzkopf in the desert: "Schwarzkopf would call him in and tonguelash him morning after morning, like he was trying to vent his frustrations." In his defense, Schwarzkopf was working under extraordinary pressures, both in terms of time and to build a vast, multinational fighting force, but he seems to have made the work as difficult as possible for those around, under, and over him.

In managing Schwarzkopf, Powell had two advantages that wouldn't have been available to him during the Vietnam War. One was telecommunications. Powell has banks of secure lines in both his office and second-story living quarters at Fort Myer that can connect him instantly with the president, Secretary of Defense, and all the joint commanders—including, during the Gulf War, Schwarzkopf's Riyadh redoubt. In addition to meeting face to face numerous times in Washington in the early days after the Kuwait invasion and in the desert as the hostilities drew near, Powell and Schwarzkopf talked at least once a day every day that Schwarzkopf was in Saudi Arabia.

"All in all, the war ran smoothly," says one Pentagon officer, "but keep in mind that we have communication capabilities we never had before. Stormin' Norman would pick up the phone and say, 'All right, Colin, Dick, this is what I intend to do,' and if Powell or Cheney heard any inflection in his voice, they could ask him about it."

(Alma Powell says that although her husband never discussed classified information with her, she was able to use the phone line to Riyadh as an early-warning system for breaking news: "Colin's master bank of telephones upstairs rings here as well as at the office," Mrs. Powell said in an interview with the author at her Fort Myer home. "It would start ringing furiously, and I'd look over, and if I saw that it was Norm Schwarzkopf calling, I immediately turned on CNN to see what was going on.")

In dealing with Schwarzkopf, Powell also had the advantage of the Goldwater-Nichols Act, which had invested his position with a level of real authority missing before 1986. "If you're the chairman and you've got the backing of the Secretary of Defense and the President, you can pretty much tell Schwarzkopf what to do," says Washington *Post* reporter and military historian George C. Wilson. "That again was one of the drives of the Goldwater-Nichols Act. In the old days before Goldwater-Nichols the Chairman of the Joint Chiefs was like the interlocutor in a minstrel show. He could 'left' and 'right' and 'left' as the chiefs of the services sang their songs. If they sang the same song he could tell the President what it was. If they sang different songs he had no corporate advice from the chiefs to give the President. Powell was empowered by Goldwater-Nichols to give his military opinion to the President, no matter if the chiefs agreed with it or not. That made the Chairman *the* military adviser to the President in fact, not just in theory." Former Defense Department official Lawrence Korb says: "I hate to think how we would have fought the Gulf War if we'd had the system that prevailed during Vietnam. [Gen. William] Westmoreland was in charge of running the ground war. You had an admiral in Hawaii running the naval war, and whenever they had a dispute they had to send it back to Washington for the Joint Chiefs of Staff to vote on."

Even beyond the powers granted him under Goldwater-Nichols, Powell seems to have an instinctive feel for the exercise of authority, for the fine pressure points and subtle signs that reinforce a hierarchical structure. Powell, says another Pentagon official, "was probably the best thing that ever happened to Schwarzkopf. Powell understands in his genes the power game, and he handled Schwarzkopf well. There was never a *moment* of doubt who was in charge. It was like the alpha wolf in a pack. He doesn't have to bite the other guy; he just has to look at him and he knows. If Schwarzkopf hadn't had Powell, he would have self-destructed."

Just as George Bush seems to have been determined not to micromanage the Gulf War—and Bush gets high marks for it—so Powell also seems to have been determined not to try to run it from the safe haven of the Pentagon. More than anything else, that may have been what Norman Schwarzkopf needed. "There were a couple of times during the war where Powell had had it up to his nose with Schwarzkopf," NBC's Fred Francis says, "and he had it out with him a couple of times on the phone. He tolerated—and that is the word—some of Schwarzkopf's arrogance because he firmly believed that the commander on the ground should run it."

And as Powell said of his reconfirmation hearing before Sam Nunn's committee, "All's well that ends well." But did the Gulf War end well? That really may be the $64,000 question, and it may well take years to answer.

"The only reason to go to war is to remove a government that's doing something you can't accept," says Adm. Thomas Moorer, chairman of the Joint Chiefs of Staff during the latter part of the Vietnam War. "When [Lyndon] Johnson said we're not going to overthrow Ho Chi Minh, I said, 'Oh, hell, what are we doing there?' '' The same logic, Moorer says, applies to the Persian Gulf War: "I wanted to get rid of Saddam. He was the problem, and he's still there." Indeed, although the United Nations mandate under which the Allied force was operating never called for the ouster of Saddam Hussein, his continued presence in Baghdad does remain the problem in any evaluation of the success of Operation Desert Storm.

The Gulf War presented the Bush administration with three interrelated public-relations problems. Chief among them was how to paint Saddam Hussein as sufficiently evil so that the American people would be willing to risk their sons' and daughters' lives doing battle against him. Saddam would make his own great contribution to that cause, but the overwhelming success of the effort and Saddam's subsequent survival as the Iraqi head of state left many with the impression that the war was, as the title of the *U.S. News & World Report* history of it says, a "triumph without victory."

Powell has maintained that though Saddam survives, he survives in such a diminished state that he is a threat only to his own people. "I don't know how much longer he's going to stay in power," he told CNN's Wolf Blitzer in a January, 1992, interview. "I think the world would be better off and, most important, the people of Iraq would be better off were he to leave power. He is not in as strong a position as some of these one-year retrospectives would have you believe. He no longer has an army that's capable of generating an offense that would threaten its neighbors. Although he is someone who is still pursuing a nuclear option, thank heavens Desert Storm came along last year to stop that nuclear option for now . . . He is an irritation as far as I'm concerned. He is not causing me a great deal of stress."

But that, says Ret. Col. David Hackworth, is not enough: "The point of the exercise was that, had you had a warrior general rather than a political general, he would have said to the president your objective doesn't make sense. You've got to whip the guy if you told the country he's an Adolf Hitler. What Colin Powell did was go along to get along." In a January 20, 1992, column for *Newsweek*, where he is a contributing editor, Hackworth went further: "As a military man, Gen. Colin Powell . . . should have insisted to President Bush that halfway measures don't work in war. Gen. George Marshall told President

Franklin D. Roosevelt at the outbreak of World War II that the goal had to be unconditional surrender and the destruction of enemy military capability. It's impossible to imagine him agreeing to stop the fight when the Nazis left France. George Bush's generals should have made the same demands. The president could then have told the United Nations that only the elimination of Saddam Hussein would justify Allied soldiers climbing out of their foxholes.''

The second public-relations problem was to paint the Kuwaiti sheiks who had lost their tightly controlled land as worthy of the risk of American lives. The challenge was considerably more difficult than representing Hussein as a Hitler. ''Public opinion was necessary,'' says author and Ret. Lt. Col. William Corson. ''Where the fuck is Kuwait? Is it down near the Chevron station or what? We had to make these nepotic assholes into freedom-loving democratic types. How do you do that? You don't have William Randolph Hearst around to demonize the dirty Spaniards. In this case we have to humanize the dirty Kuwaitis, so you go to [the public-relations firm of] Hill and Knowlton, and everybody gets a tear in their eye.'' (Hill and Knowlton was paid a reported $8 million to represent Kuwait in the months after the Iraqi invasion. Among the public-relation firm's senior executives who managed the Citizens for a Free Kuwait account was Craig Fuller, who had been chief-of-staff to George Bush when he was vice-president.)

The third public-relations problem, hinging the success of the other two and an inevitable lesson of the Vietnam experience, was to assure that whatever was undertaken in the Gulf be accomplished quickly, with as little loss of American lives as possible. ''We could sustain two thousand casualties on the battlefield,'' Corson says. ''Hell, two thousand casualties is nothing in military terms. But we couldn't sustain it here in the streets of the United States.'' Yet—and here is the double-bind of the public-relations strategy—going to Baghdad to satisfy the heightened lust for revenge against Saddam Hussein not only was opposed by the Arab members of the alliance but almost certainly would have extended the American casualty list to the limits of the tolerable or beyond. Saddam had not committed all of his army to the Kuwaiti theater of operations. Nor, as Manuel Noriega had demonstrated in Panama, is it always easy to find a head of state, even one with total military control. Just as significant, removing the head of state in a nation torn by ethnic strife—Saddam's more moderate Sunnis, the pro-Iranian Shiites, and the long-suppressed Kurds—is only the beginning of the geopolitical problem. And Colin Powell understands geopolitics.

"It is clear to me that if we had gone all the way [to Baghdad] we would have had a quite different set of problems," says Ret. Adm. Elmo Zumwalt. "We would have been rid of Saddam, but we would have had the Shiite problem, and that would have upset our allies, the Saudis. We would have had the Kurd problem, and that would have upset our allies, the Turks. Not to mention the most important thing of all—that we would have lost two to three thousand more American boys in the fighting." The carping about the outcome of the war, Zumwalt says, "is to be expected in a presidential election time. If we had gone all the way, they would be attacking Powell for that—for breaking up the alliance and so forth."

Ironically perhaps, given the emphasis on keeping Allied casualties to a minimum, it was the mounting death toll on the enemy side—and particularly the ghastly images of the so-called Highway of Death running north out of Kuwait City—that seems to have been the clincher in bringing the war to a sudden end. For that decision, Powell seems to bear the major responsibility. It was after viewing such images, *Newsweek* reported in its January 20, 1992, retrospective on the war, that Powell argued in an Oval Office meeting against pressing the attack further. According to *Newsweek*'s account, Powell said that doing so "would be un-American and unchivalrous." "The way Colin presented it, to have pursued the campaign beyond where we did would have been just a massacre," an administration aide recalled—and another official, among those present in the Oval Office that day, says there was no real disagreement with Powell's conclusion. The next day Bush took Powell's advice and announced the cease-fire. Although he had planned a 144-hour ground war and although he later told interviewer David Frost that his recommendation had been to "continue the march," Norman Schwarzkopf seems at least to have agreed that the carnage was getting out of hand. Questioned by Sen. John Warner at a postwar hearing of the Armed Services Committee, Schwarzkopf answered: "I would tell you, Senator, quite frankly that some of my subordinate commanders have told me that they're thankful that the war was stopped when it did because we were really at a point where we were really wreaking great destruction on the enemy, and we were taking a lot of lives that didn't necessarily have to be taken.''

Did Colin Powell in any way help let Saddam Hussein survive? In a sense, perhaps. His strategy seems to have been a combination of hope and see—hope that Saddam was killed in the aerial pounding of Baghdad, some of it directed at his known command installations, then see if the Iraqis would rise up themselves and do the job. But as Schwarzkopf testified before the Senate Armed Services Committee, ''The legitimacy for our being over there was the United Nations resolutions, and none of those United Nations resolutions called for us to invade Iraq. We could have invaded Iraq easily. We could have taken the whole country . . . [but] that was not our charter. That's not what we were asked to do. That was not our military mission. Our military mission was to kick Iraq out of Kuwait, and that's exactly what we did.''

Did Powell influence George Bush to call a cease-fire too soon? The *Newsweek* retrospective on the Gulf War argues that Powell, perhaps armed with questionable information, assumed that Allied forces were in place northwest of Basra to strip Iraqi soldiers of their weapons and equipment as they marched back to Baghdad in defeat. At a critical juncture in history's most high-tech war, communications somehow appear to have broken down.

Was Powell made overly squeamish by the photos coming from the Highway of Death? ''That did repulse him,'' David Hackworth says, ''and then he made a political decision: 'My God, we're going to be called an army of murderers.' Well, war is a bloody thing. As Sherman said, war is hell.''

But one highly placed official who knows Colin Powell well suggests that his decisions in the closing days of the Gulf War ought to be placed in the context of an obscure little book entitled *Every War Must End*, first published in 1972 by the Columbia University Press. The author is Fred Iklé, with whom Powell worked in the Weinberger Defense Department, and according to this source, Powell had several chapters of the book photocopied and sent to a number of generals before the offensive against Iraq began. "In part, governments tend to lose sight of the ending of wars and the nation's interests that lie beyond it, precisely because fighting a war is an effort of such vast magnitude," Iklé writes near the beginning of his book. "Thus it can happen that military men, while skillfully planning their intricate operations and coordinating complicated maneuvers, remain curiously blind in failing to perceive that it is the outcome of the war, not the outcome of the campaigns within it, that determines how well their plans serve the nation's interests. At the same time, the senior statesmen may hesitate to insist that these beautifully planned campaigns be linked to some clear ideas for ending the war, while expending their authority and energy to oversee some tactical details of the fighting. If generals act like constables and senior statesmen act like adjutants, who will be left to guard the nation's interests?"

Colin Powell is a rare combination—a soldier with a diplomat's touch and the training of a White House insider. If that makes him less a warrior-general than a political, or more appropriately, a geopolitical one; if it causes him to look at the interplay of nations as much as he looks at the clashing of armies; if it makes him acutely mindful of the need not to let a war get too far in front of the public's tolerance for the carnage of war, the nation ultimately may be the better served because of it. The limits of military power in achieving lasting peace have been well documented, particularly in the swamp of competing interests that is the Middle East.

"There's criticism everywhere in this town, and people always like to do the Monday-morning quarterbacking," Powell told "Good Morning, America's" Charles Gibson in January of 1992, "but at the time there was no question in my mind that the president was making the right decision [in calling a ceasefire when he did]. I gave him that recommendation; it was the recommendation of all his commanders and advisers. One year later, reflecting back, I have no reason to think that recommendation was incorrect. We had achieved our military mission. We had achieved the political objective we had been assigned, and it was time to stop the killing, and I have no second thoughts about that . . . It was not our intention to totally decimate the entire Iraqi army; it was not our intention to go to Baghdad; and had we done that we would have gotten ourselves into the biggest quagmire you can imagine, trying to sort out two thousand years of Mesopotamian history.''

John Kester's comment on Powell bears repeating: ''[Colin] is not a Hamlet.'' Brooding introspection and second-guessing himself are not his style.

CHAPTER 16

Holding On for a Hero

Barring the unforeseen—a military return to Iraq, some new flash point on the globe—the remaining work for Colin Powell during his second term as chairman of the Joint Chiefs of Staff does not seem the stuff of hero-making. Powell came to prominence as National Security Adviser when there was still another superpower intact and at the tail-end of the massive peacetime military buildup that began with Jimmy Carter and accelerated throughout the early and middle years of the Reagan administration. He leaves the chairmanship of the Joint Chiefs of Staff at midnight on September 30, 1993, as the highest-ranking military officer of the only remaining superpower. Until then, his work stands to be largely downsizing the vast military machine he helped to create—to shrink the armed forces without hollowing them and to do so in the absence of the one global fact that has driven U.S. defense policy and sustained military budgeting for nearly half a century: the 800-pound bear of the former Soviet Union. It is no small trick Powell or the service chiefs face. To their benefit and their credit, though, they have had a running start at the problem.

A restructured military began to be talked about seriously in late 1988, according to former Army Chief of Staff Carl Vuono. The following year, Vuono says, the outline of what would come to be known as the "Base Force" concept began to take shape. Indeed, one of the minor ironies of the Gulf War is that on August 2, 1990, Powell and Dick Cheney were to give their first closed-door briefing to selected members of Congress on the new lean military. The meeting took place as scheduled, but restructuring never came up—August 2 was the day Iraq invaded Kuwait; for the next half year, big would again be beautiful. From the first, too, the restructuring plan seems to have recognized that although the Soviet Union might endure, its days as an adventuresome global military power were numbered. For that, says one Pentagon planner who has worked on the restructuring, Powell and his predecessor as chairman, Adm. William Crowe, deserve credit—if not for pure prescience then at least for listening to unpopular news. Both seem to have been willing to contemplate a New World Order well before it was ever called that, back when the Pentagon and the military-industrial-political complex still were heavily invested in superpower status quo. "He and Crowe both deal very well with bad news," this planner says, "and they were both making some tough decisions when it wasn't popular. A few of us were running here saying, 'The Russians *aren't* coming! The Russians *aren't* coming!' There were people all around Washington who wouldn't deal with it—it was just suicide to do so. But Powell was dealing with it in secret. He was dealing with reality when the others were not."

Still, the new order Powell does envision and the Base Force he says is necessary to deal with it both pay a form of homage to the old order in refusing to ignore the remnants of the Soviet Union and in refusing to back away from the need for overwhelming U.S. military superiority. In a March, 1992, appearance on "The MacNeil/Lehrer Newshour," Powell laid out his Base Force. Inherent in it is his view of the post-dual-superpower world—a world in serious respects almost as threatening as the one it replaces.

"First of all, we have to have an adequate level of strategic nuclear power, offensive power, to deter the Soviet Union, Russia, the Ukraine—whatever you wish to characterize it as these days," Powell told co-anchor Jim Lehrer. "They still have twenty-seven thousand nuclear weapons in that land of eleven time zones. Until we have negotiated them all out of existence and until they have actually been destroyed, I will never allow the strategic nuclear forces of the United States to ever be second best to any nation that has similar weapons which can destroy our way of life in thirty minutes. That's a given.

"Second, we have made a judgment that in the foreseeable future it would be wise and prudent for us to remain forward deployed with some forces in Europe, in the Pacific, [and] in southwest Asia . . . We've also made the judgment that it would be very wise for the United States to have the capability—the air, land, and sea capability—to perform another Desert Shield/Storm-type operation in that part of the world, not against an Iraq but just against a potential threat that might emerge from that part of the world. We've also made a judgment that we should have the capability to deal with another crisis in the Pacific, in northeast Asia. One of the most destabilizing things we could do is to cut our forces so much that if we're tied up in one area of the world such as southwest Asia and we are not seen to have the ability to influence another area of the world, we might invite just the sort of crisis we are trying to deter." Add it all up, Powell said, and it comes out to the Base Force—"about one million people less than we have now, going down to a significantly reduced portion of the federal budget and with a significant reduction in the claim we are making on our gross national product."

Asked by Lehrer if that doesn't mean the United States will still have by far the most powerful military force in the world, Powell answered: "I think that's just fine. I think it is very, very useful for world peace and in order to steer ourselves into the future we're all hoping for, for the United States to be seen as a very powerful nation—politically powerful because of our value system, economically powerful, and, yes, militarily powerful. I don't think we should apologize for that. And people are not afraid of that military power. In fact, our western allies in Europe want us to stay in Europe with part of that power. Our new friends in Central and Eastern Europe are looking toward that power. Why? Because it's power that can be trusted. It's power that does not seek to seize anyone's sovereignty or to take land from anyone. It's power that rests on democratic values and will not be misused."

That, in a nutshell, *is* the world according to Colin Powell: trust us to do the right thing, give us the military power to do it with, and the world will beat a path to our door. As Powell says in his standard stump speech for the Base Force concept, "We've heard it again and again: America cannot be the world's policeman. Yet . . . when there's trouble, when somebody needs a cop, who gets called to restore peace? We do.''

On paper, in concept, the Base Force has the elegance of simplicity—a finely honed fighting force overseen by a new, slimmed-down unified command, and all for less money; in effect, addition by subtraction. In the real-world give-and-take of Congress, where the budget pressures for a domestic "peace dividend" are immense and where constituent-driven decisions often outrank any larger considerations, holding the restructuring plan together will be a harder task, perhaps most especially on the subtraction side. Every senator and representative is for base closings until the proposed base is in his or her district; all of them are for trimming the reserve force until the first fifty phone calls come in from back-home voters who will be losing a supplemental paycheck. That is politics. And as Chicago *Tribune* defense correspondent David Evans notes, even under the Base Force plan "we're still carrying eight lanes of programs on a budget carrying four lanes of money.'' When the base line for cutting involves the $250- to $300-billion budgets allocated to defense for nearly a decade, less expensive is still very expensive. Buying into the armed force that Powell foresees for the mid-1990s and beyond almost demands accepting his vision of the need for substantive superiority over a vaguely defined enemy. Yet Powell does seem determined to make the Base Force plan his legacy to the military; he is not a man easily dissuaded or discouraged, and as he has proven time and again, he does know politics in a way that to some can appear almost unseemly for a soldier. Nor should his built-in clout on Capitol Hill be underestimated, says veteran defense correspondent Charles Corrdry. "I don't know if it's true on the Senate side, but in the House Armed Services Committee they really try to separate Powell from Cheney and try to call it the Cheney force, the Cheney budget. They tell me quite frankly they don't want to take on Powell, and I believe it. He comes pretty close to being—invulnerable is a pretty strong word, but I don't know any way to get at him.''

Perhaps the tougher part of shrinking the armed forces—tougher psychologically if not strategically for Powell—is the human side of the equation. "He's got to figure out how to bring the force down without breaking it,'' says a Pentagon official. "I mention that for a reason—because he's a good guy and he understands the personal pain of letting go some of the best men and women we've ever had in the service, of sending them home and saying we don't need you anymore. That's not easy to do without breaking all kinds of systems."

Of necessity, a smaller military means fewer troops, and if Powell is inordinately proud of any one thing—if he is guilty of the tragic flaw of *hubris* on any front—it is the pride he takes in America's troops and in the military's role in shaping their future lives. "We provide one heck of a social service to this country," he told *Washingtonian* magazine in 1990. "We will be taking in a couple of hundred thousand a year—I don't have the exact number in mind—[but] usually the principal reason for coming in is they hope to better themselves, hope to get some education, or hope to put money aside and get the benefits of GI plans to allow them to go to college. They might not otherwise be able to afford to go to college. Two, three, or four years later we turn out and discharge back into American society most of them. They tend to be much more responsible. They have a better sense of order in their lives, a better sense of self-discipline, self-appreciation, knowing who they are. They tend in very large percentages to be very, very fine citizens once they go back into civilian life."

The measure of the military's success—and the measure perhaps of the lack of opportunity elsewhere in American society— is that "nobody's waiting to get out. There are no conscripts to be discharged," Powell said. "The story I like to tell is at the end of World War II, Congress was receiving 80,000 letters a week saying, 'Send my son home now.' We aren't getting any letters for anybody to come home. Congress is getting letters saying, 'Am I going to lose my job? What about my career you guys promised me?' So the greatest danger we have and my greatest concern as a manager as opposed to a strategist is allowing us to bring the armed forces down at a manageable rate so that you don't take this very, very high-quality, professional, proud force of some two million active and another million reserves, all of whom have signed contracts and volunteered for this, and suddenly start to do terrible things to that force and break their spirit, break their pride, and break all those contracts. That's my concern."

And, of course, to an extent Colin Powell is also talking about himself. Where Powell would be today without the Army is an imponderable. He says that he might not have stayed in college had it not been for the ROTC. He acknowledges that the Army gave his life a sense of order, and he probably couldn't have landed in an organization more ready to put black Americans on the fast track toward the top, an organization more inclined in his favor. But Powell made his own luck; he had the attributes. As retired Col. Ben Willis says, Powell would have made it to the top "if he was purple." It is no reflection on Powell that he walked into the Army in a crease in time when all the auguries were pointed in his favor. Now to be involved in partially closing that door must work a personal pain on him; to do so with a force that is twice as black as American society generally can only make the pain more personal. Powell never forgets his roots. Nor, one suspects, can he avoid involving his own sense of honor in the battle to preserve as large a fighting force as possible. As Gen. Benjamin Davis, the first black graduate of West Point in this century, says, "There's an element of break- ing the faith—the recruiting promises made many years ago. For a lot of people they will not come to fruition; they will be reneged upon." Even if it is unavoidable, breaking faith with the armed forces, and especially with black fighting men and women, must be very near to Powell's own vision of Hell.

Where will Colin Powell be after September 30, 1993? There is, in fact, no statutory requirement for Powell to leave the chair- manship after two terms. The Goldwater-Nichols Act allows chairmen of the Joint Chiefs of Staff to serve up to six years, or eight years if the president deems it in the national interest, or for an indefinite period in time of war. In theory, too, there is one last military job Powell could take without diminishing his reputation—Supreme Commander of NATO. Gen. Lyman Lemnitzer followed that route in 1962 after John Kennedy nudged him out of the chairmanship in favor of Maxwell Taylor. In a way, it is a job almost ideally suited for Powell—a combi- nation of military expertise and international diplomacy. Two terms, though, has been the custom for chairmen, and with the collapse of the Soviet Union, NATO is a less glamorous posting. Powell, too, makes it clear that October 1, 1993, is the end of the line for his military career; almost certainly, it will be for him a deeply wrenching moment.

"There have been opportunities over the last several years

since I was National Security Adviser to leave the Army and go out and undertake a speaking career or go into private business," Powell told C-Span's Brian Lamb. "There were other opportunities as well, making a lot more money than I am now. And every time I have faced up to this choice, I just find the satisfaction of being a soldier and the love of my profession overwhelming and more important to me than making a great deal of money or doing something I may not like as much as being a soldier . . . I also knew that one day I would have to retire, probably at the end of this term—I'm quite sure at the end of this two-year term—and I can turn my attention to private matters. But I've never in the past thirty-four years found any other line of work, profession, or any other livelihood that appealed to me more than being a soldier."

Powell's consolation, if he needs one, is that "the world will be his oyster," says Ron Walker of the executive-recruiting firm of Korn/Ferry International and a friend of Powell. "He's got any number of options. First and foremost, he will be very sought after as a speaker, very sought after as a potential outside director for any number of Fortune 100 companies. I can't imagine he doesn't have one or more books in him, and I think he could also move out and run a Fortune 100 company. There may be a caveat in that, because his entire career had been in the military, there would be some concern about whether he understands how the private sector works, profit-and-loss sheets, that kind of thing, but that can be mastered in a hurry . . . It's my understanding that General Schwarzkopf is getting between $50,000 and $75,000 a speech, but I think that has a lot to do with timing—he got in at a high point. It's hard to say what Colin would make, but I think it would be in that range." As for board-of-directors slots, Walker says, "The pay range is anywhere between $25,000 and $50,000, but there are an awful lot of add-ons. You're on various committees and you get additional fees for that. You get stock options, meeting-day fees, and it ranges across the board."

Historically, says one corporate executive who served high up in the Reagan administration, high-ranking military people have done very well upon retirement as professional corporate directors. "They don't know beans about finance, but they do know ethics, they have the ability to size people up and make rational decisions, and they do have judgment." For Powell, all that seems to go double, and, this executive says, Powell brings one added factor to the mix that makes him almost irresistible: "From the point of view of the private world, I suspect he's a two-fer. Not only is he good on his own, he's a minority. They get quality, and they get a minority director."

There is also the distinct possibility that Powell will remain on in some other line of government service. He has the background to be a secretary of defense or of state, and remember that George Bush had once offered him the directorship of the CIA. Becoming head of the Federal Bureau of Investigation also seems well within reach, should Powell want it. Like Dwight Eisenhower after World War II, Powell could become president or chancellor of a major university (in Eisenhower's case it was Columbia University), or perhaps head of one of the nation's leading foundations. He has "drawing power." Like Alexander Haig, he could set up shop as an international consultant in his own right; his Rolodex is diamond-studded. Powell has dined with prime ministers and kings; he is an old hand at global summitry. Powell's friend and mentor Frank Carlucci undoubtedly would be overjoyed to have him bring his sterling reputation and long list of impeccable contacts to the Carlyle Group, the international investment house where Carlucci toils lucratively as vice-chairman. It would seem the world is Colin Powell's oyster.

And then there is politics, elective politics. It is a question frequently asked of Powell, yet divining his intention on this front, if he has formed one, would take a team of CIA cryptologists on a very lucky roll.

Asked in July, 1990, by Sam Donaldson on ABC's "Prime Time Live" if he would like to be "the first black on a national ticket," Powell answered, "I have no political ambitions at the moment, Mr. Donaldson. I just want to be the best chairman I can be." A year and a half later, on NBC's "Today" show, Katie Couric chewed the same bone: "Is it safe to say now, having heard some of your past interviews, you have no political aspirations, period, end of discussion?" Powell's answer was of the sort that doesn't let hope die easily for those who would like to see a President or a Vice-President Powell: "I have no political aspirations at the moment," Powell said. ". . . I don't know that it's required of me to say what I might do when I'm seventy-five years old.'' A few days before the "Today" segment, CBS's "60 Minutes" showed a Vancouver, Washington, high-school student asking Powell, "Do you have any plans to participate in presidential politics in 1996?" "I plan to vote, yeah," Powell answered with a laugh. "Do you have any thoughts of being a national candidate in 1996," the student persisted. "No," Powell answered, "I don't anticipate that will be the case. . . . I'm a soldier. I know who I am." Even that statement holds out hope for his followers. Life is full of the unanticipated.

Perhaps the most complete answer Powell has ever ventured to the elective-politics question came in the interview with Brian Lamb that first aired on C-Span in April of 1992. "As long as I am in the uniform of the armed forces of the United States, I always am uncomfortable with any suggestions of political life or political career," Powell said. "It's anathema to a soldier to allow his career or his image to be pushed in a political direction, and so my response has been, honestly, I enjoy being a soldier and chairman of the Joint Chiefs of Staff. I have no political ambitions. I have no political fire burning in my stomach. I want to finish this tour as chairman, then enter private life and find a way to make a living for my family as well as to find something I can enjoy and be good at. And I have seen no indication that politics would be the correct route for me . . . I think people have been generally pleased by the way the military has performed during recent crises, and so they think that is instantly transferable, that performance is instantly transferable into a civilian political environment. I'm not sure it really is." And then, as Powell so often seems to do when confronted with the question, he threw in one last kicker that appeared to leave the door at least slightly ajar: "I very much hope that after I leave the military I will have something that will permit me to support my family, but I'd also like to have the opportunity to serve this nation in other ways . . . I think my life would be incomplete if I was not serving the nation and our society in some way. Everybody wants to talk about politics, but I believe there are other ways to serve the nation than embarking on a political career."

Perhaps. But Gordon Kaiser, a retired Marine colonel and author and director of operations for the Naval Institute, recalls a story about Army generals Douglas MacArthur and Dwight

Eisenhower. "They knew each other well," Kaiser says. "Ike had been MacArthur's aide, his military secretary, when he was in the Philippines. Eisenhower still hadn't gotten out of the Army yet, and one time when MacArthur had come back to visit him, he said, 'What is it, Ike, I hear about this business of your running for President?' Ike answered, 'Oh, General, I'm completely nonplussed. I have no idea what any of this is about.' MacArthur looked over his glasses and said, 'That's the way to play it, Ike.' ''

The "Black Eisenhower" tag, indeed, has been much hung around Colin Powell's neck, with all that implies about life after the military. Leave aside the fact that it is historically inaccurate. Powell wasn't the field commander in the Persian Gulf War; he is, if anything, much closer to the "Black George C. Marshall," the soldier-statesman who helped run World War II from Washington. And, of course, Operation Desert Storm was, in the final analysis, no more than a hundred-hour ground war preceded by an aerial pounding of what proved a relatively undefended nation of some nineteen million. As the Washington *Post*'s George C. Wilson says, "You can make almost anything work for one hundred hours. It was a magnificent deployment operation, but Desert Storm was a one-of-a-kind war. We had the best airfields in the world—those in Saudi Arabia—to use as launching pads and repair centers for our aircraft. Allied nations provided about half the shipping to get our stuff from here to there. Iraq did not oppose our massive buildup and gave us five months to complete it. Hussein's army, when the ground war started, chose not to fight. It had lost its cohesiveness. Its leaders had taken off. Saddam had been rendered virtually deaf, dumb and blind by our air power before the ground war started. When the ground war did start, leaderless Iraqi privates and corporals said what the hell and gave up, usually without firing a shot. The American Army and Marine Corps, which fought the ground war, were tested and showed they could move fast and effectively, but they were not stressed." World War II, it was not; nor, surely, was it the equivalent in duration, human cost or historical significance of the American Civil War, another conflict that a general (Ulysses Grant) rode into the White House.

Still, there are parallels with Dwight Eisenhower not to be

ignored. Like Eisenhower, Powell has been proposed for national office on both tickets. Early in 1992 liberal white columnist Martin Schram suggested Bill Clinton make Powell his running mate; a year earlier black conservative columnist Clarence Page had suggested George Bush make Powell *his* running mate. Asked by the author if he had any reason to believe Powell was, in fact, a Republican, Page answered, "None whatsoever. A lot of folks thought Eisenhower was a Democrat, and we could fall into the same thing now. There's probably good reason to believe Powell's sensitivities might lie toward the Democratic party. I think he could go either way." Politically, at least if and until he declares himself, Powell is a man for all seasons; so was Ike. Like Eisenhower, Powell also seems to hold out the promise of restoring dignity to electoral politics. He has shown little capacity for the low blow or the dissembling that so often seems to be at the heart of campaigning. Like Eisenhower, too, Powell is almost bulletproof. That last quality, more than anything else perhaps, Powell would put at risk by entering elective politics, but if he has as he says no "fire in his stomach," he does have raw guts, fortitude.

"It's hard to think of a figure who has been involved in more controversial matters and been criticized less, and a figure in a Republican administration who has been criticized less by Democrats," says Elliott Abrams. "I attribute that to his very winning personality and, in part, to race. Democrats seek to avoid criticizing such a prominent black unless he is a conservative. And I want to add another factor to that: I think partly it's the hope that he will turn out to be a Democrat. I think if Powell would announce now that he's a Republican and will be running for the Senate in this state or that or for the presidency, the Democrats would start shooting at him."

Inevitably, too, there is the issue of whether America's voters are ready to elect a black man or woman, *any* black man or woman, to the presidency. Tony Brown, the conservative black host of PBS's "Tony Brown's Journal," says they are not. "As long as Powell is the chairman of the Joint Chiefs of Staff, he's working for the Secretary of Defense and the president. Then he can be as military as he wants. But if he was in the Oval Office with the Black Box, I think a lot of people wouldn't be able to handle it psychologically because he's black. In a fair world, General Powell could easily become president. He could do that if we didn't have this little problem of racism, but racism is here, and even a Colin Powell is its victim.''

Nor, were Powell to enter politics, could he avoid committing himself on the bitterly divisive issues of the day. Part of Powell's seeming invulnerability to criticism has come about ''because he is not engaged in much risk,'' says Jesse Jackson. ''On a day-to-day basis, he isn't covered much in the press. When he surfaces, he's testifying about budget appropriations. There's nothing controversial about that. Or he's leading the military in the most popular war we ever fought.''

Frank Carlucci, Powell's longtime mentor, says that politics ''is not [Colin's] cup of tea. He's used to a different world, a fairly crisp world where you don't have to compromise. I asked him once what he thought about abortion. He didn't have any particular stand on it because he hadn't been required to take one.'' But, Carlucci adds, ''he's a very attractive person; he's articulate and has good presence. He's got all the outward tickets, and God knows, I guess people are desperate for quality candidates these days. They should be.''

And that is, perhaps, a large part of the point. America is a nation starved for heroes of substance. Especially in the political arena, Americans are starved for people they can hold up to their children. In explaining why Powell attracts so little criticism, Lawrence Korb, who worked with him in the Weinberger Defense Department, says, ''He's a decent, honest, open person. People give you the benefit of the doubt if you're decent and honest and open. The other thing is that he's a role model, and, heaven knows, we have so few role models, we don't want to knock down the ones we have.''

For Colin Powell to make the transition to elective politics would involve extraordinary practical difficulties. He has no in-place political machine; he's never won an election at any level; as of fall, 1993, when he presumably gives up the chairmanship, he drops off the national radar screen; and particularly on the national level the old boss-system is defunct in both parties. Nominations aren't given, they are earned, and primaries are grinding work with an intense focus on the sorts of issues that Powell has been mostly mute on. Also, the political landscape is littered with generals who would have liked to be president—Alexander Haig being perhaps the most notable modern example. However, John McCain, a Vietnam War hero who became a senator, says that Powell is not cut of the usual mold of generals. ''The thing that he has acquired through his work in the Pentagon and especially in the National Security Council is how to deal with people. In the military you grow up with generally a single sort of philosophy, a same view of the world and the issues, which are usually defined in national-security terms. But I think Colin's experience has qualified him enormously [for elective politics].'' And McCain is not alone in his evaluation.

Former Assistant Secretary of State Elliott Abrams says that Powell will be, if he chooses, ''a great pol. Natural political ability is hard to define, but he has it. He is quite articulate. He can make people feel at ease with him. He is more natural in public than almost any official I've come across. He has the ability to talk to people in a way that indicates self-respect and respect for them, the ability to project competence. His briefings on the U.S.-Iraq war, particularly the early ones, I would say are among the two or three best briefings I have ever seen any official give on any subject ever. They were unbelievable. I think you can easily foresee him as a contender for the vice-presidency in either party in 1996, and you can easily foresee him going someplace and running immediately for the Senate—Virginia [where the Powells have lived most of the time since 1969], for example, or New York [still Powell's official residence].'' For the record, Abrams, a conservative Republican, says that, ''My guess is Powell's a Democrat. The decision to be a Republican is one taken by black leaders like Clarence Thomas only after a very lengthy evolution of their views towards a conservative, free-market view on domestic policy. Those issues haven't preoccupied Powell, and there is no evidence he has moved toward that view on domestic policies. On foreign policy, I'd say he's a Clinton-Gore type of Democrat.'' But, says Democratic Rep. David McCurdy, in a sense the ambiguity of Powell's political affiliation is one of his greatest assets: ''Part of what is his strength is that he's not identified as either a Democrat or a Republican. He's an American and a patriot . . . He could have it on either side—at least the number-two spot [on a national ticket] probably.'' Unlike many generals and admirals, Powell also understands the press. "He works the press very hard," says Kenneth Adelman. "He kids with reporters, jokes with them, calls them up. He has no great allergy to the press, which is exceedingly unusual for the military." The press doesn't win elections for candidates, but a press favorably disposed to a candidate is a great comfort on the campaign trail.

Ben Willis, who served as Powell's executive officer in Korea, says of Powell's future plans, "I've given this a little thought—what I'd do if I were he. He doesn't have a great deal of money. He's put three kids through college on Army pay, and he's just totally honest. He couldn't have very much money because he's not a crook, and you just can't amass any kind of personal wealth in the Army. My guess is he'll probably retire and sit on some boards and build up an estate. In his situation, in two or three years he can build up a reasonable stake for his family. Then after that he might start getting into politics."

That would be roughly 1996, and as Alma Powell says, she would just as soon stay in Washington, even in civilian quarters. "My husband always says he doesn't care where he lives," Mrs. Powell says. "But Washington is nice, and I'm too old to start going and looking for the shopping centers and dry-cleaners and dentists and all those things you have to look for when you move. I don't want to do that, so, hopefully, I will not have to."

It's a thin thread to hang a prediction on. There are a lot of things to do in Washington other than run for and serve in elected office. Mrs. Powell also says that as the wife of the Chairman of the Joint Chiefs of Staff "You essentially become a public person and belong to everyone whom you meet." Being the wife of a president or vice-president would make her belong to everyone still more, and there is no indication that she, any more than her husband, has a desire for that. Indeed, there may be some counterindication. NBC Pentagon correspondent Fred Francis says that Colin Powell has "almost no political ambitions. I think that would be different if Alma were interested, but she's not. She's just flat not interested, and he feels he owes her an awful lot." But Francis adds, " 'almost' is a qualifier; things may change." Another soldier who served with Powell and has known him well for many years says: "Left to his own devices, he and his family would prefer to do something less in the public eye and give themselves a little more time with each other. [But] if someone were to show him where his participation in the political process could really do something for the country, I think he could probably be persuaded to run."

Appearing on ABC's "Prime Time Live" segment on Powell in July, 1990, Rep. Les Aspin, the chairman of the House Armed Services Committee, said, "The black who will make it on a national level as a vice-presidential candidate or as a more serious candidate for the president will be somebody who comes out of law enforcement—either the military, FBI, something like that. That is the black candidate that's going to make the big breakthrough." For the moment and for the foreseeable future, Colin Powell dominates that horizon. Indeed, he *is* that horizon. Perhaps the largest question of all—and it's only speculation—is how much Powell sees himself involved in and at the service of history. Like any black who has risen to the top of American society, Powell finds himself defined willy-nilly in terms of "firsts": first black National Security Adviser, first black chairman of the Joint Chiefs of Staff. There is perhaps one last "first" tantalizingly within his reach. Even if he doesn't want it, Powell may feel compelled to pursue it, not for himself and perhaps least of all to fulfill personal ambition but simply because it is there and history seems to have defined him as the person most apt in his generation to achieve it. Powell is a dynamic man; he has spent more than half a decade near the national pulse beat; and fifty-six years old, the age he will be when he leaves the military, seems too young for him to settle back into the relatively dull twilight of amassing an estate.

"I don't know what the future holds" for Powell, his friend Harlan Ullman says, "but I would tend to be of the school that the future holds something far, far greater."

Whether or not Colin Powell enters national politics, whether he ascends to the presidency or the vice-presidency, becomes a senator or a university head, or simply amasses an estate and settles into the trappings of wealth, he already has served history. Arguably Powell has helped to perform a kind of double exorcism—of modern American history, particularly of the Vietnam War, and of the totality of American history.

Colin Powell did not win the Persian Gulf War, nor has he ever claimed to have done so. He wasn't on the ground when Operation Desert Storm began; he never fired a shot or led a tank charge across the Iraqi desert. Certainly Iraq was, in baseball parlance, a Triple-A opponent at best. Perhaps the very ease with which the war was won sends its own dangerous lesson—in George C. Wilson's words, "that war is relatively painless. It never has been and never will be. . . . The national interest should be compelling before we ask teenagers to die to do what the diplomats could not do." Perhaps, too, the war wasn't even won. "In all the post audits I've seen and read on Desert Storm," Wilson says, "this question has never been raised: 'If the American Army during World War II had kicked Hitler out of Czechoslovakia but Hitler remained in Berlin as a threat to his neighbors—as Hussein, whom Bush called Hitler, has remained in Baghdad—would Eisenhower and Marshall have run victory parades like Schwarzkopf and Powell did?' Of course not." But the adulation that fell upon Powell and Norman Schwarzkopf as the two most visible manifestations of the American military during the war was beyond any doubt real and deeply felt. Embedded in it was the recognition that an armed force which more than two decades earlier had been sent to fight a war for which there was no valid plan for victory—an army that had been mustered with terrible, almost criminal inequities in the draft system; that had returned from Southeast Asia to the scorn of its countrymen and had been nearly broken in the aftermath—was the same armed force no more. Like the U.S. troops who fought in Vietnam, the Desert Storm troops were disproportionately black, disproportionately from the bottom of the economic ladder, but even if economics drove many of them into the military, every man and woman who fought in the desert had joined up of his or her own volition. As happened in Vietnam, there were too many American deaths in the Gulf from "friendly fire"—war is hell, wherever it is waged—but it was an army that did its job quickly and well and stopped short of wreaking total mayhem on the enemy, an army informed, so it seems, by moral imperatives as well as by geopolitical ones. All that is in large part the work of Powell, Schwarzkopf, and their whole generation of officers who stayed in the military after Vietnam and worked to fix it. "I think we were always reasonably confident about ourselves," Powell told "Today's" Katie Couric, "but we've been subjected to a lot of abuse. Our weapons wouldn't work; our generals perhaps weren't up to standards; we didn't do anything right; the toilet seats cost too much . . . It felt good for a change to demonstrate to the world that the United States is blessed with a very, very competent armed force."

Intuitively, one suspects, the crowds who cheered the returning Desert Storm veterans knew that and were sharing in Powell's joy. The military remains a central element in American society and in the nation's image of itself. Intuitively, too, one suspects that many of those cheering the Desert Storm troops realized they were serving another, larger purpose. "In a way I think all the celebrating after the Gulf War came from the national consciousness of how badly the Vietnam veterans were treated," says Gen. Hank Emerson. Powell addressed the matter in his Memorial Day, 1991, speech at the Vietnam Veteran's Memorial on the Mall in Washington.

"If you're a veteran of Vietnam, you will be at every parade and at every celebration," Powell said. "You will be there in person or in the hearts and minds of all Americans. The parades [for the Desert Storm veterans] will be for you, too. But you won't be there to redeem yourself. You need no redemption. You redeemed yourself in the A Shau Valley. You redeemed yourself at Hue. You redeemed yourself at Dau Tieng, at Khe Sanh, in the South China Sea, in the air over Hanoi or launching off Yankee Station, and in a thousand other places.

"So you won't be in parades in Washington or in New York or anywhere else in this great country for the purpose of redemption. You'll be there to share in the adulation, to accept some of the applause you were denied, and to be recognized for the true and brave patriots that you are. The parades and celebrations are not needed to restore our honor as Vietnam veterans because we never lost our honor. They're not to clear up the matter of our valor because our valor was never in question. Two hundred and thirty-six Medals of Honor say our valor was never in question. Fifty-eight thousand one hundred and seventy-five names on this Wall say our valor and the value of our service were never in question.

"Today, my friends, we are very, very proud of our Desert Storm heroes. They fought brilliantly. They put their names in the record book of American arms . . . And we are equally proud of the heroes of Vietnam. Although those didn't get a parade, the Wall shows that they earned America's love, America's respect, and our devotion to their memory. The Desert Storm parade may also serve to finally, as Lincoln said, bind up the wounds of Vietnam." And, perhaps, to expunge it finally from its dominant role in modern American memory. That, too, seems to be part of the legacy Powell intends to leave behind from what will be his thirty-five years in uniform. As Lincoln also said, Powell noted, citing the Gospel According to St. Mark, " 'A house divided against itself cannot long stand.' I believe this government cannot endure permanently half slave and half free." For a quarter century, Vietnam has been the immediate American divide. Since nearly the beginning of American history, race has been the nation's abiding schism, its inner continental divide.

Race—its role in shaping his life and career and in shaping the public's perception of him—is perhaps the hardest thing to measure with Colin Powell. One prominent Washington academician says that the fact that Powell is black "gets everybody warm and fuzzy, but it also is one of several sources of his enormous political strength. It's virtually impossible to criticize him. His race, his charm, his political experience and sophistication—all those make him extremely formidable and probably in a way that is not entirely healthy." A newspaperman who has covered the military and defense issues for many years says that the part race plays in protecting Powell from criticism "is one of those unreportable questions we all wonder about." Indeed, in such a politically correct time, Powell may well get something of a free ride: America is starved not only for heroes and role models but also for good news about blacks. The test of the hypothesis is what has been suppressed or downplayed, and the answer to that seems to be—not much. He may have had a larger role in the Iran-contra affair than has generally been reported, but he was a second banana in those days, a soldier under orders from the Secretary of Defense. He has perhaps been, as another reporter contends, "at the cutting edge of conventional wisdom" in downsizing the military, but while Powell seems willing to work within a reduced budget, he clearly favors a continuing, towering, and global American military presence. There's no secret about it: What you hear from him is what he believes. Much of the criticism seems to be nibbling at the margins.

In a sense, Powell makes the issue of his race easy to ignore. He is fair-skinned; his voice has no particular ethnic or even regional inflection. One photographer with twenty years of professional experience says that Powell "doesn't put off a black vibe at all. He's like a whole bunch of other generals I've [photographed]. He's seemingly not aware of race so much as he is of stature." Judging Powell by the content of his character, not by the color of his skin, is easier physically with Powell than it is with, say, Jesse Jackson. Yet Powell seems determined—and perhaps more so since he has risen to such prominence—not to make forgetting his race easy. When the "Today" show's Katie Couric tried to turn Powell's attention to "one of your heroes," Dwight Eisenhower, during a January, 1992, interview, Powell answered briefly, then took the question in his own direction: "Martin Luther King, I'd like to note as we come upon his birthday, I think he's a great American, a great American hero; the black soldiers who went before me but who did not have the opportunities I had, are heroes in my eyes," he said. "America's full of heroes. My teachers were heroes, my ministers were heroes. [There are] lots of heroes, all you have to do is look for them."

Beyond much argument, Powell is an example of what Roger Wilkins calls "black exceptionalism." So long as a Colin Powell is the nation's highest-ranking military officer, so long as his name can be seriously advanced as a vice-presidential or presidential candidate, it is easier for some to ignore or avoid the fact that black Americans are seven times more likely than white Americans to die of tuberculosis, six times more likely to be murdered, and three times more likely to die of AIDS; that the black infant mortality rate is more than twice the rate for white infants; that while blacks make up about twelve percent of the population, they earn about five percent of all medical and law degrees; that a black American family is more than four times more likely than a white one to be living below the poverty line; that blacks, who in 1950 accounted for less than a third of the nation's prison population, now make up about half of it and about forty percent of all prisoners on death row; and that one in five black males will spend at least some part of his life incarcerated. Going on a century and a half since slavery was abolished, America still is, as the title of Andrew Hacker's book puts it, *Two Nations: Black and White, Separate, Hostile, and Unequal.* (It is from Hacker's compelling study that the above statistics are drawn.) Powell's résumé, the trust that has been placed in him by two presidents, the authority he has been given to exercise are subject to misuse by those who do not wish to face up to the harrowing statistical portrait of black America. As Powell himself says, ''A lot of white people salve their consciences'' by citing his success. Which is hardly his fault. Indeed, it seems a strangely incomplete way to view a life, and a uniquely unfair way to view Colin Powell's.

Perhaps what especially distinguishes Colin Powell are not his achievements—considerable as they are—but his sense of duty and responsibility. And perhaps if his life to date offers one diamond-hard lesson, it is that only through the exercise of individual duty and responsibility can the nation's abiding wounds be healed.

''We must all reach back, we must all reach down,'' Powell told the 1992 graduates of predominantly black Fisk University in Nashville, Tennessee. ''We must all work together to pull our people, to pull all Americans out of the violence, out of the dank and soul-damning world of drugs, out of the turmoil in our cities. As we climbed on the backs of others, so must we allow our backs to be used for others to go higher than we have . . . The other evening Alma and I were privileged to be with Maya Angelou. She talked about her upbringing in Stamp, Arkansas. She told us something her grandmother had said to her many years ago. Her grandmother had said, 'Girl, when you cross this threshold, you're going to be *raised*.' So raise your children. Treasure them. Love them. They are our future. We cannot let the generation in front of us go to waste.''

''Raise strong families,'' Powell urged the graduates, and ''as you raise your families, remember the worst kind of poverty is not economic poverty, it is the poverty of values. It is the poverty of caring. It is the poverty of love.''

The Colin Powell story is one of grit, drive, determination, and talent. It is a story that sweeps through many of the defining events of American life in the last half-century. It is the classic tale of the immigrants' child, pushed by his parents to exceed the outward accomplishments of their own lives. It is a West Indian story and a Bronx story, an Army one and an American one. Most of all, perhaps, it is a story of another sort of exceptionalism, one too rare and one ignored at great risk: human exceptionalism, the irregular capacity of the species—black, white, or yellow; male or female—to rise above the norms and leave a lasting mark. With Colin Powell, that really should be the bottom line.

APPENDIX

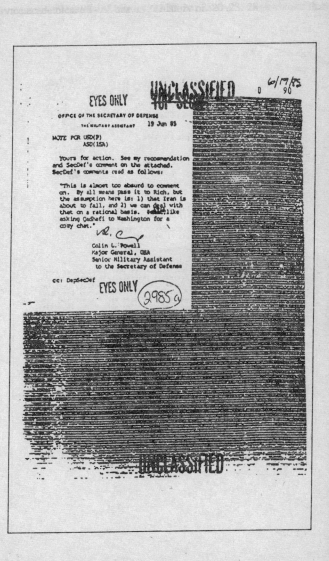

60/19/85
D   90

EYES ONLY ~~TOP SECRET~~

OFFICE OF THE SECRETARY OF DEFENSE

THE MILITARY ASSISTANT   19 Jun 85

NOTE FOR USD(P)
ASD(ISA)

Yours for action. See my recommendation
and SecDef's comment on the attached.
SecDef's comments read as follows:

"This is almost too absurd to comment
on. By all means pass it to Rich, but
the assumption here is: 1) that Iran is
about to fall, and 2) we can deal with
that on a rational basis. It's like
asking Qadhafi to Washington for a
cozy chat."

Colin L. Powell
Major General, USA
Senior Military Assistant
to the Secretary of Defense

cc: DepSecDef

EYES ONLY

2985 c

UNCLASSIFIED   6/17/85

THE WHITE HOUSE

WASHINGTON

D   91

June 17, 1985

SEC DEF
HAS SEEN

JUN 18 1985

~~SECRET~~/WITH
~~TOP SECRET~~ ATTACHMENT

MEMORANDUM FOR THE HONORABLE GEORGE P. SHULTZ
           The Secretary of State

           THE HONORABLE CASPAR W. WEINBERGER
           The Secretary of Defense

SUBJECT: U.S. Policy Toward Iran (S)

The Director of Central Intelligence has just distributed an SNIE
on "Iran: Prospects for Near-Term Instability", which I hope you
have received. This SNIE makes clear that instability in Iran is
accelerating, with potentially momentous consequences for U.S.
strategic interests. It seems sensible to ask whether our
current policy toward Iran is adequate to achieve our interests.
My staff has prepared a draft NSDD (Tab A) which can serve to
stimulate our thinking on U.S. policy toward Iran. I would
appreciate your reviewing the draft on an eyes only basis and
providing me with your comments and suggestions. I am concerned
about the possibility of leakage should we decide not to pursue
this change in policy with the President. If you feel that we
should consider this change, then I would refer the paper to the
SIG(FP) in preparation for an NSPG meeting with the President.
(S)

Robert C. McFarlane

2985 b

~~SECRET WITH~~
~~TOP SECRET ATTACHMENT~~   UNCLASSIFIED

UNCLASSIFIED

NSC/ICS 4026

THE WHITE HOUSE
WASHINGTON

DRAFT

TOP SECRET

D   92

NATIONAL SECURITY DECISION
DIRECTIVE

U.S. Policy Toward Iran

Dynamic political evolution is taking place inside Iran.
Instability caused by the pressures of the Iraq-Iran war,
economic deterioration and regime infighting create the potential
for major changes in Iran. The Soviet Union is better positioned
than the U.S. to exploit and benefit from any power struggle that
results in changes in the Iranian regime, as well as increasing
socio-political pressures. In this environment, the emergence of
a regime more compatible with American and Western interests is
unlikely. Soviet success in taking advantage of the emerging
power struggle to insinuate itself in Iran would change the
strategic balance in the area.

While we pursue a number of broad,
long-term goals, our primary short-term challenge must be to
block Moscow's efforts to increase Soviet influence (now and
after the death of Khomeini). This will require an active and
sustained program to build both our leverage and our
understanding of the internal situation so as to enable us to
exert a greater and more constructive influence over Iranian
politics. We must improve our ability to protect our interests
during the struggle for succession.

U.S. Interests and Goals

2985c

The most immediate U.S. interests include:

(1) Preventing the disintegration of Iran and preserving it as
     an independent strategic buffer which separates the Soviet
     Union from the Persian Gulf;

(2) Limiting the scope and opportunity for Soviet actions in
     Iran, while positioning ourselves to cope with the changing
     Iranian internal situation;

(3) Maintaining access to Persian Gulf oil and ensuring
     unimpeded transit of the Strait of Hormuz; and

(4) An end to the Iranian government's sponsorship of terrorism
     and its attempts to destabilize the governments of other
     regional states.

UNCLASSIFIED

UNCLASSIFIED ~~TOP SECRET~~

~~TOP SECRET~~ 2

DRAFT

D 93

We also seek other broad and important, if less immediately urgent, goals.

(1) Iran's resumption of a moderate and constructive role as a member respectively of the non-communist political community, of its region, and of the world petroleum economy;

(2) continued Iranian resistance to the expansion of Soviet power in general, and to the Soviet occupation of Afghanistan in particular;

(3) an early end to the Iran-Iraq war which is not mediated by the Soviet Union and which does not fundamentally alter the balance of power in the region;

(4) elimination of Iran's flagrant abuses of human rights;

(5) movement toward eventual normalization of U.S.-Iranian diplomatic consular and cultural relations, and bilateral trade/commercial activities;

(6) resolution of American legal and financial claims through the Hague Tribunal; and

(7) Iranian moderation on OPEC pricing policy.

Many of our interests will be difficult to achieve. But given the rapidity with which events are moving, and the magnitude of the stakes, it is clear that urgent new efforts are required. moving forward, we must be especially careful to balance our evolving relationship with Iraq in a manner that does not damage the longer term prospects for Iran.

Present Iranian Political Environment

The Iranian leadership faces its most difficult challenges since 1981. The regime's popularity has declined significantly in the past six months, primarily because of intensified disillusionment with a seemingly unending war, the continued imposition of Islamic social policies on a population increasingly reluctant to accept such harsh measures, and a faltering economy brought on primarily by declining oil revenues. The impact of these problems is intensified by the realization that Ayatollah Khomeini's mental and physical health is fragile, which in turn casts a pall of uncertainty over the daily decision-making process.

UNCLASSIFIED

322

TOP SECRET   D   94

Unless the acceleration of adverse military, political and
economic developments is reversed, the Khomeini regime will face
serious instability (i.e. repeated anti-regime demonstrations,
strikes, assassination attempts, sabotage and other destabilizing
activities throughout, increasingly involving the lower classes)
This condition will sap officials' energies and government
resources, intensifying differences among Iranian leaders as the
government tries to avoid mistakes that would provoke popular
upheaval and threaten continued control.

While it is impossible to predict the course of the emerging
power struggle, it is possible to discern several trends which
must be accounted for by U.S. policy. As domestic pressures
mount, decision-making is likely to be monopolized by individual
representing the same unstable mix of radical, conservative and
ultra-conservative factions that now control the Iranian
government. The longer Khomeini lingers in power, the more
likely the power struggle will intensify, and the greater the
number of potential leaders who might affect the outcome of the
struggle.

The ultimate strength of various clerical groups and the power
coalitions they may form are not known. However, the weaknesses
of various opposition groups -- inside Iran and abroad -- are
evident, especially the lack of a leader with sufficient stature
to rival Khomeini and his ideas. The most likely faction in a
power struggle to shift Iranian policy in directions more
acceptable to the West -- should their influence increase -- are
conservatives working from within the government against the
radicals. Radicals within the regime, and the leftist
opposition, are the groups most likely to influence the course of
events in ways inimical to Western interests.

The Iranian regular armed forces represent a potential source of
both power and inclination to move Iran back into a more
pro-Western position. Representatives of every faction inside
and outside the regime recognize the potential importance of the
military and are cultivating contacts with these forces.
However, as long as the Army remains committed in the war with
Iraq it will not be in a position to intervene in Tehran.

The other instrument of state power, the Revolutionary Guard, is
becoming increasingly fractured. It will probably come apart
following Khomeini's death, and might even engage in a major
power struggle before then. In any scenario, the Guard will be
at the center of the power struggle.

DRAFT

~~TOP SECRET~~

4

D 95

The Soviets are well aware of the evolving developments in Iran. They will continue to apply carrot-and-stick incentives to Iran in the hope of bringing Tehran to Moscow's terms for an improved bilateral relationship that could serve as a basis for major growth in Soviet influence in Iran. Moscow will clearly resist any trend toward the restoration of a pro-Western Iranian government.

Despite strong clerical antipathy to Moscow and communism, Tehran's leadership seems to have concluded that improvement of relations with the Soviet Union is not essential to Iranian interest. They do not seem interested in improving ties with us. This Iranian assessment is probably based on Tehran's view of what Moscow can do for -- and against - Iran rather than on an ideological preference to conduct relations with Moscow. The USSR already has much leverage over Tehran -- is stark contrast to the U.S.

Moscow views Iran as a key area of opportunity ▐▐▐ In return, Moscow is certain to offer economic and technical assistance, and possibly even military equipment. While they have heretofore balked at providing major weapon systems, the Soviets might relax their embargo if the right political opportunities presented themselves. While Moscow would probably not act in a manner that severely disrupts its relations with Baghdad, given Iraq's dependency on the USSR for ground forces equipment, Moscow possesses considerable room for maneuver if it senses major openings in Tehran for the establishment of a position of significant influence.

Moscow may also pursue a strategy based on support of separatist movements. The Soviet Union has had ample opportunity to cultivate the ethnic groups that cut across the Soviet-Iranian border. Most ethnic groups are unlikely to challenge the central government in Tehran as long as they fear severe reprisals. But in the areas of Iran adjacent to the Soviet border, the Soviets can provide a security umbrella to protect rebellious ethnic groups from reprisals.

The U.S. position in Tehran is unlikely to improve without a major change in U.S. policy. The challenge to the U.S. in the post-Khomeini period will be severe. Any successor regime will probably seize power in the name of Islam and the revolution and

~~TOP SECRET~~

DRAF

~~TOP SECRET~~

D 96

can be expected to have a built-in anti-American bias. ~~A more conservative regime, still Islamic, might lessen the emphasis on revolution and terrorism and could move cautiously toward a more correct relationship with the U.S.~~ On the other hand, radical ~~forces~~ will try to ~~exacerbate~~ anti-American feelings to strengthen their own positions at the expense of the conservatives.

Our leverage with Iran is sharply reduced by the current degree of hostility that springs from the ideology of the radical clergy, especially as it serves their foreign policy goals. Moreover, the moderate and conservative elements of the clergy may also share the radicals' belief that we are inveterately hostile to the Islamic government, making accommodation with the U.S. impossible. The clerical regime continues to believe that the U.S. has not accepted the revolution and intends to reverse the course of events and install a puppet government. This perception has been reinforced by our restoration of diplomatic relations with Iraq, efforts to cut the flow of arms to Iran, as direct threats of military action in retaliation for Iranian-inspired anti-U.S. terrorism.

U.S. Policy

The dynamic political situation in Iran and the consequences for U.S. interests of growing Soviet and radical influence, compel the U.S. undertake a range of short- and long-term initiatives that will enhance our leverage in Tehran, and, if possible minimize that of the Soviets. Particular attention must be paid to avoiding situations which compel the Iranians to turn to the Soviets. Short-term measures should be undertaken in a manner that forestalls Soviet prospects and enhances our ability, directly and indirectly, to bar U.S. and Western influence in Iran to the maximum extent possible in the future. Planning for the following initiatives should therefore proceed on a fast and longer-term track. The components of U.S. policy will be to:

(1) Encourage Western allies and friends to help Iran meet its import requirements so as to reduce the attractiveness of Soviet assistance and trade offers, while demonstrating the value of correct relations with the West. This includes provision of selected military equipment as determined on a case-by-case basis.

~~TOP SECRET~~

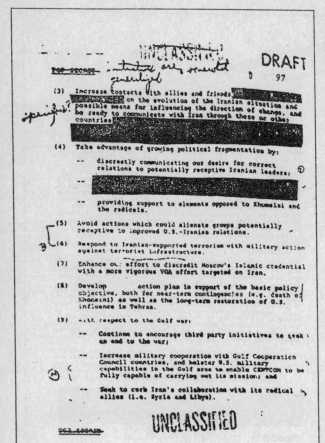

DRAFT

D 97

(3) Increase contacts with allies and friends ▓▓▓▓▓ on the evolution of the Iranian situation and possible means for influencing the direction of change, and be ready to communicate with Iran through these or other countries ▓▓▓▓▓

(4) Take advantage of growing political fragmentation by:

-- discreetly communicating our desire for correct relations to potentially receptive Iranian leaders;

-- ▓▓▓▓▓▓▓▓▓▓▓▓▓▓▓▓▓▓▓▓▓▓▓▓▓▓

-- providing support to elements opposed to Khomeini and the radicals.

(5) Avoid actions which could alienate groups potentially receptive to improved U.S.-Iranian relations.

(6) Respond to Iranian-supported terrorism with military action against terrorist infrastructure.

(7) Enhance our effort to discredit Moscow's Islamic credential with a more vigorous VOA effort targeted on Iran.

(8) Develop action plan in support of the basic policy objective, both for near-term contingencies (e.g. death of Khomeini) as well as the long-term restoration of U.S. influence in Tehran.

(9) With respect to the Gulf war:

-- Continue to encourage third party initiatives to seek an end to the war;

-- Increase military cooperation with Gulf Cooperation Council countries, and bolster U.S. military capabilities in the Gulf area to enable CENTCOM to be fully capable of carrying out its mission; and

-- Seek to curb Iran's collaboration with its radical allies (i.e. Syria and Libya).

UNCLASSIFIED

~~TOP SECRET~~

UNCLASSIFIED   D   98

_____ ways to establish contacts with "moderates" _____ seek
who play important roles in the administration of Islamic
rule but who also favor policies more favorable to US
and Western interests.

Political

-- Through contacts with allies and friends, we should discreetly communicate our desire for correct relations to
   potentially receptive Iranian leaders based on their
   renunciation of state-supported terrorism, their willingness to seek a negotiated settlement to the Iran-Iraq war,
   their non-interference in other states' affairs, and their
   cooperation in settling US-Iranian claims in the Hague
   Tribunal.

-- Maintain our neutrality in the Iran-Iraq war while encour-
   aging third party initiatives to end the conflict and increasing political-military cooperation with Gulf Cooperation Council countries.

-- In light of recent evidence that our allies continue to
   permit sporadic transfers of militarily useful equipment
   to Iran and that negotiations may be taking place between
   commercial firms and Iranian officials, we should increase
   the pressure on our allies by considering public statement
   and possible sanctions.

Public Diplomacy

-- Our public statements on Iran should bring pressure to
   bear squarely where it is needed--on the current Iranian
   regime. In tone, our public position must avoid casting
   Iran as a country and the Iranian people and culture, as
   well as Shia Islam, as the enemy, but should emphasize
   opposition to the policies of the present Iranian governm
   and the corrupt mullahs inside the government. Our statements should aim to encourage those elements in Iran who
   disagree or oppose regime policies.

Economic

-- A full range of US export controls are already in effect.
   _____ we
   should reassess the effectiveness of present controls in
   curbing all but strictly civilian exports.

UNCLASSIF

D   99

-- In conjunction with discreet political contacts proposed
above, we could suggest to the Iranians that correct relations would include relaxation of current US trade
restrictions and normal trade relations with an Iranian
government that is not hostile to US interests.

(TS) I concur with the balance of the recommendations in the
draft NSDD in so far as they support current US policy. My recommendations reflect my very strong view that US policy must remain
steadfast in the face of international lawlessness perpetrated by
the Iranian regime. Changes in policy and in conduct, therefore,
must be initiated by the Iranian government. By remaining firmly
opposed to current Iranian government policies and actions, yet
supportive of moderation and a longer term improvement in relations,
we can avoid the future enmity of the Iranian people and develop the
leverage necessary to counter a possibly very dangerous increase in
Soviet influence. In particular, we need to be prepared for a
possible period of turmoil as the regime begins to change, by
building up effective instruments of influence and access to people
and organizations within Iran, so as to counter a Soviet attempt to
promote a pro-Soviet successor regime.

cc: Secretary Shultz

INDEX